Korean Traits (K-DNA)

That cultivated Korea's prosperity

Written by **Shin, Bohyun**

DAEHAN

Introduction

On July 4, 2021, the United Nations Conference on Trade and Development (UNCTAD) unanimously announced Korea's status from a developing country to an advanced country. It was the first case since 1964, that a country's status changed in this way. The decision is made only when all countries participating in the conference agree to a change in status. Considering Korea's gross domestic product (GDP), the world's 10th-largest, Korea should have risen to the ranks of advanced countries early on. However, the change of national status at the UNCTAD is not determined by the scale of the economy alone.

Since the middle of the 20th century, Korea has achieved phenomenal economic growth. This is why countries around the world are paying attention to Koreans. The Republic of Korea was a fledgling democracy established after World War II with UN approval in the southern part of the Korean Peninsula. Less than two years after the government was established, the Korean War erupted with a surprise invasion of the south by the communist government established in the north. The war broke out well before Korea's status as an independent country was properly established. During the Korean War, the country was nearly destroyed in ruins. The war ended with the Korean Peninsula divided into South and North Korea as it is now due to an armistice agreement. South Korea, which was invaded by a surprise attack in a defenseless state, suffered severe damage from the war and fell into becoming one of the poorest countries in the world. Even so, Korea rose up again only with human resources. Koreans first achieved self-reliance on staple foodgrains through the dual green revolution of increased food production and reforestation. Because of this, Korea succeeded in becoming a global role model of reforestation. In addition to this, in 1960s, Korea had the lowest per capita income of any poor countries in the world. However, from 1962 to 1996, through a total of 7 rounds of the 5-year national economic development plans, Korea achieved rapid economic development. It is said that the economic development achieved by Koreans cannot be explained by any economic theory. Entering the 21st century, Korea has not only gone beyond the model of economic development but achieved political democratization. Most recently has sparked a craze all over the world with unique Korean cultural contents products and industry contents technologies such as Korean dramas and movies, K-pop, K-food, K-semiconductor, K-ship building, K-construction, and K-defense. Now, it is widely accepted that Korea has reached the level of strong power in terms of culture and technology, wielding soft powers to its advantage.

I was born during the Korean War and I grew up in one of the poorest countries in the world. I have personally lived through the evolution of Korea becoming a developed country. In the 1980s, I studied abroad from the 1990s to 2004. I had many interactions with people from other countries, overseeing defense industry and military diplomacy affairs as a national public official. During this process, I personally experienced the change in the attitude of foreigners of Korea based on the heightened national status following the growth of Korea's economy. As Korea's status continued to rise after the 2010s, I began to question, "How on earth have we Koreans been able to achieve Korea's prosperity today?" This could be the same question for those who want the prosperity of their country around the world. Isn't it said that Korea has now become a role-model for national development for many people in developing countries? I believe that the general characteristics of Koreans and the DNA of Koreans which are thought to have contributed to Korea's prosperity were inferred and presented under the agenda of 「DNA of Koreans who have made Korea prosperous today」.

The book is composed of two parts. Part 1 deals with the

characteristics of Koreans today, such as general personality, lifestyle, and behavioral patterns. First, it was presumed that a person's innate personality is formed by collective memories or thoughts imprinted in genetic factors as they evolve generation after generation under the influence of the environment around them. The background of characteristics formation was divided into environmental, historical, ideological, religious, cultural, and complex influences. Based on specific facts for each influencing factor, the background of the internalization (DNAization) of the personality, life attitude, and behavioral style inherent in many Koreans today was described without addition or reduction.

Part 2 presupposes that Korea's prosperity today was 'possible because of economic development' and the agenda was set as 'the key factor that led to Korea's economic development'. Also the leadership of national leaders, environmental/social conditions, and the unique characteristics of Koreans (K-DNA), can be said to be the DNA of Koreans who have made Korea prosperous today. I hope it will be of some help to those who are interested in Koreans or who want to know how Koreans developed their country into an economic powerhouse or advanced country.

Dec. 2022. at Bulgwa-Jung East Hongcheon
Bo-hyun Shin

Table of Content

Part 1 Characteristics of Koreans
(Personality, Lifestyle, and Behavior)

Part 2 Key factors driving Korea's economic
development

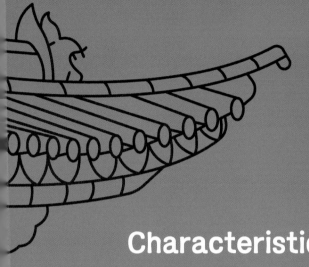

Part 1

Characteristics of Koreans
(Personality, Lifestyle, and Behavior)

We generally refer to the characteristic traits of most members of a nation, that is, the habits and inclinations, and the attitudes and behaviors derived from them, as the characteristics of the people. Therefore, in the first part of this book, I classified and presented the environmental, historical, ideological, religious, and cultural influences of most Koreans today, and the personality that is thought to have been formed by the complex influence of such influencing factors, and the corresponding lifestyle and behavioral patterns.

Modern psychology defines 'personality' as a unique psychological characteristic of an individual that consistently appears to adapt to the environment in a way that is unique to them. However, human personality and the behaviors induced by it are very complex and stem from a variety of reasons. In addition to this, the bio-psychological and social psychological factors are related to personality. Therefore, it was assumed that a person's personality is formed by maturing as a whole through adapting to a social environment which is inherited to the next generation.

The premise is that "the typical structure of consciousness that determines attitude towards life and behavior of people included in the same community based on the innate personality traits of community members, the living environment, historically important events experienced by ancestors, and the long-term ideological influence that has dominated them" makes a logical analogy possible. Terms such as a person with the 'temperament of an island nation' or a person with 'temperament of a peninsular' prove this.

These genetically endowed temperamental characteristics develop into an integrated whole under the influence of various environments such as direct and indirect experiences, will to cultivate character, education, human relations, organizations to which individuals belong, social community spirit, ideology and culture, and they form the personality which is the frame of basic behavioral tendencies. Koreans have settled and lived on the Korean Peninsula for at least thousands of years. It was presumed that the character of Koreans was largely formed by environmental (geology, topography, geopolitics, climate), historical, ideological, religious, and cultural influences, and sometimes formed through a combination of the factors mentioned above. Under this premise, I classified and arranged collective characteristics of today's most Koreans such as their general personalities, life attitudes and behavioral patterns, under the factors. I also provided specific facts such as memories, collective unconsciousness, lifestyle habits and tendencies formed by the experiences of ancestors that are passed down from generation to generation.

Characteristics shaped by environmental influences

Environmental factors can be classified into geology and topography, geopolitical characteristics, climate of where Koreans have lived. Characteristics shaped by such environmental influences refer to characteristics such as character, life attitude, and behavioral pattern, that can be inferred from their ancestors who have been living on this land for generations.

The habits and tendencies of the elderly are inherent in many Koreans.

In many Koreans, the habits and tendencies of the elderly are inherently influenced by the geology and topography of the Korean Peninsula. When the elderly pass away, Koreans will say that they "went back". To Koreans, when a person dies, it means that they return to their original position. It also coincides with the meaning of the Bible, which says that "since man is made of dust, all will return to dust." It means that man is born from the soil and returns to the soil. Based on this, it can be assumed that the character and characteristics of people living in a certain area are related to the characteristics of the area where the ancestors of those people lived for generations. Based on these assumptions, we may infer that the habits and tendencies of today's Koreans are believed to have been formed under the influence of geology and soil.

More than 70% of the geological foundation of the Korean Peninsula was formed from the beginning of the Paleozoic to the end of the Mesozoic period. The rest of the Cenozoic strata are only locally distributed.[1] The geological structure consists of sedimentary basins formed from sedimentary rocks or geosyncline sedimentation, making the ground extremely stable. The soils of the Korean Peninsula are mostly gneiss and granite as a foundation rock formed before the Cenozoic Era.[1] It is a reddish-brown soil that contains a lot of iron. It does not contain much organic matter and is considered to be a soil with poor productivity.

More than 70% of the geological foundation of the Korean Peninsula, the home of Koreans, was formed during the Archean period. Change and development stopped a long time ago, and its change has plateaued throughout. The soil is an old soil, mostly ocher with poor productivity and lack of organic matter. The water flowing through the Korean Peninsula is always blue, except for the water from the Tumen River, which forms the border with Manchuria. People can drink it or at least can easily purify for human consumption. These facts indicate that the soil is old. The water flowing through the young, fertile land has a turbid black color. It contains a lot of organic and inorganic substances, so it is unsuitable for human consumption.

As for the topography of the Korean Peninsula, more than 70% of the country is mountainous terrains with a height of less than 1,000m. Low hilly areas corresponding to old age terrain are widely distributed. There is no mountain that emits

---

1) Rocks that make up the foundation ground

smoke on the Korean Peninsula and no fire-breathing volcanic craters. There is also no earthy brown valley water flowing down the mountain. Vibrant earthquakes that would break down mountains, divide the land, and stir the seas seldom appear. The people who had lived in an environment of geology and topography in old age is different from the people who had lived in an environment of geology, topography, and soil in young age.

Due to the effects of more than 70% of the land being affected by the geology, topography, soil, etc. of the old age, the majority (70% or more) of Koreans have a static and docile tendency inherent in them, which is also a characteristic of the elderly. They are also characterized by a calm and peaceful nature. Prefers the status quo rather than change. Rather than taking risks, they would rather settle down. They are reluctant to actively step forward and show a tendency to passively contemplate circumstances. It seems that people called Korea "the land of the morning calm" in the 20th century because of those characteristics of Koreans.

The term "The Land of the Morning Calm" comes from an article of Joseon called "Corea, The Hermit Nation" written by Griffith, American missionary, in 1882. 『Korea, the hermit country』 originally meant 'a country closed to Western civilization and Christianity,' nevertheless, the author introduced the name of the book as meaning 『The Land of the Morning Calm.』 Since then, the term "land of the morning calm" has long been used as a symbol of Korea. Koreans are docile in character. The mountains and rivers of the Korean Peninsula, where Korea is located, are always calm and stable. It is thought that people viewed Korea as the country of the morning calm because people agreed with these sentiments. Korean Air's in-flight magazine 『Morning Calm』 is also meant to express Korea as a land of calm mornings. It is a term used to describe a calm Korean morning with no wind after the land breeze that blows toward the sea all night on the Korean Peninsula stops and before the sea breeze blows toward the land during the day.

It is said that Japanese who stayed for an extended period of time in Joseon under Japanese colonial rule in the early 20th century, tended to have reduced dynamic properties compared to people living in Japan. There is a record[2] that, after living in Joseon for many years, returning to Japan and coming into contact with the Japanese landscape, he/she felt a kind of excitement mentally without realizing it, and felt a sense of waking up from the tranquility of being in Joseon. Even today, many Koreans say, "Now that I'm back home, I feel alive." Of course, it may be that one feels that way because one has returned to his/her homeland. However, it also could be that it feels so comfortable to return to where the geology and topography are calm and stable.

It is also possible to prove that many Koreans have temperamental characteristics similar to those of the elderly by using Sasang medicine theory. Sasang medicine is a field of medicine recognized by the World Health Organization (WHO). According to Sasang Medicine, about 70% of Koreans are Eumin (Yin-person), a combination of taeeumin (strong Yin-person) and soeumin (weak Yin-person). Yangin (Yang-person), a combination of Taeyangin (strong Yang-person) and Soyangin (weak Yang-person), accounts for the remaining 30%. The temperamental characteristics of a Eumin (Yin-person) are similar to those of an elderly person. They are typically quiet, calm, stubborn, and timid. The temperamental characteristics of Yangin are similar to those of young people. They like to come forward and brag about it, and they are lively and entertaining. According to Sasang Medicine, the composition ratio of Eumin (Yin-person) and Yangin (Yang-person) in Koreans is approximately 70:30. This 70:30 ratio of Eumin (Yin-person) to Yangin (Yang-person) in Koreans are the same as the geological and topographical ratio of the

Paleo-Mesozoic to the Cenozoic that constitutes the Korean Peninsula. There is a time difference of about 130 years from the present when Sasang Medicine determined the composition ratio of Koreans by predisposition. However, assuming that people's innate temperamental characteristics would not change significantly after 130 years, it is possible to prove the inference that about 70% of Koreans have temperamental characteristics similar to those of the elderly, influenced by the geological foundation and topography of the land. In addition to this, there is a geopolitical characteristic that it is a peninsula where Koreans live. As a result, the temperamental characteristics of the elderly that are inherent in many Koreans are transformed and appear in various forms.

The peninsula states are destined to play a bridging role between the continental and maritime powers. In particular, a country located on a small peninsula, such as the Korean Peninsula, is an environment inevitably affected by continental and maritime forces. It is because the power of a small peninsula nation is relatively weak. The people living in the Korean Peninsula had to face war at times depending on the rise and fall of the Mongols and Manchus who lived in the Northern Asia, and as national power grew in the eastern and southern Japanese islands, they had to resist whenever they looked outside to find a vent. If the continental power in the north and the maritime power in the east and south are strengthened at the same time, the Korean Peninsula inevitably becomes a point of conflict between the two powers. Due to these geopolitical conditions, the Korean Peninsula had to endure countless stormy days between continental and maritime forces. When one force invades and retreats, another force invades soon after. Sometimes another force invaded again even before one force could retreat. The ancestors of Koreans are those who survived this constant national crisis.[3] As a result, it can be said that today's Koreans have the geopolitical temperament of the peninsula that has been handed down from generation to generation.

The feudal state system is a state system that emerged in a situation where it was difficult for the central government to exercise its normal governance power due to the large territory. On the Korean Peninsula, where Koreans live, there has been no feudal state system that inevitably emerges in the process of national system development. Because the Korean peninsula was so small, the feudal state system that most countries experienced was not established.

Turkey, Spain, and Italy, which are well known peninsular countries, had built great empires beyond their territory of peninsula. The peninsulas which those countries occupied were large enough to absorb various cultures at the junctions of continents and then make those cultures of their own and carry their strength outward. This made it possible to build a great empire. On the other hand, it can be seen that the size of the Korean Peninsula is so small that a feudal state system could not arise and the nation's strength could not reach that level.

The national power formed on a small peninsula had to have a limit to its power. Inevitably, Korea in a small peninsula was more influenced by the surrounding powers connected by the peninsula than the powers formed on the large peninsula. The Korean Peninsula, the home of Koreans, protrudes south on the periphery of the Asian continent and faces the Japanese archipelago, which is more than twice its size. Because of its location on the periphery of the Asian continent, until the mid-19th century, exchanges with foreign countries were limited to China, which was connected by land, and Japan, which was connected by the sea. Korean ancestors lived in a relatively smaller territory than those of their neighbors, almost cut off from the outside world, and sustained an agricultural society of their own for a long time. Because of this geopolitical environment, it has been invaded by continental and maritime powers more than any other peninsula countries. In the process of resisting such a number of external aggression, the static and docile habits and inclinations of Koreans, which were formed under the influence of old-age geology and soil, were bound to be transformed. Sometimes it appears to be strong, sometimes weak, and sometimes in a completely opposite form.

Koreans tend to reject changes, and prefer to wait-and-see rather than to come forward.

Many Koreans internally tend to reject changes in religion, ideology, learning, institutions, customs, and habits once they have been accepted. Koreans don't like to come forward either. This is also a pattern that appears under the influence of the geology and topography. Koreans generally have a strong tendency to stick with a certain ideology once they accept it as their own. They hold on tight and willingly settle under its authority. It doesn't matter what the motive was at the time of accepting any ideology. Once accepted, they do not try to accept any new ideas.

Buddhism was introduced to the Korean Peninsula around the 4th and 5th centuries. There are records in the history books that most of the sects maintained their Jongji[2] from the time of introduction, until the government started to reject Buddhism during the early Joseon Dynasty. The fact that Jongji has been preserved as it was at the time of its introduction for nearly 1,000 years proves the tendency of Koreans to reject change. The same is true for Confucianism. During the reign of King Chungnyeol of Goryeo dynasty, Zhu Xi's compendium from China was brought in and taught Zhu Xi school of neo-Confucianism at Taehak. After that, until the end of the Joseon Dynasty, for more than 600 years, no schools of Confucianism other than Zhu Xi's Neo-Confucianism could set foot. This is the result of the fixation tendency of Koreans who refuse to change. There is a similar case in the case of Christianity. Most of the Koreans whom the American missionaries encountered at the end of the Joseon Dynasty were poor and ignorant. The missionaries determined that addiction to alcohol and tobacco was one of the causes. It was said that this is why they forbade alcohol and tobacco to church members. There is nothing in the Bible forbids this. More than 100 years have passed since then. Even though some Christians in Korea may not know the taboos mentioned in the Bible, alcohol and cigarettes are certainly seen as taboo. Koreans have enjoyed wearing white clothes for thousands of

---

2) the sect's creed, tenets, etc.

years since the days of Buyeo before the Three Kingdoms period. This habit of wearing white clothes is also a case that proves that Koreans do not want to change the habit once they have accepted it.

The fixation tendency of Koreans means that they are obsessed with the past. This implies reminiscing and reproducing the past rather than planning or preparing for tomorrow. In preparation for the future, this plays a role in thoroughly blocking the will to change or reform the ideas set in the past in line with the present. What will happen to the country if its leader clings to the past? A prime example is the political reform of Daewongun, who came to power with the accession of the 12-year-old King Gojong in 1863. His reform drive preceded those of Japan's Meiji Restoration which was launched in 1868, by five years. Even so, he ignored the international situation at the time and pursued retrospective reforms towards the early Joseon Dynasty. On the other hand, Japan promoted national modernization toward society of the first industrial revolution, which was the major global topic at the time. In less than 10 years since Japan promoted reform, the results of reform began to surface. Joseon succumbed to armed threats and a fleet show of force preceded by warship Unyo-ho of Japan, which was a product of national modernization. In February 1876, a humiliating treaty was signed between Korea and Japan, and after that, Joseon became a victim of their imperialist territorial expansion policy.

Many older generations in Korea in their 50s and 60s still have a fixed mindset. It means that they have more conservative and static personality traits rather than forward thinking or dynamic ones. Such Koreans do not try to change anything once they become their own. They have a strong tendency to resist change. They are reluctant to take on challenges or adventures that try to do something first. There is a strong tendency to regard watching from behind as a virtue.

Rather than challenging the absolute authority of the state, they are obedient.

It is also one of the habits and tendencies that appear under the environmental influences of old age geology and topography. Many Koreans who own a cautious personality prefer to keep a wait-and-see attitude rather than coming forward. As a result, Koreans are characterized by active cooperation and follower-ship when they sympathize with strong national policies promoted by the state for a cause. Historically, Koreans had shown a strong resistance to change. Nevertheless, they actively cooperated with the government's innovative policies without resistance as long as it contains a right cause. In particular, since the 1960s, the low illiteracy rate of less than 1% of the people and the high level of education have greatly contributed to understanding and actively participating in the correct policies promoted by the state.

Prime examples include the Saemaul movement, miracle on bare mountains, and reforestation, which were implemented by the Korean government in the 1970s at the pan-governmental level that set a global example. This became a model for national development in developing countries. In addition, examples include the separate garbage collection campaign, toilet cleaning campaign, and no-smoking campaign in public places that successfully settled among Koreans in a short period of time in the late 20th century. The docile nature of Koreans and their high level of education played a decisive role in the success of the government-wide public participation movement. This is one of the tendencies of Koreans who played an important driving role in creating today's Korea. Just as flexibility overcomes strength, Koreans' benevolence, gentleness, and high educational zeal have served as the basis to build today's Korea.

Koreans have a wisdom to adapt to the signs of the times (時勢).

It seems that Koreans are conscious of the wisdom of acknowledging and accepting reality as it is in order to survive. It is a lifestyle learned to survive in a barren environment with the pressure and aggression of neighboring powers for a long time. They settled in the barren soil and made a living through farming. Korea has a natural environment with four distinct seasons, hot like the equatorial region in the summer and cold like Siberia in the winter. It was an environment where even with extreme droughts and floods, they could not leave the place of life in search of a better place. If there was a way to survive in such a harsh reality and an environment with no place to escape, it was to accept and adapt to reality as it is. It is the logic that as a result of Koreans living a life that adapts to the harsh natural environment for generations of their ancestors, their ability to adapt to the environment and survive has become stronger. In addition, while experiencing frequent foreign invasions for a long time, they also experienced that they must know how to adapt in order to survive. It is the opinion that Koreans have acquired the wisdom to adapt to the signs of the times through the hardships of such a life.

Koreans are very calculative. For that reason, Koreans are

excellent at overcoming difficult environments. Nonetheless, Koreans were not absorbed by other powers between the relatively enormous continental and maritime powers. They created and maintained their own unique culture and easily overcame international financial crises such as the IMF and mortgage loan crisis. Although their cohesion seemed weak in their daily lives, they bond was incredibly strong in crisis. Others thought they would give in to the powerful, but they also showed a behavioral pattern in which they risked their lives to resist. The characteristic of Koreans adapting well to the times is their life attitude to protect themselves.

As mentioned earlier, Koreans have a strong tendency to reject changes and prefer to maintain the status quo. Nonetheless, in Korea, policies at the government level are well implemented in seamless order. These cases such as the Saemaul movement, the volume-based garbage disposal system implemented at the national level, the no-smoking campaign in public places, the government-wide PC and internet distribution and computerization of government systems, the digitization of the infrastructure of national operations, and the recent mask wearing mandate against COVID-19 are the examples that the national policies were successfully accomplished in a short period of time. I believe that this was possible because of the low illiteracy rate and high level of education mentioned above, as well as the wisdom to adapt to the times and the strong patriotism that was ingrained in them. Koreans have the wisdom to adapt to the times, so they actively participate in the implementation of correct policies at the national level. That is the reason why the right government-led policies have been able to easily settle in Korean society and drive national development to this very day.

For Koreans, imitation and fixation are evident in their ideology for many generations.

For most Koreans, due to the geopolitical influence of the Korean Peninsula, the home of their lives, their ideology clearly shows tendency of imitation and fixation. Until the 19th century, trade relationship with foreign countries by the dynasties formed within Korean peninsula was limited to China and Japan. It also heavily relied on China. Simply put, on the Korean Peninsula, people-to-people exchanges and visits by foreigners were extremely limited. In such a situation, it was very unlikely that home grown ideologies would surpass those ideologies that naturally appeared in China, where many people's diverse cultures were intertwined with each other. At the beginning of the 14th century, when the Joseon Dynasty was established, the Korean peninsula had a population of only one million.[3] This is the reason why there was no choice but to imitate the religions or ideologies that were introduced through China.

The Korean Peninsula was an environment in which there was no choice but to imitate ideas and religions introduced from China. Koreans have a tendency to strongly reject changes due to geological and topographical influences. For that reason, it is the opinion that ideas or religions internalized by Koreans had long been unchanged and fixed. It is the logic that Koreans have a strong adherence to ideology and religion, displaying habits and tendencies that generally appear in old age of animals and plants due to the influence of the geology and topography of the Korean Peninsula. It is said that there was a proverb in the Joseon Dynasty, "Do not try to change the old law, and do not try to establish a new law!" It is also a phrase that indicates that many Joseon people typically had the characteristics of the elderly. There are many examples of how strongly Koreans adhere to their ideology. One of the prime

---

3) Looking at the population of Joseon based on the annals, the result of the census in the 22nd year of King Sejong (1440) was 692,000, 4.16 million in the 38th year of King Jungjong (1543), 5.24 million in the 4th year of King Sukjong (1678), and 13.12 million in 1910.

examples is that recently, Chinese scholars who aims to restore Confucianism visited Korea and are learning related contents in Korea. Sungkyunkwan Daeseongjeon in Korea still commemorates Confucian saints and sages, including Confucius, who was born in China about 2,500 years ago. From the early Joseon Dynasty to the present, their mortuary tablets are enshrined and Seokjeon Daeje is held every spring and fall to honor their virtue. During the Cultural Revolution of 1968, China had destroyed temples and shrines across the country. Then, a while ago, in order to restore records of the Confucian tradition, Chinese scholars had collected data for the traditional ancestral rites and related contents from Sungkyunkwan, where the memorial services for Confucius have been held since from its foundation. This is because Korea preserved the original Confucian traditions and its contents from its beginning. Looking at this, one can easily see how strong the imitation and adherence of Korean to the ideologies are.

The adherence to ideology can also be explained by the Seonbi (scholarly) spirit that remains strongly at the base of most Korean consciousness. The Seonbi (scholarly) spirit is still acting as a restoring force to a just society in Korean society. For many Koreans, some historical perceptions remain that Joseon was a negative country where factional strife and Sadae ideology (toadyism) were prevalent. Some think that such negative perceptions of Joseon is due to the influence of Japanese colonialism. The Joseon Dynasty was a small country geopolitically sandwiched between China and Japan. Nevertheless, it was a strong dynasty that lasted more than 500 years, established in 1392 and maintained for 518 years until 1910, one of a few in the world. In my view, it was possible to maintain it for more than 500 years because the basic ethics of Neo-Confucianism and the Seonbi (scholarly) spirits had been maintained at the base of society. It was possible because the Seonbi (scholarly) spirit that values uprightness, integrity and fidelity, and the moral standards of Neo-Confucianism, the mainstream Confucianism at the time, that includes benevolence, righteousness, courtesy, wisdom, and trust were firmly rooted in Korean society. The Joseon Dynasty adopted Confucianism as the basis of its governance and adopted the policy of reject-Buddhism and worship-Confucianism as its founding ideology. In early Joseon dynasty, the Seonbi (scholarly) spirit was naturally embedded to scholars and government officials. The spirit of Seonbi, who value noble character as the value of life, became the life-oriented aim point for bureaucrats who were also Confucian scholars.

The image of a scholar they sought was a honorable man with noble character. They were highly educated, had good behavior and manners, valued loyalty and principles, and did not covet official positions or wealth. Japanese samurai were not engaged in productive work. No matter what the lord thought or pursued, blind loyalty was the greatest virtue. On the other hand, Seonbi of Joseon is expressed by the word principle. Their main characteristic is their uprightness, which did not yield to what they considered right even in front of the king. It seems that such a Seonbi spirit remains as a standard for a righteous life at the base of Korean consciousness due to the ideological fixation tendency of Koreans. It is my opinion that Seonbi spirit is working as a underlying strength to lead Korean society into a just society.

Koreans have excellent strong viability.

About 70% of the soil on the Korean Peninsula is old and mountainous. Most of them are granite grounds and are acidic barren sandy soils with a lot of quartz sand. There are many rocks in the mountainous areas, and any potential arable lands contain many pebbles of various sizes. Since it is old soil, it has been washed away by rain over time and contains almost no organic or inorganic matter. Most of them are poor soils where farming does not provide high return.

There is a big difference when comparing the animals and plants that live in old geological foundations, topography, and barren soils with those that live in ever-changing young geological foundations, topography, and fertile soils. In the case of former, generally, there are few species and they grow slowly. They don't grow into a lush forest. However, they contain strong viability. Characteristics of the typical native animals and plants of the Korean Peninsula such as crucian carp, pine trees, and grass. Found in almost all rivers on the

Korean peninsula, carp are omnivores. It is a fish with excellent adaptability to changes in the environment. Pine trees, which grow in almost all areas of the Korean Peninsula, are heliophyte. It has green leaves all year round. It takes root deeply and grows well even in barren places where other trees are difficult to grow. Korean grass, which is a completely crawling type and widely distributed in the Korean Peninsula, also has a strong sideways crawling nature. It withstands well the pressure of stepping on it. It is resistant to pests and pollution making it easy to manage. As such, common native animals and plants inhabiting the Korean Peninsula have one similarity: their strong ability to survive and adapt to the environment. Its characteristic is that its shape or color is not flashy or beautiful, but it is almost unchanged throughout the four seasons.

People whose livelihood is farming usually settle in one place. They have a conscious awareness that they can live by farming as long as they have land to cultivate. They think they can reap as much as they put in effort. People who have lived in barren soil have a stronger sense of this tendency. Most of the soil on the Korean Peninsula is very barren. Disasters such as droughts and floods are frequent. Korean ancestors lived while adapting to such a dynamic environment. In the modern era, the population has increased explosively, and there has been reckless logging without accounting for planting. It was a series of vicious cycles in which mountains and fields became more barren and farmland became less fertile. As a result, entering the late Joseon Dynasty, their lives became more difficult. Such a vicious cycle continued until the early 1960s when Korea fell into the position of one of the world's poorest countries. The descendants of those who survived such adverse conditions are today's Koreans. It is natural that they, like the typical native animals and plants inhabiting the Korean Peninsula, have strong viability to the environment.

Koreans have strong adaptability to environmental changes.

Koreans have a strong ability to adapt to environmental changes. Adaptability refers to the ability to adapt to a changing environment. In other words, Koreans have an excellent adaptational characteristics to suit changes in the environment. These characteristics are thought to be one of the genetic factors that have become habitual to Koreans in the process of fighting for generations to survive in the Korean Peninsula where the living conditions were not comfortable at all.

When the environment changes and life becomes difficult, people abandon the place where they used to live in search of a better living environment. Or they seize from the outside whatever that may help them survive. Otherwise, people have to adapt to the changed environment by disasters or calamities. At this time, an indomitable will to survive may be required. It is said that the early ancestors of Koreans were northern horsemen who were active, sometimes aggressive, and fluid. Nevertheless, whenever faced with a difficult environment of life and death, Koreans did not try to solve the problem externally. It is not clear whether the reason was because they were innately a peace-loving people, because they liked agricultural life, because they did not have the ability to do so, or because they were afraid of adventure. Rather, they tried to overcome disasters or calamities from within by themselves. In the course of extreme struggle against natural (天災) or man-made disasters (人災), the ability to adapt to sudden environmental changes determines life and death. 「Fluidity」, which is referred to as one of the habits and inclinations of Koreans, is used in the process of adapting to survive sudden environmental changes. It seems that Koreans have developed excellent adaptability to environmental changes in order to survive in the process of resolutely fighting against sudden natural disasters, man-made disasters, and aggression from neighboring countries.

In 2011, the International Institute for Management Development (IMD) in Switzerland conducted a survey on people's acceptance of change. It was indexed by asking foreigners residing in each country to rate the respective people's acceptance to changes. According to the released data, Koreans' "acceptance to change index" was 6.96, the second highest only after the United States, which recorded 7.22. This is an objective proof that Koreans are highly adaptable to environmental changes.

Let's enumerate a recent case related to the adaptability of Koreans to environmental changes. In 2019, the Japanese government took retaliatory action against the South Korean Supreme Court's ruling in a forced labor lawsuit against Nippon Steel, as well as a ruling ordering the company's assets to be seized and sold if the company wouldn't compensate. Japan immediately took retaliatory action and amended the export control regulations to Korea. Export restrictions were imposed on three key items, including the photoresist used in the process of semiconductors and display production. It was intended to deal a blow to the semi-conductor industry which has supported the Korean economy accounting for about 20% of Korea's total exports and about 10% of the country's total manufacturing output. Such a move by Japan was an act of breaking trust in the supply chain coming from Japan. Also, since the measure was a retaliatory in nature, it violated international law, and the Korean government first protested Japan's unfair actions. But above all, to solve the problem, the Korean industry quickly turned to domestic and other foreign markets. At the government level, in the mid- to long-term, a policy to reorganize the value chain of semiconductor materials, parts, and equipment centered on domestic industries was established and implemented. As of 2021, Korea has significantly lowered its dependence on Japan for key materials by implementing a localization policy and diversification of supply chain. As a result, for the three key materials that Japan intensively blocked from exporting, the supply chain was stabilized by reducing imports from Japan, using alternative materials, and securing new suppliers. According to government data, the scale of major semiconductor materials imports from Japan in 2021 compared to 2019 was reduced to 1/6 of high-purity hydrogen fluoride and 1/2 of photoresist. The Japanese government's intention to hurt the Korean economy was completely missed. Rather, it served as an occasion for Korea to diversify its dependence on other foreign countries for its major industrial raw materials and to lead the localization of its materials and equipment industry. It strengthened Korea's industrial base. On the contrary, Japan suffered a major blow to its home materials, parts and equipment industry.

In the Analects of Confucius, it said, "If a person is agile, it can be a strength."[4] It seems like a word that represents Koreans responding to changes with agility and achieving unexpected results. As in the case above, whenever difficult conditions arose in the course of economic growth, Koreans used the crisis as an opportunity by displaying agile adaptability to environmental changes. Taking it as an opportunity to grow one step further, Korea has achieved prosperity that no one thought of today. It is my opinion that it was possible only because Koreans have strong adaptability to the changing environment.

Most Koreans are very settled and diligent.

This is also the influence of living in an agricultural society in a place where the four seasons are distinctive. To cultivate land and farm in a certain area, you must stay there for a

---

4) The Analects of Confucius, Part 6

certain period of time. This is because it takes a certain period of time from planting the seeds to harvesting the fruits. Crops must be tended continuously until harvest. As one gets to stay like that, one will get used to the local environment and adapt. Unless there is a complete disaster that forces them to move, rather than moving to another place, they stay in the place where they have been farming and continue farming. As this cycle is repeated, people in agricultural societies naturally form the disposition to settle down and live in the place where they have been farming. This also means that even if, due to unavoidable circumstances, they had to move their place of living to another place to start farming, they would have to immediately adapt to the environment there and settle down.

The ancestors of Koreans settled on the Korean Peninsula from B.C. and made a living through agriculture. The Korean Peninsula is surrounded by the sea to the east, south and west except for the rough north being connected to Asia. Their livelihood was not a condition where they could escape by moving to another place even if a disaster occurred. They have lived by overcoming and adapting to the natural disasters that occur in such topographical conditions. Maybe because it has become a habit, even today, most Koreans seem to have a strong tendency to settle there rather than searching for or moving to a better place once they get to live in one place.

I would like to introduce a case[4] showing the settlement of certain Koreans about 100 years ago. This is part of the report on the 「Koreans in the Yeonheukryonggang region」 of the Russian Imperial Decree published in 1912. The report mentions the settlement of Koreans who were hired as laborers at the Blagoveshchensk alluvial gold placer in Siberia. The report said "Workers include Chinese, Japanese and Koreans. Usually, Koreans build houses surrounded by logs at their own expense. In the case of people with families, Korean wives receive wages for sewing or washing clothes for other Korean or Chinese workers while their husbands are out for work. Koreans are generally well-behaved and good-natured. They also get along well with Russians. They drink, but they don't do violent things under the influence of heavy drinks. They don't like to make a fuss. They do not gamble or take opium. Unlike the Chinese, they do not harm their compatriots or foreigners for the purpose of robbery or murder. The disease rate among Koreans is very low compared to that among Russians. This is because Koreans are clean. However, what is unusual is that even if they are sick, they are rarely treated by a doctor, and usually resort to treatment with home medicine. Korean workers rarely move or fluctuate in numbers. This is because they became accustomed to living in the jungle around the alluvial gold placer while working for a long time and are reluctant to move. Most of them settle in one place to grow vegetables or breed horses. At first, only cabbage and radish were grown. In recent years, sweet potatoes and other vegetables are also grown. Gold miners gave Joseon people yeonmaek, a kind of oat, and they cultivate it in the hollow of the placer and sell the harvested yeonmaek as food for the horses in the placer."

From the point of view of the person in charge of the placer, the Koreans were evaluated as the best among the yellow people. As an only negative factor for Joseon people, they point out that they tend to be indigenous and settled. However, the indigenous Russian people believed that the settlement of Koreans around the placer did not harm the regional interest of Russians. It is written that the reason for this was because the placer farm was in the jungle and surrounded by the marshland, making it difficult to move and live. It has been a record that even the indigenous Russian people could not migrate and live in that land, but the Joseon people cultivated and achieved satisfying results. And it also mentioned that the indigenous people also benefited from locally procuring products that had previously been procured from afar. Looking at this record, it is truly amazing to see how strong the settlement tendency of Joseon people had been.

Unlike hot regions where farming can be done in all seasons, the Korean Peninsula has four distinct seasons. If you want to farm in an area with the four distinct seasons, you must not miss the timing. If you miss the time to sow, there is nothing to reap. If the weeding season is missed, the harvest will be reduced. If you miss the timing of harvesting, farming can be ruined. it's an environment where you can't survive if you're not diligent. This is the reason why people living in agricultural societies in regions with four distinct seasons are diligent. In addition to this, Koreans have enjoyed wearing white clothes from generation to generation, but white clothes have a downside that is difficult to maintain. In order to weave white fabric, a bleaching process is required. It takes a lot of work to take care of bleached fabric so that it doesn't become filthy. Koreans have always worn white clothes the most, even though they have lived in a farming environment with dust and sweat. It would have been impossible if Korean grandmothers and mothers were not diligent. It can also be said that the well known habitual diligence of Koreans is due to the influence of these four seasons and the preference for wearing white clothes.

Koreans have a strong passion for higher places.

One of the characteristics of Koreans is their intense passion for higher places. This, too, is one of the characteristics uniquely shaped by environmental influences. In a competitive environment, it is natural to have a strong comparative psychology and competitive spirit. As mentioned earlier, Koreans have lived in an agricultural society in the Korean Peninsula, where geology, topography, climate, and geopolitical factors were extremely challenging. For those who make a living by farming on limited farmland, when the population grows exponentially and the number of mouths to feed increases, they instinctively seek a breakthrough for survival. Externally, they may attack other countries and plunder food. Internally, even a palm-sized piece of land will not be wasted, and even mountainous areas will be reclaimed and used as farmland. I don't know if it was because Korean ancestors were a people who loved peace. They did not try to solve the problem of eating and living externally, but instead have tried to solve it internally while adapting to the environment.

As mentioned above, according to records such as the Annals of the Joseon Dynasty, the population of the Korean Peninsula was less than 1 million at the time of the founding of Joseon in the 14th century. At the beginning of the 20th century, there were more than 10 million people, more than tenfold in 500 years. In just 40 years from 1910 to 1950 when the Korean War broke out, the population of North and South Korea reached 26 million. The population had increased exponentially. This might be due to advances in medical technology. Such an increase in population on a small Korean peninsula meant an increase in the number of hungry people in inverse proportion. It is no exaggeration to say that the ancestors of Koreans, who lived mostly through agriculture, with the exception of a few landlords and bureaucrats, always lived in hunger as population increased. Among many North Korean compatriots today, there are many people who would say that "I wish I had eaten a lot of rice with meat soup!" Most of the ancestors of Koreans in the past may have lived like their North Korean compatriots today. Let's apply psychologist Maslow's 5-level theory of human needs to Korean ancestors. According to his theory, human needs form a series of stages in order of importance, from the most urgent to the least urgent. It is said that the first need is stronger than the need to achieve at the next level, and only when urgent need is satisfied, it is transferred to the next level of needs. Korean ancestors lived without satisfying the physiological needs to avoid hunger and maintain life, which is the first-level physiological need that humans must satisfy most basically for survival. It can be seen that the satisfaction of physiological needs to avoid hunger to maintain a normal state of the body was the highest priority in life among the basic needs of food, clothing and shelter. The lower the level of need, the more intense it appears. This represents that Korean ancestors have always lived with intense desire, with the first priority being the satisfaction of the basic need to solve hunger in order to survive. They had always lived with a strong desire to eat well in the midst of hunger. For this reason, it seems that Koreans have a passion for a higher place, hoping for a better life than the reality. In modern terminology, 「Hungry spirit」 is defined as "the attitude of working hard at anything with the mindset of having nothing to loose, like being poor and hungry." It can be said that most Koreans still have such an attitude. I wonder if Korea became an advanced country today because of the hungry spirit inherent in Koreans.

Characteristics shaped by historical influences

The basis for the claim of 5,000-year history of the Korean people first appeared in 『Samguk Yusa(三國遺事, Memorabilia of Three Kingdoms)』 written by monk Il-yeon during the reign of King Chungnyeol of Goryeo. Also, in the Book of Wei (魏書), a Chinese history book, there is a record that says "2,000 years ago, there was a man named Dangun Wanggeom (檀君王儉), who set up the capital in Asadal and established a country called Joseon, at the same time as King Yao of China." From these references, we can assume that the myth of Dangun, which explains the process of formation and growth of Gojoseon, is based on the historical facts. This is because the historical facts of mankind had developed into myths in the process of being relayed orally for a long period of time. Gojoseon was invaded and perished by the Han Dynasty of China in 108 B.C. Then the era of three kingdoms began. The history of struggle between the three kingdoms of Goguryeo, Baekje, and Silla, which were founded at around at the end of B.C., battled against each other until the middle of the 7th century. Eventually, after unification by Silla, Silla dominated the Korean Peninsula until the middle of the 10th century.

Goguryeo, which expanded its influence to Manchuria and Liaodong before the unification of the three kingdoms, was so strong that it was inevitable to cause armed conflict with the unified dynasties of China. At the end of the 6th century, the Sui Dynasty, which unified China, invaded Goguryeo, but was defeated and the dynasty was eventually perished. In the Tang Dynasty that followed Sui, the emperor himself directly invaded Goguryeo in the middle of the 7th century. In the end, he was defeated and withdrew. At the time of Goguryeo, the northern Korean people had successfully stopped the invasions of the Sui and Tang dynasties, the great unified empires of China, with their own abilities. Since the unified Silla, the history of the Korean people has been unilaterally invaded by neighboring countries except for a few minor incursion cases. Every time the balance of power in their neighboring countries changed, they were invaded and their land was destroyed. The people suffered miserable humiliation, being slaughtered or taken as slaves. It is reported that during the period of Joseon and Goryeo dynasties, there were 128 invasions during the Goryeo Dynasty and 56 invasions during the Joseon Dynasty, totaling 184 invasions.[5] For 993 years, from the foundation of Goryeo in 918 to the collapse of Joseon in 1910, Koreans were invaded every 5.4 years on average by foreign countries. How horrible it must have been with such intensely frequent foreign invasions?

Korean ancestors fought against Mongolia, which was the most powerful dynasty in the world during the 13th century, for 40 years. Although Goryeo's mountains and rivers were devastated, they survived by resisting with guerrilla tactics and field clearing tactics. In the late 16th century and early 17th century, it was invaded by Japan and the Manchus. The capital, Hanyang, was occupied, the palace was burned down, and the entire country was devastated. Every corner of the country was depopulated by looting, murder, and arson, but it managed to survive. Then again, in 1910, Joseon finally collapsed and became a colony of Japan. Due to the policy of plundering land and forests by Japan, most of the peasantry were forced to become serfs of landowners. Around the end of the 1920s, many people were unable to withstand the harsh Japanese exploitation and abandoned their hometowns and left for places such as Manchuria. The ancestors of today's Koreans are those who never left the Korean Peninsula. They are people who have survived harsh trials while maintaining their own culture. That's not all. After liberation in 1945, the fratricidal war, which began with North Korea's invasion of the South in 1950, continued for three years and one month until the armistice was signed in 1953. The Korean War was one of the most disastrous wars in history. In both South and North Korea, about 2 million people lost their lives. The material damage was also severe, and more than a third of houses and social overhead capital were destroyed. Today, Koreans are the people or their descendants who have survived tenaciously without dying in an impoverished situation where there is literally nothing left.

Koreans are proud of being a single nation with a long history of Hongik-Ingan ideology.

For many Koreans, the Hongik Ingan (弘益人間, Humanitarian Ideal) ideology seems to be cherished as an incredibly important value in their lives. This means that most Koreans' values act 'to benefit human society' as mentioned in the founding myth of Gojoseon, Dangun, who they consider to be their founder. The myth of Dangun that Koreans are proud of reflects the historical fact that Gojoseon was established during the Bronze Age. In the myth of Dangun, Gojoseon was founded by the union of the Hwanung tribe, who claimed to be descendants of God, and the bear tribe, who worshiped the bear as their totem. The perception of Dangun Joseon has changed over time. During the Three Kingdoms Period of Goguryeo, Baekje, and Silla, Dangun was not considered the origin of our nation. In fact, each kingdom had their own version of the nation was founded. Later, when Silla emphasized the unification of the three kingdoms, the idea that the three Korean dynasties became one for the first time began.

At the end of the 13th century, Goryeo, as a sister state of Mongolia, was partially ran by Mongolian dispatched supervisors. At that time, Lee Seung-hyu, a civil minister and scholar, wrote the history book 「Jewangungi(帝王韻紀)」. In it, he incorporated the myth of Dangun, which had been handed down as a myth until Korean history suggested that the Korean people built up one nation with Dangun as its founder. In addition, by emphasizing that the Korean people were unique and independent, making it distinct from the Han people in China. Here, he induced each citizen to be prideful and mindful. It was to unite the people by instilling national consciousness in order to stand against Mongolia's political interference. Later, the question of "Who is the founder of Koreans?" was raised. In the early Joseon Dynasty, Dangun was confirmed as the founder of the Korean people. The name Joseon is also derived from the name of Dangun Joseon.

Joseon tried to control regional sentiment under the banner of a single nation by putting Dangun as the founder of the Korean people. King Sejong built a Dangun Shrine in Pyongyang and held ancestral rites. On Manisan Mountain in Ganghwa-do, there is Chamseongdan, which is said to have been built by Dangun to hold ancestral rites to the heaven. During the Goryeo and Joseon Dynasties, national ancestral rites were actually performed for Dangun. In this way, from Goryeo to Joseon, nation-wide events were held on the premise that Dangun was the founder of all Korean people. The belief that Dangun was the founder of Korea naturally became true for all Koreans.

In parallel, research on Gojoseon was actively conducted after the 13th century. Since then, whenever the country faced difficulties due to foreign invasion, the leaders of the nation widely emphasized the historicity, longevity, and unity of the Korea to the people in order to overcome the national crisis. At the end of the Joseon Dynasty, when the Japanese invasion began in earnest, Daejonggyo, which deified Dangun, appeared and spread the faith of Dangun. During the Japanese colonial period, the faith of Dangun served as the spiritual pillar of its national movement. In order to mobilize national capabilities, some politicians, scholars, and journalists at the time emphasized the unity of Koreans across the nation. As a result, many Koreans today have come to think that they are descendants of the same ancestor with a long history.

When was Gojoseon founded? Also on the Korean Peninsula, agriculture began to develop during transitional period from the Neolithic Age to the Bronze Age. The influence of the Bronze Age culture led to the creation of private property and created a gap between the rich and the poor. It naturally led to the development of class system and the emergence of ruling class. A society that was different from the previous egalitarian one was created and new social order was established. It is estimated that Gojoseon was founded during this time period. It is said that the founding ideology of Gojoseon was Hongik Ingan (弘益人間).[5] During the reign of King Sejong, research on Gojoseon was actively conducted. Since then, Hongik Ingan, the founding ideology of Gojoseon, has been handed down from generation to generation as the prime ideology for the politics and education in Korea. The term Hongik Ingan comes from 『Samguk Yusa』 which read that Gojoseon made this its founding ideology. Hongik Ingan was also adopted as a

---

5) The word Hongik Ingan is a word that appears in the contents of the founding process of Gojoseon in Gojoseonjo of 「Samguk Yusa」 and Jeonjoseongi of 「Jewangungi」, and it means "broadly benefiting the human world."

formal educational ideology for Korea. According to Article 1 of the Education Act, enacted and promulgated on December 31, 1949 (currently Article 2 of the Framework Act on Education), "Education is for all citizens under the ideology of Hongik Ingan... Its purpose is to contribute to the realization of the ideal of co-prosperity for all mankind." At the time, the Ministry of Education said that Hongik Ingan was an ideology consistent with the basic spirit of democracy, and that it was an educational ideology, considering it as an ideal of all mankind that was in line with the spirit of philanthropy in Christianity, benevolence in Confucianism, and mercy in Buddhism. In the hearts of Koreans today, the ideology of Hongik Ingan aims to contribute to the realization of the ideal of co-prosperity of mankind by benefiting human society widely, the highest value in their lives. For that reason, many Koreans are proud of the fact that they are a single ethnic nation based on the Hongik Ingan ideology, with Dangun as its founder.

Koreans have a strong sense of indomitable resistance to foreign powers.

Even an insignificant creature desperately resists to survive when faced with danger. How much more would people do!

The history of Koreans has been a series of national crises due to its geopolitical environment. For generations, Koreans have been acutely aware of the fact that when the country is weak, the people get harassed. Koreans have resisted foreign invasion with an indomitable sense of resistance. Goguryeo did not succumb to the enormous pressure of China's Sui and Tang dynasties and fought back and confidently defeated them. Goryeo stubbornly resisted the invasions of Khitan and Mongol on several occasions. During the 40-year war with Mongolia, the incompetent government fled to Ganghwa island for their own safety, but the people stood up and resisted. In Joseon people united and stopped the numerous invasions of the country by Japanese and Manchu forces. In particular, during the Imjin and Jeongyujaeran, monks and righteous civil soldiers willingly sacrificed their lives to stop the Japanese army. Even under Japanese colonial rule, Koreans took part in the March First independence movement risking their lives against the Japanese military forces. The cases presented above show how strong the Korean people's indomitable sense of resistance to foreign aggression is. Then, what is the psychological background that gave Koreans an indomitable sense of resistance against foreign invasion?

Koreans have prided themselves on being a nation with a

long history like China. Independence spirit was strong with being a single nation that has a long history with Dangun Wanggeom of Gojoseon as its founder. As a result, Goguryeo defeated large Chinese invasions twice and Silla also confidently defeated Chinese interference after the unification of the Three Kingdoms. Since then, it appears that the consciousness of being a nation that inherited the strength of Goguryeo and the independence of Silla seems to have been embodied in the ancestors of Koreans. In addition, judging from the fact that Hongik Ingan was set as the founding ideology of Gojoseon in the Dangun myth, the belief that Koreans are the people who follow the reason and order of nature to widely benefit the human world seems to have been transmitted.

This is backed up with the following historical facts. In 1270, Goryeo reconciled with Mongolia, who had been fighting for nearly 40 years. However, Goryeo became their son-in-law's country, and the independence of the Korean people was in danger of being greatly damaged due to the stripping of their culture and political interference. Then, in order to overcome this, Il-yeon's 「Samguk Yusa」 and Lee Seung-hyu's 「Jewangungi」 appeared to describe Korean history on an equal footing with Chinese history. Even under the Japanese colonial rule in the early 20th century, when the independence of the Korean people was greatly damaged, Park Eun-sik's 「Korean Tongsa」 and Shin Chae-ho's 「Chosun Sanggosa」, which were compiled to awaken the sense of independence, appeared. These are examples showing that Koreans thought that they had the same level of longevity as the Chinese, had an equal history, and had a strong sense of independence with Hongik Ingan as their identity.

The followings are press reports from Korea under Japanese colonial rule.[6] Koreans evaluated themselves as"Koreans are docile and without cruelty. They are not barbaric and consider ethics and morality as the highest virtue. They are superior in terms of health. They have both continental, maritime, and island characteristics. Peaceful but they are full of courage. Simple, but never foolish." This suggests that Koreans thought that they were "those who benefit the human world according to the order of nature".

As such, it can be seen that Koreans have lived with pride as being part of a nation that benefits the human world and has strong autonomy due to the historical longevity and homogeneity with Dangun Wanggum as its founding father. They have had a strong sense of resistance against foreign aggression that has damaged their self-esteem. In addition, it is my opinion that the view of the state of Confucianism, which was introduced from China, further strengthened the consciousness of indomitable resistance to foreign powers. Confucianism, which was introduced to the Korean peninsula during the Three Kingdoms Period, had been established as an ideology of the ruling class since the Goryeo Dynasty. By the way, one of the highest values pursued in Confucianism is "GyeonRiSaEui GyeonWiSuMyeong (見利思義 見危授命)."[6] For Confucian scholars and students, when the country is in trouble, the greatest virtue is to sacrifice one's life to protect their country. As such ideas became clear, Koreans rose up resolutely and resisted, regardless if they were rich or poor whenever their country was in trouble. At the end of the Goryeo Dynasty or the late Joseon Dynasty, even though the government was helplessly incompetent, bureaucrats were corrupt, and people's lives were ruined, massive uprising to overthrow government did not occur. Even if a uprising occurred, it was easily subjugated even by weak government forces because it could not get a justification from people. Koreans have been resisting foreign aggression for a long time from generation to

---

6) As part of the content in the 13th section of the Analects, it means "If you see a profit right in front of your eyes, you should think about whether it is right (Gyeonrisaeui), and if the country is endangered, you should sacrifice your life to protect it (Gyeonwisumyeong)."

generation, and it seems that the indomitable sense of resistance to foreign forces and the idea of "viewing the world" are imprinted in their minds.

Their self-protection tendency is strongly inherent.

In the 1920s, Japanese commented that Koreans lacked courage, are cowardly, and good at the art of self-protection.[7] Even today, many Koreans hesitate to come forward with words and actions that hold them to be responsible. They would rather wait for someone to speak and act first. Then, trying it after examining the circumstances is considered as a wisdom of life.

It can be said that words and actions of Koreans' strong self-protection tendency and their reluctance to step forward are due to the geology, topography, and soil of the Korean Peninsula. It is similar to the habits of the elderly. I believe that it is a characteristic that has been imprinted due to historical events that occurred in the Joseon Dynasty. During the Joseon Dynasty, there were incidents in which the courageous words and actions of scholars or politicians sometimes brought about the disaster of self and the extinction of family. These events casted a great shadow on the political history of the Joseon Dynasty.

The ruling ideology of the Joseon Dynasty was Neo-Confucianism. In Neo-Confucianism, power itself was the goal and the highest value. Confucian ideology has the tendency of dividing only right from wrong. Such attributes have led to divisions among bureaucrats into those who are right and those who are not. With this ideological background of Confucianism, struggles to gain power occurred in the Joseon Dynasty from the beginning of its founding. The 1st and 2nd prince's rebellion to gain power, King Sejo's Gyeyujeongnan, who executed Sayuksin (Six Dead Loyalists) who rose against him, and the four major factional wars[7] during the reigns of Yeonsangun and Myeongjong are examples of such events. Every time a power struggle incident occurred, many bureaucrats were harmed. In order to maintain their power, they brutally killed or exiled the opposing forces just because they were political opponents. In the process, so many people suffered unjustly. The desperate death in prison from the expulsion of political opponents led to a vicious

---

7) During the 47 years from the 4th year of King Yeonsangun to the years of King Myeongjong, the four major factional wars between the Hungu faction, which emphasized Chinese literature and task guidelines necessary for passing the civil service exam, and the Neo-Confucian faction/Sarim faction, an emerging political force that emphasized the realization of royal politics and Confucian classics, resulted brutal executions and purges of the opposition.

cycle in which more deaths in prison were evoked when the tide was reversed. Factional conflicts or wars arose in this process.

In the late 16th century, Sarim faction took the realm. As the number of yangban, ruling class, who wanted to enter the political arena increased, competition, confrontation, and antagonism among the yangban were inevitable. It was an environment for the inevitable emergence of Bundang (factional) politics in a colonial perspective. Early on, Bungdang politics still recognized the opposing political factions as critical but balancing power. As time passed and the confrontation between the factions of Bundang intensified, it degenerated into an all-out war to remove the opposing political forces from the political stage altogether. The prime example was the Hwanguk (State Affair Turnover, 還國), the process of three consecutive factional leadership changes during the reign of King Sukjong (1674-1720). Chaos in state affairs had begun as they all pursued only personal or family interests. The power struggle gradually intensified into a "life or death" battle. The people who seized power survived, and the yangban who were driven out perished. Through these political conflict, the Yangban class walked the path of self-banishment.

Since the middle of the 18th century, the Bungdang politics had degenerated into a one-party despotism, and the kingship became unstable. This is the reason why Tangpyeongron, the equal opportunity policy, came to the forefront. As royal authority weakened after Sunjo, the era of Sedo politics began, in which the maternal family monopolized state affairs. A very small number of people from a specific family monopolized power and ran the country for the benefit of their own family. The political order began to fall into rupture. It had become a society where the Sedo family monopolized high-ranking government posts and engaged in trafficking of official posts. The trafficking of the high-ranking positions led to the trafficking of low-ranking positions. In the end, it was a structure in which only the innocent people located at the bottom suffered. The people had to pay all sorts of outrageous taxes. They were arrested for the sins they never committed and they had to pay a fortune to get released. This was the picture of Joseon society in the 19th century, where justice was completely missing.

After obtaining positions, officials who led politics in the Joseon Dynasty made a distinction between enemies and comrades in order to survive. They rallied their faction through the abuse of power. It didn't matter how high or low the position was or whether or not they contributed to the country. Simply because they were against to the opposing faction, they were falsely accused with the causes and ethical standards that the opposing faction created. Removal from office, exile, exclusion, isolation, even beheading and bestowal of poison, were carried out without hesitation. As a result, there were numerous cases where the whole family had been annihilated for being in the wrong line with opposing point of view. There were even cases where ordinary and insignificant words or actions became a source of trouble, causing the person to be exhumed and posthumously executed, and his descendants suffered severely. How many innocent people must have suffered unjustly in the process of killing or exiling of opposition removal?

Those who were pushed out by the opposing forces for asserting their will in the political arena should feel less unfair. There were many cases where people were killed or exiled simply because they had a relationship with someone such as a family member, a relative, or a colleague. In some cases, they were degraded to slaves. There were many people who worked hard for the yangban in hopes of help and took on sins they did not bear, going through difficult labor. Most of the people who watched such a situation from the side are the ancestors of today's Koreans. How did those situations look in their eyes? How would they interpret the behavior of the victims? It's natural to think that 'It is better to avoid any potential words and/or actions that could be problematic. It is better for you not to step in before someone else does. it's a smart way not to show your feelings.' It is my opinion that these historical events in Joseon's politics further strengthened the habit of Koreans' self-protection tendency.

Koreans have a strong attachment to their possessions, and the behaviors as a socially underprivileged person still remain.

People who live in a certain areas and live on farms have a strong desire to own land. They are different from nomads who herd their livestock seasonally. The national land system of Joseon, which was represented by the Gwajeon Law[8], was changed to the landlord's system[9] and the joint farming and half return system[10] after the 16th century. As a result, most

---

8) A system in which all lands were divided into two categories by the government: public land in which the state guarantees farmers the right to cultivate and receives tax from them, and private land in which the state gives individuals the right to collect tax.
9) After the middle of the Joseon Dynasty, as land acquisition, purchase, and reclamation became active, the economic system consisted of landlords who owned land and farmers who rented it for farming.

farmers lived as tenant farmers tied to a small number of field owners or even served as servants of field owners. As the population continued to grow, the exploitation of the peasantry by the wealthy landlords intensified. Nevertheless, it became more and more difficult for tenant farmers to borrow fields. Naturally, the wages of servants continued to decrease. This vicious cycle continued until the collapse of Joseon, the Japanese occupation, and the beginning of industrialization in Korea after 1960. Most Koreans have made a living by borrowing other people's fields or becoming servants of landlords in difficult living environment for generations. Having their own lands was a longing and a dream for those who made a living by borrowing from other people's fields as a farmer or for those who lived as servants of landlords for a long time. It seems that the long aspirations and wishes of such Korean ancestors have been accumulated in the minds of their descendants. The strong attachment to the land for farming in the 1950s and 1960s and the strong attachment to a house (apartment) owned by Koreans today tell us this.

In addition, there is a common characteristic among people who have lived as tenant farmers or servants for a long time.

---

10) A system in which landlord's land is rented and cultivated under the landlord's system, in which ownership of land is recognized as an individual, and half of the harvest is given to the landlord

This is that they were not grateful to the person who lent the land or the master who provided the conditions of work. it's because they always thought they were on the losing side. Of course, everyone is fundamentally self-centered and calculating. Before one thinks about how he/she is treating the other person, one first thinks about how the other person is treating themselves, while always putting their needs first. So, from the point of view of the person receiving help, he/she always feels that "Little more help would be nice!" This is why people who receive help always think they are on the losing side. They never thanked their landlords for lending them the land or providing them with a job. They thought that the contract between them and the landlords was fundamentally unequal as a contract between the haves and the have-nots. In addition, since they got paid for their hard work, they see absolutely no reason to be grateful. As mentioned above, most of today's Korean ancestors lived difficult lives as tenant farmers or servants. From generation to generation, the habit of being an underdog has become habitual in the bottom of the mind, and most Koreans have a strong innate tendency to be very calculating and ungrateful. It is my opinion that there are still socially underprivileged Koreans who do not know how to thank even those who helped.

Koreans are conscious of the self-centered idea of equality.

For Koreans, the idea of equality is strongly conscious through the period of political chaos under Japanese colonial rule and post-liberation, land reform in 1950, the Korean War, and expansion of educational opportunities. Nevertheless, because it has been influenced by Confucianism for a long time, their sense of equality is quite self-centered. Joseon was thoroughly ruined while going through the Japanese colonial rule. The existing authority of the ruling class, such as the royal family or the yangabn, was not recognized. Moreover, with the liberation, western culture was introduced and modernization was promoted in a rapid pace. In the process, the existing social order fell into chaos. Perception of traditional culture, gentry, and existing intellectuals was disparaged. As Korea went through a period of social chaos with colonial rule, liberation, and the indiscriminate flood of Western culture, many remnants of pre-modern inequality disappeared in Korean society.

Immediately after the outbreak of the Korean War on June 25th, Korea was ruled under communist occupation, albeit for a short period of less than three months, except for some south eastern Gyeongnam regions including Busan. While under communist rule, many people's statuses were reversed up and down. The communist occupiers put forward people from the lower classes as the communist proxy. Also, during the war, 3 million people, or three-eighths of North Korea's population, came down to South Korea. Without knowing each other's past identities, they mixed with South Koreans and lived on an equal footing. It was an opportunity to eradicate feudal remnants, such as the Bansang (班常) class system, which divided Korean society into yangban and low class, which had dominated Korean society for a long time. The Korean War caused enormous loss of lives and properties. However, it also served as an opportunity to thoroughly remove the remnants of pre-modern traditions and social order that no kind of internal revolution would achieve.[8]

The land reform implemented by the Syngman Rhee regime in 1950 aimed at democratizing rural areas and rationalizing agricultural production and distribution. To this end, owner-ship of the land was transferred from the absent landlords to farmers. The impact of land reform, which focused on protecting farmers engaged in farming, was substantial. The landlord class disappeared, and most tenant farmers were replaced by independent farmers. This also served as an opportunity to remove invisible class remnants between the haves and the have-nots. In addition, following the implementation of President Syngman Rhee's national education priority policy after the Korean War, many citizens received democratic higher education, and the idea of equality took root in Korean society following the spread of the ideology of liberal democracy.

True democratic equality refers to the equality that respects the equality of others. This is a social equality concept, which means that the freedom and rights of the other person should be respected as much as I want my freedom and rights to be respected by others, and that I fulfill my responsibilities that stem from my freedom and rights. But unfortunately for Koreans, as the ideology of equality was being embodied in the 20th century, it was established against the background of differential Confucianism. As a result, the idea of equality embodied in them is self-centered and self-advantageous. This is also a tendency that has been instilled in them through fierce competitions for survival from generations in the past. Koreans' self-centered ideology of equality literally claims that everyone is equal, claiming only their freedom and rights. They have no regard for their own obligations that they have to abide by. They are not interested in the freedom or rights of others. At the same time, it strongly demands the observance of the duty of others. That is the proof that Koreans' ideology of equality is self-centered and self-advantageous. But still, it is also true that the consciousness of equality among Koreans has played a large role as a driving force for the success of the Saemaul movement and political democratization.

The past generations of Koreans were transformed into today's Koreans with strong passion and conviction through the Saemaul movement.

A 'yeopjeon' is an old round coin made of brass with a square hole in the middle. Until the 1970s, some Koreans even demeaned themselves by labeling them as Yeopjeon. Koreans disparaged themselves, and they used the word Yeopjeon a lot in the sense of self-torture by saying "Yeopjeon did it, and that's the limit isn't it?, I really don't like it!, No matter how hard I try, but that's what it is!"

This may be due to the influence of instilling a colonial view during the 36-year Japanese rule. Perhaps this is due to the many restrictions and restraints on the rights that Koreans should have if they were citizens of a sovereign state under Japanese colonial rule. No matter how hard they worked to develop their abilities and master their skills, they were not in a position to unfold their will normally. Even if one had the ability and the skills, there was no way at all to unfold them. What would happen when one hits a wall where one cannot pursue their will and gets frustrated? People fall into a state of desperation. It is my opinion that such a vicious cycle had continued and became ingrained. Moreover, many believed that things would get better after liberation in 1945, but the country was divided into South and North Korea. The intensifying of the ideological conflict between the East and the West further plunged politics and society into chaos. In the end, the foundation of life was ruined by killing and destruction while going through the Korean War of fratricide. It was an almost hopeless life on the ruins. It was the life of a citizen in the world's poorest country, which made it difficult to find anything to eat. I believe that those are the reasons why the self-torturing sense of self-desperation thinking dominated most Koreans at the time.

Until the early 1960s, Korea's main industry was agriculture. In societies based on agriculture, if agricultural productivity does not increase proportionally with population growth, hungry people are bound to get hungrier. As mentioned earlier, since the mid-Joseon period, farmers, most of whom were tenant farmers, had to pay more and more fees over the years in order to rent the same size of tenant farmland. The vicious cycle of reduced wages for wage earners continued. Korean ancestors had to fight more fiercely to survive. Seriously, at the end of Joseon dynasty, even though they knew that the fate of Joseon would get worse like a candle in the wind. If Japan won at the Russo-Japanese War, why would many Koreans greatly blessed Japan's victory? Some even said that most of the Joseon youth did not oppose the deprivation of sovereignty in 1910. Some went further saying that they agreed to build a new Joseon culture under the auspices of Japan.[9]

Contrary to such expectations by some, the ordeal of colonial rule that befell on the Joseon people became more and more brutal. Japanese colonial rule led to military control (1910s), cultural control (1920s), and national obliteration control (1930s and afterwards). They first took the land from the Koreans via land survey project (1912~1918), then took the rice from them via the rice production improvement plan (1920~1934). Finally, they took away everything via national mobilization. The Allies' victory freed Korea from Japanese rule. They were liberated but politically and ideologically chaotic society awaited them. Instead of unification, Korea was divided into communist North and democratic South. The three-year Korean War, which broke out with the invasion of the South by the communist regime in the North, destroyed most of life. All that remained of Koreans were the ruins of their lives and the painful scars of fratricide. It was a desolate and miserable environment in which no one could see any hope. Those who survived and their descendants are today's Koreans.

In the early 1960s, the May·16 military regime initiated national economic development centered around cities. Subsequently, 「Saemaeul Movement」was adopted to literally raise the income of rural areas to the level of cities. This Saemaul movement was a 'rural modernization movement' proposed by then President Park Chung-hee on April 22, 1970. Since then, the Saemaul movement had developed and been implemented on a national level. The Saemaul movement originated from the Rural Modernization Promotion Act announced on November 1, 1969 for the modernization of rural areas. The Saemaul movement is based on Hyang-yak[11] in the Joseon Dynasty. With the people at the center, they were

---

11) During the Joseon Dynasty, a promise made among rural villagers to uphold the Confucian ethics of encouraging each other for good things, scolding for bad things, sharing correct servitude, and helping each other in disasters and difficulties.

induced to lead the social reform movement by organizing voluntary associations. On April 21, 1972, President Park Chung-hee composed and wrote the lyrics for the Saemaeul Song and disseminated it nationally, further vitalizing it.

The Saemaul movement started in the late 1960s as a small farmhouse income boost project, such as widening farm roads, weaving bales, improving roofs, and reforestation projects during the off-season. However, it laid the foundation for Korea's tremendous economic development today. It was the basis for achieving unprecedented economic growth in the world. The Saemaul movement revived the rural economy. It gave people hope that if they worked hard, they could live better. With the opening of the Gyeongbu Expressway, logistics transportation had been accelerated and the national economy began to recover. This Saemaul movement and the 5-year economic development plan became a starting point, and the Miracle on the Han River was realized today. The forest reclamation project for bald mountains was also successful. People were able to overcome the drought and flood damage that they had to endure every year. Now, Korea had become a dense forest country and the government had to spend money on thinning. As such, the pan-governmental Saemaul movement, which began in 1973, spread and developed into a nationwide movement. The Saemaul movement not only laid the groundwork for today's economic growth in Korea, but also gave Koreans the confidence that "we can live well if we work hard" and just as much the diligence to work hard "quickly and quickly".

The government-led Saemaul movement in the 1970s had turned Koreans with a strong sense of desperation and self-torture who used to say "What can we do? That's it. It's over", into Koreans with confidence and strong sense of responsibility who work passionately to achieve their goals and say that "We can do it. We have to work quickly to fulfill our responsibilities and we can achieve our goals if we do our best".

Confidence that we can do it has become a habit.

There is a Korean proverb that goes, "Even a mouse hole has a sunny day." It is thought to be a proverb that came about in the process of living through a historically harsh living environment. It means that even if it is impossible to come true, it is better to be optimistic. Compared to the early 1960s, Korea these days can be said to be more than a case of sunlight in a mouse hole. For a long time, Koreans lived their lives comforting themselves with an unachievable hopes and vaguely saying that "There will be sunny days even in a rat hole!" However, the Saemaul movement became an opportunity to feel hope and confidence that even if there was no land to farm, they could live well if they worked hard.

The Saemaul movement, which was the "consciousness reform movement" of Koreans, is being introduced as a rural village development strategy to the international community. It was a mental movement that inspired Koreans who had no hope at all to believe that they could do it too. The basic idea of the Saemaul movement was to create a better tomorrow's Saemaul (New Village) than yesterday with the spirit of "diligence, self-help, and cooperation". This also coincided with the "goal of the modernization of motherland", which was the ideology of the time to achieve national development and national revival along with the improvement of individual life and growth. Through the Saemaul movement, Koreans began to believe that "We can make it happen. We can do it." In addition to such confidence, in the 21st century, it has now laid the foundation for Koreans to have the spirit of spreading out into the world, saying, "We can become the best if we work hard." Now, some Koreans even believe in the saying, "Those who believe they can do it become like that, and even those who believe they can't do it also become like that."

It has become a habit to work quickly in order to complete the task.

The word "bballi, bballi (quickly, quickly)" seems to have become synonymous with Koreans. This is because what many foreigners say when they think of Koreans is "quickly, quickly." However, one thing to be clear is that Koreans were not innately quick-tempered. It is due to the influence of 「Saemaul movement」, which was carried out nationally in the 1970s, that in today's culture has become habitual to Koreans that even foreigners know the phrase 'quickly, quickly'. During the Saemaul movement, they rushed 'quickly, quickly' in order to finish what needed to be done in a timely manner, so it became a habit in their daily lives. In the process of implementing the Saemaul movement, Koreans had to work 'quickly, quickly'. It was because at the time, they had to simultaneously do the things they had to do by participating in the Saemaul movement for village development and completing the tasks they needed to do for their own livelihood. If they didn't hurry up early in the morning, they couldn't finish all the things they had to do. That's how 'quickly, quickly' has become a habit.

Koreans are generally seen as "being sentimental and having high emotional ups and downs." Referring to Ryu Seong-ryong's Jingbirok (Book of Correction), Koreans at the end of the 16th century were generally very impatient. It was a characteristic that whatever they do could not last long. What about now? In the eyes of foreigners, the typical temperamental characteristic of Koreans is their hasty personality of "quickly, quickly". Both are similar characteristics. On the other hand, how were Koreans seen by foreigners 100 years ago? There is a record that says, "They are easy-going, not in a hurry, and have a Yujang[12] temperament."

The following are the temperamental characteristics of Koreans observed and recorded by the Japanese between 1910 to 1924. The record[10] said that "They are relaxed, bold and calm. They have a slow-tempered personality, a personality that values a duty, and an optimism that knows how to find comfort even in tension." "Koreans do not express their emotions

12) Calm and slow-tempered

violently. Neither bitter nor frightening. There is room for all the joy and sorrow. They are mild and warm like a spring breeze. They move leisurely and unhurried. Even their gaits are relaxed and dignified, which is admirable." These attributes were mainly displayed in those who did not have to face the difficulties of living such as yangbans, landlords, and powerful families in Gyeongseong or other regions at the time. However, the book also pointed out that even if all Koreans are compared with all Japanese, these attributes of Koreans are more obvious. At that time, there were only a handful of Koreans living in Gyeongseong with an affordable livelihood plan. Most of them were living in a dangerous situation, walking downhill into poverty. The appearance of their garments or palanquins was worn out. However, their attitudes and appearances were not afraid when compared to the Japanese in similar situations. It is said that they had little or no nervous temperament.[13] Farmers in the countryside had lived in poverty for hundreds of years during the Joseon Dynasty, and the barn had been always empty due to exploitation by government offices and landlords. Nevertheless, they observed that Koreans had the same or even higher optimism and laid-back spirit than

---

13) A state of being ashamed or anxious about and noticing about belittling oneself for one's shabby or pitiful appearance

Japanese farmers. Then, it went on saying that all Koreans are generous and free-spirited. At least it seems that they had the attitude and appearance. This spirit was highly evaluated as a beautiful temperament and an advantage of Joseon people. Interestingly, the phrase "Joseon people are not in a hurry and are relaxed in everything" was also mentioned in several records of Westerners who visited Joseon 100 years ago.

But what about now after 100 years? Koreans today cannot wait patiently and they don't work with leisure. Moreover, it is far from working while waiting in consideration for the other person or resting with others. How about at work? In particular, when one is in competition with someone else, he/she is described as always rushing 'quickly, quickly' as if he/she is being chased by someone. It's not surprising that foreigners wittingly say 'quickly, quickly' when they see Koreans.

What is the reason why Koreans appear differently after the end of the 16th century, the beginning of the 20th century and the middle of the 20th century? It is a general belief that the original temperamental characteristics of each individual, naturally endowed as a human being, usually do not change.[14] But the objective temperamental characteristics of the people who make up a country are not fixed and unchanging. I think

---

14) The basic principles of Doctor Lee Je-ma's Sasang medicine

this is because it is expressed differently according to the historical experience of one's ancestors in the midst of social and environmental changes and the experiences of one's own life. In October 2000, I experienced this in the course of supervising test evaluation and negotiations for a national level large scale weapon system acquisition project with people who lived under the communist system until the mid-1980s, and I would like to share it below.

The time I met them was after more than 15 years had passed since the communist regime collapsed in their country. Nevertheless, they had no desire or attachment to the work given to them. They never acted or said anything that might entail a commitment or duty. They were only seeking self interest. It seemed that they did not feel any responsibility to the organization or country. No one was interested in test evaluation results or negotiations that might benefit their country. My colleagues and I were puzzled by their unexpected response. Having lived as a servant under the privileged minority of the communist party for nearly 70 years, I came to the conclusion that it was because the traits of a servant were engraved in them. In this way, each person's temperamental characteristics can be expressed differently by the experiences of their ancestors' life for a long time and their own experiences. Also, I think it can be seen differently depending on the viewer.

Let me summarize what has been said above. At the end of the 16th century, Joseon people seemed to be in a hurry and then quit halfway. On the other hand, Koreans in the 1910s and 1920s were laid-back and bold, and they looked relaxed. And since 1970, modern Koreans seem to be in a hurry as if they are being chased by everything. In this way, the temperamental characteristics of Koreans appeared completely different according to the times. And the way they were perceived was different.

Mr. Ryu Seong-ryong in Jingbirok (Book of Correction) criticized the Joseon people being in a hurry but quitting midway. As a leader of the government at the time, I wonder if this is what he experienced with most of government ministers during Imjin Waeran, the Japanese invasion of Korea in 1592. At that time, the so called the government ministers did not try to come up with constructive suggestions or measures to solve the problem in an emergency situation for the survival of their country. They were busy trying to read King's mind by just observing King's eyes. Depending on the situation, they just acted as if they were in a hurry. No alternatives were presented to overcome the situation. At the same time, people with the same interests formed factions to denigrate and oppose even constructive proposals from other factions. I think those were his observation watching the ministers of the government for a long time at that time.

In the early 20th century, about 300 years after that, how could the Koreans be seen by the Japanese as having a laid-back, relaxed and beautiful temperament? Japanese at the time recorded the reasons as follow.[11] First, it said that it was due to the fact that Joseon people have a character of Yujang (悠長)[15] and are not rich in emotional rage. There was a Joseon proverb that says, "the length of a Joseon people's face, pipe, and vigor reaches up to three feet." This could be an expression of the long, relaxed and calm emotions of the Joseon people, who always felt pleasure in safety. Second, it said that it originated from Joseon's extreme emphasis on courtesy at the pan-national level. As explained before, Koreans have lived with pride in the fact that the country they lived in is an "Eastern country of Courtesy." The root of courtesy lies in being generous and harmonious. Joseon people were accustomed to manners and their attitude towards Japanese people was confident. The spirit of Joseon people at the time was bound to be generous and relaxed. I have to agree

---

15) Calm and easygoing

that there are some agreeable insights in the Japanese evaluation on the calm and relaxed appearance of the Joseon people.

However, I think differently. In my view, it was because of the living conditions of the Joseon people at the time. It was an environment in which some wealthy and privileged pro-Japanese people could live comfortably by hiring people without incurring large expenses. There was no reason to feel rushed. Even in the position of those who worked for wages, they only had to work as much as they received. Then, what about some independent farmers or tenant farmers who accounted for the majority of the population at the time? No matter how hard they worked, most of them were plundered by landlords and Japanese. It was an environment where even if you worked hard, the reward would not come back to you. There was no reason to rush and work hard. In addition, it is my view that the "hypocritical formalism" of Confucianism, which was ingrained in the Joseon people for more than 500 years from generation to generation, also played a part in making the appearance of the calm and relaxed Joseon people.

Until the late 1960s, some Koreans greeted adults in the morning by saying "Have you had breakfast?" There was a saying that adults used a toothpick even when they left the house without breakfast. This means that the lives of Koreans at the time were so poor that they could not afford breakfast every morning. The latter can be said to be an aspect of emphasizing face saving that had been influenced by Confucian culture for a long time and had become a habit. I believe that the calm and relaxed appearance of Joseon people seen by the Japanese in the early 20th century was the result of a combination of the hypocritical face-saving emphasis culture at the time and the living environment in which there was no reason to work hard in a hurry.

Today, Koreans work in a hurry, "quickly, quickly." Koreans were really lazy and indolent until the early 1950s. Right before the outbreak of the Korean War on June 25, 1950, Korea carried out land reform to rationalize agricultural production and distribution. At that time, land reform made nearly 70% of the people's tenant farmers self-employed, which gave many people the opportunity to work for themselves. It served as an opportunity to change Koreans who were lazy, indolent, and irresponsible after being exploited by landlords for a long time into hard-working and diligent people. Furthermore, the Saemaul movement once again transformed diligent and hard-working Korean people, thanks to land reform, to people who work in a hurry "quickly, quickly."

More than anything, Saemaul movement is of great significance in that it was a mental movement that instilled the spirit of "we can do it too" onto Koreans. It was also a movement that turned Koreans into people who hurried "quickly, quickly" even though most of their living bases were rural areas. Through the Saemaul movement, people renovated thatch roofed houses in their villages, village roads were widened and they turned the village into a green hill, becoming a new village.

To do so, all the villagers had to begin work at dawn and even on holidays in order to do what was necessary to turn their village around. This was because, in addition to the work for the Saemaul movement, they had to do what they needed to do for their livelihood. If the work to build the Saemaul was not done at dawn or on holidays, the time to work for a living would inevitably be reduced. At that time, Koreans really couldn't finish their planned tasks unless they worked in a hurry "bbally, bbally" from dawn and even on holidays. Everyone got up early and worked together to build a new village while helping each other and sweating. Only then they took care of their personal things. This is the reason why the attitude of "quickly, quickly" in everything has naturally become a habit. In addition to this, helping yourself and others became a habit.

What motivated Koreans to actively participate in the Saemaul movement at the time? The government's complete and financial support acted as a catalyst. When the villagers cooperated with each other to renovate the village into a new one, the state supported all of the cement and iron bars, etc. for each village. In addition, support was expanded if the plan was successfully implemented on time. Simply put, because the state clearly compensated the people for their active participation in the Saemaul movement, the government made the people work "quickly, quickly" and the Saemaul movement was implemented successfully. This right government policy made the already industrious people into more diligent people who work "quickly, quickly" in anything.

It seems that in the eyes of foreigners, Koreans always seem to be in a hurry, "quickly, quickly." Today's Koreans are confident in everything they do, and most of them prioritize fulfilling their responsibilities rather than the rights they deserve. Koreans have been transformed into people who rushes quickly in order to finish things on time. Koreans value fulfilling their responsibilities above all else. It is the opinion that foreigners perceive Koreans to be in a hurry because of the sincere appearance of Koreans doing their best to complete their work. Westerners also value fulfilling their responsibilities. However, their rights to be enjoyed are as just important as responsibilities. They work only to the extent of their requirements of their responsibilities. During the winter and summer vacation seasons, they exercise their rights to have vacations to the extent that causes the company to stop operating normally. People living in hot regions have benefited from nature and did not have to work diligently. Even if people do not work diligently, they are provided with a minimum of food, clothing and shelter. In their eyes, Koreans who prioritize responsibility for the work over individual vacation rights are inevitably seen as working in a hurry "bbally, bbally" in everything.

Koreans are passionate about their work with a strong desire for achievement.

There is a movie titled "Die or Spit" directed by Greg Champion from 1990. In the mind of the author, who entered the military academy at the age of 19 in 1969 and served in the military until the age of 56, the phrase "Die or Spit" is a familiar phrase. Perhaps, it is because this die or spit mentality arose inside of me when I was in an unbearable training or situation at the military academy in my early 20s, when I became an officer and faced a situation that was physically and mentally difficult to overcome, and when math question was so difficult during my study in the United States. It is a concept that is invoked when one faces a situation that is difficult to endure. This is the phrase used when promising that one will overcome difficulties, adding, "I am not the type who backs down from difficulties like this!" However, seeing that such a word is also used in the title of an American movie, it seems to be a universal term.

The first record of "die or spit" may be Bae Su-jin, as mentioned in Samacheon's Hoieumhu Yeoljun. Bae Sujin refers to a camp built with the water at its back in preparation for a battle with an enemy located in the front. Soldiers were told, "Because you have your backs to the water, the only way to retreat is to die by drowning. The only way to survive is to fight the enemy head-on and defeat it. Let's all fight the enemy with all our lives and win!" In other words, it referred to a camp that was set up by generals to emphasize to the soldiers that they must fight in a "die or spit" manner in order to obtain a victory, no matter how slight the chances are, against a relatively strong enemy. As explained by Bae Soo-jin, the phrase "die or spit" is used when you have to risk your life for something with a desperate resolution.

Korean ancestors lived in an agricultural society on the

Korean Peninsula where the four seasons were distinctive for thousands of years. They have lived on farming as a means of livelihood on limited farmland, over 70% of which is mountainous. As the population grew exponentially in the process, they tried to solve the problem of survival internally by adapting to the environment. At the time, the four-character idiom representing the difficult life of Korean ancestors is the term Chogeunmokpi (草根木皮, the roots of herbs and barks of trees). How desperate the conditions must have been to eat grass roots and tree barks? Thanks to the wisdom of those ancestors who overcame difficulties with a die or spit attitude, Koreans today enjoy eating various wild vegetables from the mountains and seaweed products such as laver, brown seaweed/ kelp, sea lettuce, and ecklonia. However, in the past, they were a relief food eaten to avoid starvation. In particular, as the population of the Korean Peninsula continued to increase after the 16th century, most of the Korean ancestors, except for a few landlords, lived on farming but were always in short on food. Since they were constantly hungry, the Korean ancestors' priority in life was to find food to eat for survival. They have always lived with a strong desire to eat belly full, which is the primary survival need in life. It is the view that the strong desire for survival has accumulated over hundreds of years through generations of ancestors, and a strong desire of Koreans to pursue a better life than the present was engraved in their passion for what they do.

In addition, even when national economic development plan began in the 1960s, Koreans had to survive in fierce competition to become resources that could be used for economic development in an environment where only available resources were human workers. It was impossible to survive in the competition without ceaseless efforts for self-development. As economic development was promoted, life began in a fierce competition for survival to become a better human resource with a completely different character from the past. What a desperate life must it have been for the parents' generation who devoted their lives with the single-minded determination to have their children go to the first-class universities even if they could not afford for themselves! This was the modern life of Koreans during the early phases of the economic development policy. Because Koreans lived in a struggle to survive in such a fierce die or spit competition, Koreans have a strong sense of jealousy and competition.

Perhaps it could be said that the pan-national level Saemaul movement mentioned above succeeded because of such a fierce competition for survival. Through competition for better

Saemaul movement projects between villages and competition among neighbors for higher income, Koreans quickly turned into people who work passionately. Through such a remarkable transition, they have been transformed into today's Koreans with the confidence that we can do it too.

Koreans have struggled to survive for hundreds of years without even meeting their primary survival needs. As a result, they are extremely jealous and competitive, making the desire to achieve what they set out to do even more intense. Through the recent Saemaul movement, they gained the confidence that "if we try our best, we can do it too." In addition, the perception that only the strong can survive in the fierce competition has also been engraved into their minds. As a result, Koreans underestimate themselves. You care more about what you do wrong than what you do well. This is because they are deeply aware that in order to have a comparative advantage, they must be exceptional and flawless. For that reason, Koreans seem to take an extreme approach to anything. Whatever they do, once they start, they act as if they must see the end, either die or spit. Don't they drink like they're going to see the end?

There is a phrase in the Analects[16] of Confucius that said "the one who once said, always acts, and once acted, always

---

16) Analects, Jaro section 20

reaps results can be said to be a scholar." Among Koreans, there is a proverb that says "If a man draws a knife, he must at least cut a radish." Here is another expression of the proverb, "If you draw a sword, you don't sheath it as it is." This proverb is probably derived from the scholarly spirit mentioned in the Analects. Accomplishment refers to achieving a goal, and passion means to devote oneself to something with ardent affection. It is the view that anything can be achieved if you have a desire to achieve your work and strive passionately.

Now, Koreans have a strong desire to achieve their goals and they have the confidence that they can achieve their goals if they try their best. In other words, as a manifestation of the Seonbi spirit, deeply embedded in the mind of Koreans, which emphasizes that if once said, one must act, and must reap results, proving that they are passionate about what they do.

I would like to present a few examples. Golf was not a very popular sport in Korean society. However, in women's golf, which became an official Olympic event only after more than 100 years, a Korean female golfer won a gold medal at the 2016 Rio Olympics. As of May 2021, she held the record for winning 7 major tournaments, and is a major contributor to Korea's complete dominance of world women's golf for more than 10 years. Starting with Pak Se-ri's US Open Championship victory in 1998, Korean female professional golfers hold the record that at least 17 Korean female golfers have won a total of 34 major championships.[12] It is the result of the strong desire for achievement and passionate efforts by Korean female golfers.

The following is the case of 2022 Innovation Awards (CES)[13] won by Koreans. At "CES 2022," the world's largest consumer electronics and information technology (IT) exhibition held by the Consumer Technology Association (CTA) in Las Vegas, USA from January 5 to 7, 2022, 139 technologies and products from Korea won the CES Innovation Award and received the largest award. This year's CES Innovation Awards presented 623 technologies and products in 27 categories, and 416 Korean companies, the largest ever, participated and won 139 CES Innovation Awards (22.3%), breaking the record of winning technologies and products CES Innovation Awards (22.3%), breaking the record of winning 101 awards in 2020 and 100 awards in 2021. This was achieved by Korean companies steadily striving for technological innovation and product development to strengthen the competitiveness of their products in a rapidly changing environment despite the difficulties caused by the COVID-19 pandemic. Wouldn't it be the result of Koreans' strong desire to achieve their goals and the resulting 'die or spit' efforts? In addition, there are countless examples of Korean people's strong desire for achievement and passionate efforts to achieve their goals, such as the case of Korea's consecutive awards at the Skills Olympics and the case of the Korea Air Force's international air show, which will be discussed later on.

Koreans now have a strong belief that 'if you try your best to achieve your goal, you can do it'. And towards the desired goal, they work passionately with 'die or spit' mentality. What a beautiful human endeavor! Today Koreans are welcomed all over the world by people who sympathize with this attribute.

Characteristics shaped by the influence of ideology and religion

Confucianism contains the indigenous pantheistic ideas of the East. Many of the characteristics of today's daily life of Koreans originate from this Confucian thought. Koreans have been exposed to Confucianism for more than 2,000 years. As a result, Confucianism has had a tremendous impact on Korean life, culture, and history. For that reason, it is almost incomprehensible to separate from Confucianism to understand the lifestyle, behavioral patterns, and structure of consciousness of Koreans today.

Confucianism is an ideological and cultural tradition systematized through the process of daily life in the long history of China. In 108 B.C., the Han Dynasty of ancient China destroyed Wiman Joseon, whose main territory included parts of the Korean Peninsula, and established counties. As a result, some areas of the Korean Peninsula were once incorporated into the Han Dynasty. At that time, it is presumed that Confucianism, along with Chinese characters, was included in Jejabaekga (the ideas of a hundred schools of disciples) and transmitted to the Korean Peninsula. Later, during the Three Kingdoms period, all three kingdoms had a system for hiring talented people educated in the Confucian scriptures to become officials. Social norms were also based on the practice of Confucian ethics centered on loyalty and filial piety. Political and social systems were also built on the basis of Confucianism.[14]

Confucianism, which gradually settled in Korean society in this way, later developed into a national ruling ideology to strengthen royal authority. In the Goryeo Dynasty, Neo-Confucianism was established as the source of governing the country, and in the Joseon Dynasty, as the ruling ideology of the dynasty. As a result, Neo-Confucianism was adopted as the basic ruling ideology of the Joseon Dynasty, which ruled the Korean peninsula until about 110 years ago. The Joseon Dynasty ruled Joseon society for more than 500 years by creating a code of laws and a social system based on Neo-Confucianism. As a result, Korean ancestors were assimilated to Neo-Confucianism for many generations. The habits and inclinations that appear on many Koreans in the daily life of today's Korean society are closely related to it. Of course, it can be said that Taoism, Buddhism, indigenous beliefs, and Western Christian ideas introduced in the late Joseon Dynasty also influenced the habits and inclinations of Koreans today. However, their effects are relatively minor.

The virtues of traditional Confucianism were established by the moral code system of Samgangohryun (the Three Bonds and the Five Moral Discipline). The Samgangohryun is not content in the scriptures such as the Four Books and Five Classics of Confucianism. The Samgangohryun is the basic ideology of Confucianism and supplemented and developed as the governing ideology of the despotism for Chinese dynasties. The Samgangohryun is a basic moral code of Confucianism that was newly transformed into a life religion by absorbing some of the Legalism and Taoist ideologies to conform to the political and social environment of the Former Han Dynasty in

China. Samgang connects the important principles of nature and the fundamental relationship of human beings. The principle of heaven and earth was used to explain the relationship between a king and his subjects, the principle of yang and yin to the relationship between husband and wife, and the principle of spring and summer to the relationship between father and son. In these three most fundamental relationships of human beings, the absolute subordination of the latter to the former was regarded as a duty to be observed at all cost. In this way, Samgang is characterized by its interpretation and application as an absolute and one-sided ethics code with a clear top and bottom for the ruling standard of despotism.

In addition, the Five Discipline to be followed as human beings are the five virtues of Confucianism: benevolence, righteousness, courtesy, wisdom, and trust. Confucius taught benevolence (仁) as a virtue that human beings should have. Mencius added righteousness (義), courtesy (禮), and wisdom (智) to this, and Dongzhongseo established the Five Principles by adding trust (信) as a set of basic ethics that people must abide by.

The Samgangohryun (the Three Bonds and the Five Moral Discipline) was propagated to the ancient Three Kingdoms of the Korean Peninsula and gradually took its place as the ruling ideology of the dynasties to strengthen their royal authority. In the Goryeo Dynasty, Buddhism was adopted as the basis for morale and Confucianism as the basis for ruling the country. A new social order based on Confucianism was established. Confucian political ideology was established based on virtue, righteous governing politics and a system of civil service examinations that was implemented to select officials. The founding King of Goryeo Taejo Wang Geon recorded exemplary cases of Samgang conducts and ordered them to be passed on to future generations. As a result, the moral guidelines of Samgangohryun spread and settled as basic ethics in the lives of the people.

As the monuments and records honoring the Samgang of loyalty, filial piety, and fidelity spread widely from the Shilla to the mid-Goryeo Dynasty, and became more propagated in the Joseon Dynasty, the moral guidelines of the Samgangohryun became the basic ethics of people's lives. In particular, King Sejong of Joseon published and widely distributed <Samgang Haengsildo (Examples of Samgang Deeds)>, which recorded the historical achievements of 105 loyal subjects, filial sons, and virtuous women, and it was revised several times from the 12th year of King Seongjong to the 5th year of King Yeongjo. In addition, since King Sejong, the practice of Samgang was strongly encouraged and severe punishments were imposed on acts that violated its teachings. With nationwide implementation, the Samgang became established as basic ethics that must be observed in the lives of the people. In addition, during the Joseon Dynasty, Buddhism, which was regarded as the basis of spiritual self-training during the Goryeo Dynasty, was rejected and Neo-Confucianism was encouraged. As a result, Confucian ethical standards, as a basic guideline for life, were spread widely to scholars and bureaucrats who led society.

As for educational institutions in Joseon, Seodang was for elementary education, and for secondary education, there were Hanyang's four Hakdang, established by the state, and Hyanggyo in local areas. For a higher education, there was Sungkyunkwan in Seoul. Since the 16th century, Sarim had established Seowon equivalent to a private university in the province, which further expanded educational opportunities. In Seowon, ancestral rites were held for Confucian scholars designated by each Seowon. Its operation was also carried out independently. As a result, it served as an occasion to produce various political forces based on each school's academic traditions. Seowon had functions of education and ancestral rites. Unlike Hyanggyo, which was a state institution, Seowon also functioned as a public space where aristocrats gathered to form public opinion based on the unique autonomy and specificity of private academies. Seowon probably played a role as a foundation for forming a political faction with a person who made a successful political career at the center.

The bureaucrats who founded Joseon were scholars who pursued Confucian ideology. As Joseon society stabilized and grew, Seonbi (Scholars) developed into schools of Hungo and Sarim. Sarim (士林) is a political force that appeared around the time of King Seongjong. With social and economic foundations in Yeongnam (south eastern) and Giho (west central) provinces, Sarim grew with Neo-Confucianism, which studies human nature, as the mainstream of studies. Sarim rejected any study or ideology other than Neo-Confucianism as a heresy. Rather than a centralized system, local autonomy was pursued. Sarim, which had been in conflict with the Hungu faction, which valued Sajang,[17] took the initiative in the central political arena in the late 16th century.

As Sarim took the initiative in central politics, Neo-Confucian culture settled in Joseon society. They abolished religious events related to Buddhism and Taoism and making Confucian values part of life, and the construction of a

---

17) Practical skills required for civil service exam and administrative duties, such as Chinese literature and Simuchaek (plans for important tasks of the times)

self-governing rural community led by Hwangyak was promoted. They tried to build a society that followed the principles of Neo-Confucianism by expanding their power. As a result, any culture that was in conflict with Neo-Confucian culture was rejected as a heresy. They emphasized the moral theory and idealism of Confucianism. As a result, Yehak[18] was developed. Family rites developed into a study modeled on Zhu Xi's family rites and took root in Joseon society. They encouraged to make genealogy for each Yangban family, and developed Bohak (譜學), which recorded and memorized the history of the ancestors, as an essential culture.

Sarim established a patrilineal society centered on the patriarch under the principle of patrilineal succession. In addition, to establish Confucian social order at the national level, ethics books were compiled and disseminated, and the practice of Confucian ethics was actively encouraged. They spread the Zhu Xi Family Ceremony, which originated in the system of the clan code, and encouraged patrilineal relatives to form clans and lead rural societies. The firstborn-son centered inheritance system was also established. As a result, even today, the basic ideology of Confucius, which dominated Korean society in the past, and the life guidelines of Hyangyak

---

18) The study of Sangjangjerye (Funeral Ceremony, 喪葬祭禮)

rooted in Neo-Confucianism still remain at the base of today's Korean society. The proof is that ethical consciousness, life attitude, and behavioral patterns based on Confucian ideology are still prevalent in Korea as mentioned above and they are internalized in the consciousness of Koreans.

For Koreans, Confucianism appears consciously.

Koreans cherish worldly values and still quite a few pray for the blessing in superstition.

Kant, an educational psychologist, said, "Education for young children is like writing on a blackboard with nothing written on it. For older people, education is like finding empty spaces to write on a blackboard with many scribbles." After the introduction of Confucianism, Korean ancestors were presumed to have learned Gusaguyong (九思九容)[19] based on Confucian values from a young age. There is a historical record that shows in the middle of the 8th century, Emperor Xuanzong of the Tang Dynasty of China praised the envoy of Silla for "having the manner of JwaJakJinTui (坐作進退)[20] and

---

19) It is based on the 'nine correct attitudes' in Yegi (禮記), one of the Six Classics of Confucianism, and the 'nine thoughts that a gentleman should keep' in the 10th section of the Analects of Confucianism, and is included in Zhu Xi's Lesser Learning.
20) Methods of sitting, standing, advancing, and retreating based on the

excellent courtesy."[15] Confucianism was officially accepted on the Korean Peninsula with the establishment of the four provinces of Han around 100 B.C.[16] In Goguryeo, there is a record that they taught the Confucian scriptures by establishing Taehak (太學), a national university for the education of sons of nobles, and Gyeongdang (扃堂), a private school for the education of children of the common people in the provinces. Over time, some Korean ancestors had been exposed to the scriptures of Confucianism since childhood from about 2,100 years ago.

Confucianism, which Korean ancestors encountered for such a long time, refers to Confucius-centered teachings. Today, Koreans use Confucianism and Study of Confucius interchangeably without distinguishing the differences between them.[17] Confucianism originally refers to the teachings of the era of Confucius and Mencius, which deals with strong ethical and moral guidelines. Study of Confucius represents the Kyunghak (經學, Study of Confucius Scriptures) that theoretically systematized Confucianism since the Han Dynasty in China. The purpose of Confucianism, the teachings of Confucius, is to correct society by realizing benevolent politics and by cultivating people who make themselves sound, make peace at

teachings of Confucianism

home, govern the nation, and rule the whole world. Therefore, the goal of education is to make people have the character of In (仁, benevolence), which means love for humanity. Here, the concept is that if one abides by filial piety to one's parents and brotherhood, loyalty, trust, courtesy, righteousness, integrity, and having a sense of shame which are originated from In (仁, benevolence), inevitably spreads to all mankind. At the Confucian ideal, the purpose of personal learning is to become a good person equipped with benevolence (仁). This means growing into a person who can make oneself sound, make peace at home, govern the nation, and rule the whole world. The concept is that if one participates in real politics in this way, one will realize the rule of virtue in politics that governs the people with benevolence (仁).

What are the ideological characteristics of Confucianism? I like to introduce a discussion in the ancient Chinese Sima Qian's 『Biographical Records of History』 that mentioned Confucianism during the discussion of the hundred schools of thought.[18] According to the Book of Changes (易經), there is only one ultimate ideology in world affairs, but there are a hundred ways of thinking that lead to it, and the conclusion may be the same but the paths leading to it are different. Among them, Confucian scholars have a number of scriptures and commentaries that number 10 million. Six Sutras (六經)[21] are the foundations and even if studied for many generations, they cannot be studied completely. The Six Sutras teach people about changes, facts, and causes in world affairs. It creates harmony in the heart, contains contents that promote good-fellowship, and its range is large and wide. Although it is difficult to follow it in its entirety, it said that it was impossible to change the order of respect between the ruler and the subject and the father and son, and the distinction of ranking between the husband and wife, and the young and elderly.

Confucian thought presents a gentleman (君子) who can uprightly establish himself in the real world, serve justice in society, and establishes virtues in life that an intellectual should have. It emphasizes Courtesy (禮) as a way to realize a just society. Courtesy plays a role in preventing events through the practice of ethics and morality before they occur. However, it is difficult to outwardly see the effect because it is not visible. On the other hand, it states that the law is a criterion for dealing with what has already happened, making the effect clearly visible. This is an understandable point.

---

21) It refers to the Book of Changes (易經), the Classics of Books (書經), the Book of Courtesy (禮記), the Book of Poetry (詩經), the Book of Music (樂經), and the Spring and Autumn (春秋).

Hyo (孝, filial piety), which is the most basic need in order to cultivate one's body, is to serve parents first, then to serve the king, and to rise to fame in the end. It also mentions that it is a great filial piety to spread one's name to posterity and reveal one's parents.[22] From a Confucian perspective, the goal of training one's mind and body is to be filial to one's parents, to become a good government official, and to grow into a virtuous person. The Biographical Records of History writes that among many, the best a person can become is someone who can leave a name for future generations, gain a position, and become a person who brings glory to their parents and family. In a Confucian society, the highest value in life is to grow into a great person in society and leave a name for posterity to shine on one's parents and family.

Confucian value perceptions are based on a humanistic philosophy that focuses on human interests and ideals, where humans are at the center of everything. Most humanistic philosophies do not acknowledge the existence of a personal God alongside his divinity and inspiration. However, Confucianism is based on a pantheistic worldview that does not deny God. It does not explicitly acknowledge the god as such

---

22) From the writings left by his father Sama Dam to Sima Qian in Sima Qian's 70th episode (The Book of Confucius Taisha)

either. What did Confucius think about the existence of God? There is no special mention of God in the Analects, the log of his words and actions. However, there are records that said;"The spirits of ancestors and the gods of heaven and earth were sometimes mentioned by Confucius.", "When eating out-doors, a ceremonial rite[23] was always performed.", "If you do your best as a human being and if you respect the gods but do not get close to them, you are wise.", "Rituals should be performed with sincerity and respect rather than formality." Putting these together, it can be seen that he agreed with the pantheistic idea that God is inherently in everything. However, unrealistic, irrational, and supernatural thoughts were rejected. It can be seen that realistic and rational humanistic ideas are prioritized. Confucianism is norms of life that are necessary to live like a human being who mostly values reality.

Korean ancestors had been exposed to Confucianism for more than 2,000 years. Especially, during the Joseon Dynasty, they experienced social systems designed and operated with Confucianism as a national ruling ideology. As a result, today's Koreans still display many Confucian rituals, ideas, values, and lifestyles that are similar to their ancestors. The

---

23) An action that when a shaman performs an exorcism or one eats food in the field, one throws pieces of food to offer them to the ghosts first.

prime example is the value of life that is strongly embedded in the minds of many Koreans in their 60s to 70s, which is 'I will become a great person, shine my family, and leave a name for posterity.' Another example is the behavior of Korean Christians. Even though the Bible (Matthew 6:8-13) clearly states how to pray, "God knows what you are asking for, so pray like this!", they gather early in the morning and pray "Send my kids to a prestigious school! Give me a good job! Heal my illness! Please make me rich!" The image of Buddhists who go to a temple for the same purpose and pray even with a set deadline is also the same phenomenon. They all worship and pray for what they want in the real world rather than the afterlife. Confucian ideas that emphasize worldly values have long been embedded and passed down in the minds of Korean ancestors for generations, they are displayed even by Christians and Buddhists in Korea. For that reason, many Koreans still value Confucianism that empha-sizes worldly values, and its characteristics are strongly manifested in their faith.

Differential love is innate in Koreans.

In general, Koreans are known to put themselves and their families first and lack consideration for others. This is also due to the influence of Confucianism for generations. It is the result of the value of differential love. Benevolence (仁), the fundamental teaching of Confucianism, is defined as not giving to others what one does not wish for, loving people, being respectful and polite in governing, being generous and trustful, and being agile and having mercy.[24] It means having love for people. However, unlike Christian philanthropic love that says "Love your neighbor as yourself,"[25] Confucian love is characterized by differential love.

Differential love is an idea that is constantly flowing in the Analects of Confucianism. In the Analects, it is mentioned, "Do not make friends with those who are inferior to you, and when you are making friends, guide them faithfully, but if it does not work, quit so that you do not dishonor yourself."[26] People are classified into gentlemen and small men, adults, wise men, benevolent men, gentlemen, good men and scholars, useful friends and harmful friends, those who only know and those who like it, and those who enjoy it. This is in contrast to Christianity, which presupposes that all people are sinners from birth. In the Analects, many contents differentiate

---

24) The Analects of Anyeon section 2, 22, Yanghwa section 6
25) Matthew 22:39
26) Confucian Analects Learning section 8, Anyeon section 23

people in detail. Sometimes they even present different categories of people. Such narrative structures are effective and instructive in helping understanding. On the other hand, they let people unconsciously evaluate others differently in the process of forming human relationships with other people and treating them differently.

In dealing with enemies, Christian thought says "Love your enemies and pray for those who persecute you! When your brother sins against you, forgive your brother seventy times seven!"[27] Lao-tzu thought teaches, "Repay grudges with a grace!" Confucianism, on the other hand, says, "You cannot repay resentment with resentment, so you must show uprightness, that is, righteousness."[28] This is also a phrase that clearly tells us that benevolence (仁) and love in Confucianism is differential rather than philanthropic.

Confucianism promotes the ability to cultivate one's body with learning and virtue, so one can make themselves sound, make peace at home, govern the nation, and rule the whole world. This is the idea that man should first cultivate his mind and body, establish a right family, and then govern the country to make the world comfortable. This, too, is based on differ-

---

27) Matthew 5:43; 18:21-22
28) 36 section of the Analects

ential thought. It is a concept in which one's ability, centered on oneself, and spreads to my family, community, and country. It is the opinion that Confucianism's differential love for people is inherent in Koreans. The fact that Korea is the world's number one exporter of adopted children speaks for this. This is because people who are conscious of differential love avoid adoption because they think that other people's children can never become their own children.

For many Koreans, the upright and righteous spirit of Seonbi (scholars) is consciously conceived at the bottom of their minds.

If the Chinese have the spirit of grand cause of warring states[29] and if the Japanese have the Samurai spirit, Koreans have a Seonbi (scholar) spirit. When the mind or mental state is right and straight, it is said to be honest. When the mind is strong and straight, it is said to be upright. Every time a high-ranking public official's confirmation hearing is held in Korea, many Koreans fall into a great sense of discouragement. In general, people think that a person who is to be appointed to a

---

29) A grand cause, a set of duty or justification that a human being must protect and act, that is defined by Confucius in his historical book, <Spring and Autumn>.

high office should be different than the average person. Also, they think that anyone who wants to become a public official should have a minimum level of honesty and righteousness. Frustration is what the public feels because they are not. The fact that their lives were secular and not righteous leads to a great sense of discouragement and self-destruction. That's not all. "It was customary at the time. Didn't everyone have to do that at the time?" they said shamelessly. They were not at all ashamed of their actions of not being upright or maintaining their integrity. Rather, they displayed a confident attitude of barefaced impudence. What about people asking questions? It is a picture of a poop-stained dog scolding a chaff-covered dog. Nevertheless, their arrogant and disrespectful attitude, while pretending to be a spokesperson for honesty and righteousness, makes the people feel more anger and discouragement.

In a Christian culture that presupposes that all people are sinners, public officials are only one of the sinners. On the other hand, in the Confucian culture of Jiinjungjicjiin,[30] there is a consciousness that "a public official should be a person who has developed a different level of character than an

---

30) The idea of governing people after knowing what people are and setting myself right

ordinary person, that is, a Seonbi." It is a logical concept. The level of Korean high-ranking officials demanded by the questioners at the hearing seem to require them to be honest and upright with no defects. An example of this is the behavior of unscrupulous politicians with criminal records pointing the finger at the appointee for his/her words and actions at hearings, which are insignificant compared to their criminal records. If you ask them, "Why do you make a problem for something that doesn't matter that much?", they will brazenly explain, "Thieves do not ask their children to become thieves."

When asked about Joseon from a historical perspective, many would say that the Joseon government was preoccupied with internal factional conflicts. As a result, the people lived a difficult life to the extent that they lived only because they could not die due to the exploitation of noblemen, officials, and landlords. Externally, the toadyism was dominant under the premise that 'we cannot oppose by force.' Many would say that Joseon tried to solve everything by relying on China. People are familiar with terms such as heteronomy, stagnation, partisanship, and imitation in Joseon. Nevertheless, the Joseon Dynasty is one of the few dynasties in the world that has lasted more than 500 years. Of course, it can be said that this is due to geopolitical influences of the Korean peninsula located on the periphery. However, we should know that there was something else that helped sustain the Joseon Dynasty for more than 500 years. What has sustained the Joseon Dynasty for more than 500 years is Confucian thought of rule by virtue, people-oriented thought, and righteous politics based on morality and ethics. It is believed that it was possible because there was a ruling ideology that regarded the Confucian spirit of Seonbi (scholar) based on humanism as the value of life.

Then, what does the Seonbi spirit pursued by Korean ancestors mean? The virtues of Seonbi based on Confucian teachings can be summarized as follows.[31] First, what you say must be put into action, and if you do it, you must reap results. You should be filial to your parents and friendly to your neighbors. You should know how to be ashamed of your actions and should not dishonor your country when you travel abroad. Second, you must earnestly recommend goodness to your friends and be at peace with your brothers and sisters. As a person who loves justice, you should not think of only comfortable living. Third, even in times of need and emergency, you must keep fidelity and not commit injustice. Rather, they should be willing to lay down their lives for justice. Fourth,

---

31) The Analects of Taebaek 7, Ja-ro 20, Heon-mun 3, Wiryeong-gong 9, Ja-jang 1, Ja-han 26 section

you should not be ashamed to stand with a person wearing a worn out cotton robe, a fox coat or sable coat. You must have the confidence not to harm others or covet others' belongings. In summary, scholars are defined as "those who risk their lives when the state is in danger, think about righteousness when benefiting, respect ancestral rites, and share sorrows during funerals."

Such scholarly spirit flowed through the people of the Joseon Dynasty. That is why whenever the country was in trouble, the scholars risked their lives and took the lead in resistance to protect the country. That is what made it possible to maintain the Joseon Dynasty for more than 500 years. During the Imjin and Jeongyujaeran, righteous armies led by scholars from all over the country contributed greatly in defeating foreign enemies. In the late 19th century and early 20th century when Joseon's national fortune was dying out, it were the Korean scholars who resolutely rose up and took the lead in resisting the Japanese invasion. The attitude of such Joseon scholars was possible because of the honesty and upright Seonbi spirit[19] of these scholars. Because of the negative view of Joseon, as a failed state dominated by Confucianism, the spirit of scholars who represent Confucianism was also undermined. Therefore, it is necessary to accurately understand the positive role of the scholarly spirit in Joseon society. Andong was the region where the activities of scholars during the Joseon Dynasty were most active. It produced 326 independence fighters, the highest number in the country. Japanese imperialists burned Toegye's family home twice, judging it as the spiritual base for righteous army activities. These facts prove that the Seonbi spirit was the driving force of the uprightness against injustice when the country was in trouble.

After the Eulsa Treaty was signed, doctor Ahn Jung-geun became a righteous soldier and shot Ito Hirobumi, the mastermind behind the Joseon invasion, at Harbin Station in October 1909. In April 1932, Dr. Yoon Bong-gil surprised the world by throwing a bomb at the victory celebration of the Shanghai Incident. Behind the scenes of many independence fighters risking their lives for the independence of the country against Japan, there was a Korean scholarly spirit that believed "If the country is in danger, you have to give up your life."

Even these days, we can see content in the Korean media almost every day criticizing the ethically incorrect behaviors of rich businessmen, and not to mention, the corruption of high-ranking officials. This is because Koreans have a consciousness that if they are leaders in Korean society, they must at least have honesty and uprightness represented by the spirit of Seonbi (scholars).

Many Koreans are still bureaucrat-oriented and tend to value the humanities.

The purpose of studying for the most Koreans still seems to be aimed at government officials (powerful people). This is because people have been influenced by Confucianism for a long time. Most of the bureaucrats studied the humanities and social sciences. It was a natural result of placing more importance on humanities than science & technology. It is said that there was a proverb in the Joseon Dynasty, "If you live in the government office for 3 years, your descendants can live leisurely for 3 generations." In past Chinese and Korean societies, using Chinese characters, the bureaucrats mono-polized the culture. They taught the people, led society, and governed the country. As a result, bureaucratic characteristics were dominant in Korea until the Joseon Dynasty.

In the case of China, Qin Shi Huang (B.C. 259-210) abolished the feudal system and implemented the county system.[32] Politics by bureaucrats began. In the case of Korea,

---

32) As a local administrative system implemented in China, Silla, Goryeo, and Joseon Dynasty, in order to strengthen the sovereignty of the

King Taejong Muyeol (reigned 654-661 A.D.) from the mid-Silla Dynasty introduced and operated the bureaucratic political system of the Tang Dynasty. From then on, it can be said that Korea was under a bureaucratic political system.[20] Compared to China, this was about 800 years later. However, government officials under the bureaucratic political system of the past is different from the present in many ways. Although there are some differences depending on the era, the past test criteria for selecting officials were not job performance or the presence/absence of related legal knowledge. It was the ability to understand Confucianism and literature. The ability to write high quality sentences and poems were the criterion for selecting officials. In other words, the formula of "government official = intellectual" had been established for a long time in China and Korea, where Confucianism was the ruling ideology.

This is understandable when considering the definition of Confucianism. As explained earlier, Confucianism is not a religion, but a teaching for morality and politics. The purpose of studying was to learn and master these teachings in order to become a "gentle man," that is, a person who can cultivate his mind and body, establish a right family, and then govern the

king, local governments were placed under direct jurisdiction and officials were dispatched from the central government to govern the district.

country. In other words, someone who can correctly rule the world. The content of their studies is 'how to become a gentleman by cultivating oneself.'33) As such, in a country with Confucianism as the ruling ideology, 「intellectuals」 were 'those who study to cultivate themselves to become noble men, and to participate in politics.' Becoming an official in Confucian society was the goal and dream of those who pursued learning. This can be seen just by looking at the passage in the Analects that says, "It is not easy not to set your mind on a government post even after learning for three years!"34) Moreover, if you become a government official, isn't it accompanied by power, prestige, and a generous income? The income at the time was not due to a large salary. State-paid salaries were limited because they were paid out of state tax revenue and it was comparatively low. Most of this was made up of bribes and other forms of illegal income. This was also due to the lack of transportation and communication networks in the past, so that the eyes of the central government could not be reached. However, it was possible because it was tolerated by the bureaucratic society at the time. It was almost an open secret that bureaucrats could not

---

33) Analects Jajang section 6
34) Analects Taebaek section 12

live only on their regular salary.

In the past, officials in China or Korea had nothing to be envious of, besides power and prestige, as they were guaranteed huge incomes that could not be matched by any businessmen. Is there any job with such a blessing? This is the reason that in Confucian society, anyone who can read and write were likely to aspire to become an official. All intellectuals have either become government officials or aimed to become ones. When intellectuals are absorbed into a bureaucratic society, officials are bound to dominate and monopolize culture. In the past, people also wanted to become bureaucrats in order to become more cultural people.

In Goryeo in the past, bureaucrats shared political power with the noble. On the other hand, in Joseon, bureaucrats monopolized political power. It developed into a bureaucrat centered political system by those who had passed the civil service exam. It had also become a merit-based society. Yangin (middle class) was also given the qualifications to take the test. With this, the number of schools and educational opportunities expanded. During the Joseon Dynasty, there were legally four social classes: Yangban (nobles), Jungin (middle class), Sangmin (common people), and Cheonmin (people at the bottom). Yangban, which refers to the highest ruling class, originally referred to both scholars and military officers. Gradually, it was evolved into a term referring to Seonbi (scholars) studying Confucianism, and is recognized as such to this day. The scholars became bureaucrats and devoted themselves to studying Confucianism in order to maintain their status and pursue bureaucratic life. Rather than becoming a highly educated scholar, they devoted themselves to study in order to become government officials by passing the national civil exam. This consciousness is imprinted on Koreans today. Considering the achievements made by Korea today, there should have been a number of Korean Nobel laureates in various fields. That was not the case, but why? This is because most Koreans do not study for the development of related fields, but to become government officials and earn decent jobs.

Jungin (middle class) was the lower ruling class, such as technicians, Hyangri, Seori, Gungyo, and Seool, who were in charge of administrative work under the yangban. Ordinary people were Sangmin (common people) as Pyungmin (ordinary people) or Yangmin (lower middle class). Cheonmin who had occupations such as butchers, clowns, shamans, and prostitutes were at the lowest level. In the Joseon Dynasty, due to the priority of farming policy, most of the Yangmin were engaged in farming. As the basis for supporting the state, they were in charge of field taxes, tributes, labor and military services. Unlike the Goryeo Dynasty, they were free men who legally had an opportunity to be educated and to become government officials. However, it was a very difficult for them to become bureaucrats. This was because they could not afford to prepare for the civil servant exam over a long period of time. Nonetheless, the opportunity to take the state exam given to Yangin, who accounted for the majority of the people, gave them a big dream. Although it was very difficult, nearly impossible for many, they had the hope that they could become bureaucrats and become Yangban if they passed the national exam.

It was a great personal honor to pass the exam and became a government official. In addition to this, relatives and even the people of his hometown were proud of his passing of the exam. This made becoming a bureaucrat something of envy because it made a name for oneself. When one became a bureaucrat, there was a difference in authority depending on his role. In the case of local governors, they were endowed with administrative as well as judicial powers. Nevertheless, the contents of the test to select them tested their ability to write a poem and sentences in Chinese literature and poetry, which were judged as they were required to implement Confucian political ideology. The practical administrative ability required to govern the people in the field was not tested.

On the other hand, government offices such as Sayukwon (interpretation), Hyeongjo (judiciary), Jeonuigam (medicine), and Gwansanggam (astronomy, calendar, and yin-yang) taught the relevant technical subjects. Specially trained technicians were selected through Japgwa (various other tests). In case of Japgwa, even if one passed and entered into government service as a low-ranking official, they were not yangban, but a part of the middle-class such as Hyangri, Seori, and Gungyo. The high-ranking positions were all occupied by civil servants who studied Confucianism and passed the civil service exam. The idea of valuing the humanities over science and technology had been maintained at the national policy level for nearly 1,000 years since the Goryeo Dynasty.

In Confucian society, each individual devotes himself to cultivating character to become a gentleman. In Confucianism, only the practice and training for cultivating one's character are considered academic. In the past, the nobles of the Joseon thought that mathematics and science were sufficient if they could be used in real life. In mathematics, abstract problems such as the nature of numbers or the relationship between roots and coefficients of equations were not considered necessary.

In the Analects, it says that "No matter how small the technology, there is always something worth seeing. However, a gentleman does not do such things because he is afraid of hindering the achievement of his grand goals!"[35] This phrase, which devalued special skills by Confucius, had been handed down for thousands of years in Eastern Confucian society. I believe that this passage caused people in Confucian society decisively turn away from science and technology. It was viewed as a consequence in Confucian countries, represented by China, had become laggards in science.

For Koreans, such Confucian perceptions had been handed down for nearly 1,000 years and had become conscious. Perhaps for this reason, the current exam for high-ranking officials, which has been implemented since the founding of the Republic of Korea in 1948, was divided into administration and judiciary, which are both in the field of humanities. It is a quite similar system to the civil servant exam of Joseon. As industrialization took place rapidly after the 1970s, it became difficult for administrative officials alone to adapt to the trend of the times. Since then, the government has been implementing an engineering system. They also appoint technical bureaucrats for high-level positions in the government.

---

35) The Analects Jajang section 4

However, the reality is that most high-ranking government officials are still dominated by administrative bureaucrats.

In the past, scholars had been constantly devoted to studies due to the phrase of the Analects, "If you have the ability to afford while serving in government, learn, and if you have the ability to afford it, you should pursue the official position."[36] Sadly, however, when comparing the academic achievements of those who have passed the exam and have been high-ranking civil servants throughout their careers, with those who have been engaged in jobs unrelated to the state exam, there is a marked difference. Most of the people who passed the exam had no higher education. Could it be because of the arrogant mindset that "I passed the civil service exam, what kind of additional education do I need?" I hope… it is not one of the factors that lead the dark side of Korean society.

I would like to present another negative example of a humanities-centered society. A modern version of preparing for civil service exams in the Joseon Dynasty is being replicated today with the preparation for Gosi (civil service and judiciary examinations). Those who aspire to be government officials take the exam while in college or after graduation. Some do pass while attending school, but most of those who prepare for

---

36) The Analects Jajang section 13

the exam after graduation sacrifice everything to prepare for the exam until they pass for many years. Those who sacrificed everything show great pride in passing their exams. Passing the exam means that, in reality, government officials of the 5th grade or higher are guaranteed. It can be taken for granted. Of course, Most of them work hard with a sense of duty as much as pride. The problem is that even though they do not have the ability, they are given priority to get into high-ranking positions within the organization simply because they have passed the exam. That is what I experienced when I was working for the government. The high ranking civil servants formed an informal interest group centered on those who passed the Goshi, I think it is a natural consequence. Perhaps wasn't the bureaucratic society of the Joseon Dynasty the same? That's not all. People expect those who have risen to high positions in government, unlike ordinary people, to have an exemplary life. Of course, there are many of such people. However, many of them use their senior positions to get their children exempt from military service and commit corruption such as real estate speculation and bribery without shame. These are evidenced at the National Assembly hearings that make Koreans disappointed today.

Entering the 21st century, the world is heading for a

information-heavy society led by artificial intelligence, big data, the internet of things, and cloud systems. Society needs technological engineering support in many fields such as the development of information and tele-communication technology, the expansion of information distribution networks, the emergence of various media, and the expansion of information infrastructure. Despite this fact, the long-established value of pursuing a high-ranking government official is still of great importance to many Koreans. As a result, a bureaucrat and a humanities oriented view are more valued than science or technology. However, this value perception should be transformed into a future-oriented perspective as soon as possible.

Many Koreans value experiential intuition[37] and are accustomed to speculative thinking.

People belonging to the Chinese character culture are not good at thinking things logically and expressing things during the process of studying. This is due to the influence of Chinese characters. The form or expression of words are fragmentary and not argumentative. Chinese characters are isolated words

---

37) The tendency of directly apprehending an object without going through thinking such as experience, judgment, and reasoning

and they contain a meaning for each character. There are no inflection changes and affixes.[38] Each word has an idea and has a grammatical function based on its position in a sentence. Rather than the meaning of words, the affixes that combine and connect words are needed in logical thinking. The lack of affixes in Chinese characters is a fatal flaw when establishing logic. This is the reason why logical way of thinking is not sufficiently developed in the Chinese character culture. Therefore, experiential intuition is more important than logical thinking, and is based on intuition, metaphorical or symbolic expressions. Such expressions are also abound in 「The Analects」.

In the case of Buddhism, since the end of the Tang Dynasty, it has been handed down to the present day, with only Zen Buddhism and Pure Land Buddhism going through the rise and fall of the dynasty. The Zen Buddhism insists on direct communication from mind to mind and realization of Buddha-hood.[39] Even the Pure Land Buddhism claims that you can go

---

38) A word added to a word or to a stem to form a new word. Divided into prefixes and suffixes.

39) A phrase that represents the concept of 'not in the words' that means the truth is learned only through communication between minds, not through the medium of letters or language, and it means that true enlightenment can be obtained by intuition of the nature in the mind, and experiential intuition is regarded as the only path to the truth.

to the Pure Land by simply chanting with "Namu Amitabha."[40)] These facts also indicate the characteristics of the people who are part of the Chinese character culture emphasize simpleness and value of practice rather than theory. The Zen sect's thought of Bullipmunza (不立文字, not in the characters) had a great influence on countries with Chinese character culture, including China. Countries with Chinese character culture, including China, had outstanding technologies and inventions. Nevertheless, I believe that the reason why technology and inventions have not been developed and handed down as a well-established science or a theory in those countries is because of the influence mentioned above. It can be seen that Neo-Confucianism, which had a great influence on the countries who utilize Chinese character culture, is also based on the ideology of 'not in the characters' with an emphasys on experiential intuition.

Among the traditional ideologies, Neo-Confucianism has dominated the Korean mind and consciousness for the longest time. Confucian scholars of the Song Dynasty established the Taoist theory succeeding Confucius-Mencius Taoism. Neo-Confucianism was established as the study of a system of

---

40) It means to take refuge in Buddha Amitabha, who presides over the world of paradise.

Confucius classics[41] based on the Taoism and its philosophical basis. Zhu Xi compiled these into one. Taoism is divided into eight areas: Classical Learning, Orthodoxy, Righteousness, Neo-Confucianism, Knowledge and Conduct, Self-cultivation, Courtesy, and Governance. Among them, Neo-Confucianism presented the Taoist worldview as a philosophical theory. It is generally classified into cosmology and anthropology. Cosmology is a theory that explains the creation of the universe and all the principles of nature. Anthropology is the theory of mind, which is the system of human understanding. However, neither the cosmology of Zhu Xi in the Song Dynasty nor the theory of anthropology in Joseon Neo-Confucianism were based on experience or factual grounds. It was systematized by the Confucian scholarly method[42] and speculative thinking.[43] Even so, the Neo-Confucianism built by Zhu Xi is a philosophical system with excellent completion. However, it was not based on concrete reality or facts and was biased toward abstract ideas and

---

41) The study of interpreting or divination the meaning of the five classics of Poetry, Calligraphy, Rituals, Literature, Spring and Autumn, and the four Analects of Confucius, Mencius, Daehak, and Zhungyong
42) How to study the meaning of scriptures
43) Thinking and devising to arrive at cognition through sheer thought and not by experience.

representations. As a result, it contains a limit that is academically too ideal. In addition, the contents are aimed at the preservation and maintenance of the old order and the protection of the system. It also inherently has limitations of being conservative. In addition to this, Neo-Confucianism is strong within the studies of Confucianism and speculative thinking under the theory of 'not in the characters' that emphasizes experiential intuition. Since Neo-Confucianism was introduced at the end of the Goryeo Dynasty, Koreans have lived under its influence for many generations. As a result, Koreans still value experiential intuition rather than logical thinking and are accustomed to speculative thinking.

They tend to be conceptual, so they lack logical problem-solving skills.

Independence activist Lee Dong-hwi was one of those who resonated with Dosan Ahn Chang-ho's enlightenment ideology and devoted himself to its movement early on. After the March 1st Movement, he served as the military secretary general and prime minister of the Provisional Government of the Republic of Korea in Shanghai. Lenin's evaluation of him in Russia at the time shows a slice of what made Koreans at the time. As Prime Minister of the Shanghai Provisional

Government, he visited the Kremlin Palace to collect 300,000 yen from Lenin for communization of Koreans in Manchuria. Lenin asked him questions about the Manchurian railways and future lines that were to be built, the production capacity of Koreans in Manchuria, the state of supplies in school education, the number of banks, and the size of the nominal total capital of banks operated by Korea and Japan. However, none of his answers satisfied Lenin. According to the record, with a little anger, Lenin said, "Koreans are very eloquent, but they don't have actual contents. He speaks eloquently, saying that Joseon must be restored somehow, and that it must be done this way. However, I have never met a single person who can scientifically discuss Joseon, even now. How can a person who does not know the internal affairs of Joseon achieve any communization? Everything they say sounds like they are talking in their sleep. They must study more."[21] This is due to the influence of Neo-Confucianism. That was a typical anecdote that shows the lack of scientific and logical approach to problem solving, while being familiar with justification and righteousness.

The characteristic of people who have lived during the time of Chinese character culture is that they lack logic in their thoughts and expressions. On the other hand, they are excellent at metaphors and symbolic expressions based on experiential intuition. They value experiential intuitions and are familiar with speculative thinking, so they prefer experiential practice rather than argumentative theory. Rather than verifying things in detail, they prefer to simply check whether it is true or not. As a result, Koreans are generally accustomed to justification and righteousness. They are more conceptual rather than seeking truth based on evidence. For that reason, in the past, logical and scientific problem-solving skills of Koreans were very weak.

Many Koreans are not good at compromise.

Koreans say, "the one with the loudest voice wins the argument." This means several things. First of all, it means that the argument lacks logic. It also means to attack the flaws of the opponent's argument without thinking about the flaws in their own. It also means not thinking through the arguments of the other side, meaning that the debate is not rational and that the stronger side wins. This means that Koreans believe that what is right or wrong is not important when debating, rather that if you can raise your voice and assert strongly to break one's opponent's mentality, one could win the argument.

Koreans are bad at compromise. They are not familiar with

discussion norms in which people with different opinions on an issue come together to produce better results through debate. They have a strong adherence to their ideology, so once they think they are right, the opposing side is unconditionally wrong. They have a strong competitive spirit and never give up on their assertion, are emotional, and hot-tempered. If the other side raises an objection to their opinion, they get angry regardless of whether it is right or wrong. When the situation becomes unfavorable to themselves, such emotional characteristics become more apparent.

Koreans have a strong tendency to not admit the fallacy of their arguments, even when the evidence proves otherwise. It is a common behavior that Koreans should bring to an end. This is a behavioral pattern that appears because Koreans are conceptual and value intuitive rather than seeking truth from facts alongside logical and scientific approaches. This is because the trait of believing what one intuitively judges to be right in their heart over logical or scientific evidence is innate. Koreans strongly believe that once they claim that they are right, they are never wrong, and have a strong tendency not to change their minds. For that reason, discussion culture struggles among Koreans. How can they debate when majority of them refuse to admit that there are errors in their arguments? Most of them are consistent with fierce counterattacks and criticism even against the other person's favorable remarks. it's also common for them to escalate into an emotional fight by the end of it. It's one of the characteristics of Koreans who do not easily admit errors in their arguments and are very poor at compromising.

It seems that the moral norms of traditional Confucianism are imprinted on Koreans.

Korean has a safe society dominated by ethics.

Ethics refers to the principles and morals that form the norms for people to abide by in their lives. During the Joseon Dynasty, Confucian ideology and its moral norms, in accordance with government policy, became the biggest agenda for education and intensified educational institutions. That was not all. In families who could read and write, parents had been teaching their children from an early age as a key agenda for home education. As such, Confucian moral norms were taught by parents to their children and from teachers to disciples in school, for hundreds of years. As a result, Confucian moral norms had been embedded or become the basic ideology in the Joseon people, and had been respected as basic ethics within

Joseon society. It can be seen that the Confucian ethical norms that supported Joseon society until about 100 years ago, are still conscious or internalized deep in the hearts of Koreans, and are expressed in various forms and appearances in daily lives of Koreans today.

The social norms of Confucianism could be summarized as "Be kind in dealing with people, be honest in working, be thrifty in food, clothing and shelter, and give grace to those around you who are weak." It seems that these social norms are still strongly embedded in the consciousness of Koreans. Perhaps for that reason, Koreans believe it to be rude if the other person doesn't treat them kindly. If the rich are dishonest, they are criticized for living grand and lavish lives. If you don't practice frugality in food, clothing, and shelter, you'll be criticized as wasteful. If a person in a position to help pretends not to know, people accuse them of looking down on others due to their power. It is said that these are peculiar characteristics that foreigners observe in many Koreans. In my opinion, these unique aspects of Koreans are displayed because Confucian ethics are unconsciously embedded at the bottom of their minds and are naturally expressed in human relationships. In particular, one of the characteristics of Koreans that foreigners find difficult to understand is that "Koreans are not very grateful even when they receive financial help." This is because Koreans are imprinted with the belief that "the rich should surely help the poor", they do not show much appreciation, even if they receive financial help in difficult situations,

"If there is dust in the room and living room, you must sprinkle water and clean it, filial piety must be done with all your strength, and everything must be done with loyalty. Serve teachers like parents, children should respect elders, and those who are twice as old should be serve as fathers. When guests come, treat them with sincerity, make friends with the right people, and do the right thing yourself as well. Advise your friends when they are wrong, and when you see good deeds, follow them. The reason why people are precious is because there are three bonds and five moral disciplines in human relations, which should be observed. Be sincere in your words and work with sincerity, ask questions when in doubt, think about the consequences when you are angry, and think about what is right when you receive something. You must be honest and sincere with your words and actions, and you must display refrain when eating and drinking through self-control. Advise each other on good deeds, correct each other on wrongdoings, enjoy good customs, and help each other in disasters and

hardships. Being diligent and thrifty is the basis of raising a family, and if you accumulate good deeds, there will always be an auspicious occasion later. Disasters and blessings don't have a specific path but they are only brought in by people." The above teachings are included in Sohak, one of the must-read elementary school textbooks in Confucian society. These are the teachings that are the basis of the words and behaviors expressed unconsciously in the daily life of Koreans today.

As mentioned above, Koreans have been exposed to Confucian thought for more than 2,000 years from generation to generation. From the beginning of its introduction to the Korean Peninsula, Confucianism received active support from the dynasty as a key political idea that strengthened royal authority. It developed into a basic philosophy of governing the country as well as a foundation of moral training, became the ruling ideology of the nation later in the Joseon Dynasty. It provided an opportunity for the establishment of Confucian political ideology and a new social order based on Confucian thought. Since then, for more than 500 years, Korean ancestors have lived under the Confucian political ideology and its social system as the national ruling ideology. As a result, under the influence of Confucianism, which is the root of moral training and governance, and the social conventions that follow, Korean society has been led by ethics to this very day. It is a society in which ethics are relatively more influential than institutions and the law. The justification of helping one's colleague, which is emphasized in the Confucian society, is more important than following the rules and procedures that are valued in modern society. It is a society that prioritizes loyalty rather than compliance of regulations. This is because they believe that laws and regulations can be properly applied only when there is a cause syanding behind it. In modern Western societies, the law takes precedence over ethics. Therefore, Westerners could not understand that, in the National Assembly of liberal democratic country of Korea, why members of the minority party physically block the majority party from voting. They could not help but wonder why demonstrators assaulted the police who were simply blocking illegal demonstrations taking over the sidewalk in front of City Hall. In Korean society, it is possible to persuade them only when there is a cause that can be sympathized with. It means that only then can you get their support.

In general, societies governed by ethics are safer than societies governed by law. This is because the moral law that people must abide by is engrained in their minds. That is why you can walk through the back alleys of Seoul without feeling danger, even late at night, one of the few major cities in the world. On the other hand, this is not the case in a society where the law takes precedence. Lawlessness is committed whenever it is out of the reach of those in charge of enforcing the law. This is the reason why looting and robbery are prevalent in areas that have been swept away by an earthquake, as the law cannot be enforced. Such phenomena occur immediately in situations where the law cannot be applied. A prominent example is that personal safety is not guaranteed, even in the daylight of back alleys in large cities in so-called developed countries. However, in Korean society, ethics take precedence, so it is comparatively safe where people can come and go freely without feeling threatened, even late at night.

Koreans' patriotism is at the highest level in the world.

"Koreans can't stand being criticized for their country much more than they can tolerate being criticized themselves. The spirit of sacrifice and service of Koreans for their country may not be noticeable in peacetime but appears in a crisis." Foreigners had witnessed the true patriotism of Koreans in the gold-raising campaign of 1997 in the midst of the IMF economic crisis and volunteer campaign in 2007, in order to remove the oil spill off the coast of Taean. As a Korean, I agree with them 100%.

What was the Gold Collecting Movement? In 1997, the people voluntarily donated the gold they owned to the country in order to pay off Korea's foreign debt to the IMF. As the country became economically endangered, the people came forward to contribute at least a small amount of strength in attempts to overcome it. Newlyweds' wedding rings, children's first birthday rings, and various commemorative rings for adults poured out without hesitation. Following the National Debt Redemption Movement initiated by the people of Joseon in 1907 in order to repay national debt to Japan, it was the movement in 90 years in which the Korean people voluntarily launched a 'save the country' campaign to overcome the national financial crisis.

In addition, the Taean Oil Spill Removal Campaign was a national volunteer movement. On December 7, 2007, an offshore crane and an oil tanker collided off the coast of Mallipo, Taean, resulting in the worst marine pollution accident ever caused by an oil spill. Experts predicted that it would be difficult to return to its original state, even after decades. However, after the accident, approximately 1.23 million volunteers from all over the country gathered to remove the oil. The hands of millions that scooped the oil floating on the seawater with a bucket and wiped the oil between the rocks came together to create a miracle. Thanks to that, in 10 years, Taean Coastal National Park was certified as a national park by the International Union for Conservation of Nature (IUCN). It recovered the original ecosystem, which had excellent ecological value and excellent preservation. Taean had been reborn as a memorable world-class place of hope, symbolizing the efforts and spirit of Korean volunteers. This also became a historical symbol that shows the potential of the Korean people, that is, their patriotism.

Volunteers of the Korean gold-donation campaigns and Taean offshore oil removal volunteers are representative examples that show the world how patriotic Koreans are today. But where does the world-class patriotism of Koreans come from? In my opinion, it stems from the three facts outlined below.

First, it is due to the result of being persecuted by many foreign forces for generations because of geopolitical factors. Due to the geopolitical characteristics of the Korean Peninsula, it was inevitable that Korea had been a target for many generations when the balance of power shifted between continental and maritime powers, or when a dominant power emerged. Although, in the face of their aggression, Koreans resisted with all their might. Most of them had no choice but to endure excruciating pain in the process. What would be left? The founding ideology of Dangun, which Koreans respect as their founding ancestor, is Hongik Ingan (Devotion to the welfare of mankind). Koreans have been proud of their country of gentlemen in the East for generations. They have pictured themselves as the chosen people who did not harm other countries. I think that this may be the expression of a sense of silent resistance against the armed forces of the continent and maritime powers.

Koreans lived with the bitter ordeal they had to experience because of how their country was weak whenever approached by foreign aggression. Here are some recent examples. At the end of the 19th century, Empress Myeongseong was killed by

Japanese assassins at Gyeongbokgung Palace, where the emperor of the Joseon resided. At that time, the emperor was unable to properly protest Japan and fled to the Russian legation. How much resentment must the people of Joseon have felt in such a situation? During the Russo-Japanese War (1904-1905), Japan incorporated Dokdo, a territory of Joseon, into its territory. That's not all. Japan, which had diplomatic rights of Joseon, handed over the Gando region of Manchuria, which Joseon dispatched officials to govern, to the Qing Dynasty of China in exchange for the right to build a railway in Manchuria (1909). How much sorrow must the people have felt over the reality that the state was so weak and unable to stop enemies from plundering the national sovereign territory?

On August 29, 1910, Joseon was annexed by Japan. Shortly thereafter, the Japanese Government-General of Korea robbed farmland and forests, which were the living grounds of the Joseon people at the time, under the disguise of a land investigation project. How resentful were the Joseon people who were robbed of their livelihood? National anger exploded with the independence movement on the March 1 in 1919, to which the Japanese ruthlessly suppressed. Many people were killed and slaughtered. Subsequently, as Joseon became a food supplier to Japan, many Koreans had to abandon their hometowns. Japanese colonial policy on Joseon became more severe as the Japanese imperialist war of aggression intensified in other parts of Asia. Joseon people had to go through the pain of unbearable living conditions as colonial subjects. What did they think while enduring the sorrow of a ruined country? With the surrender of Japan on August 15, 1945, the Korean peninsula was also liberated. Japan lost the war, but it was Korea that suffered the territorial division. How unfair and resentful is this? It was the sorrow of a weak and small nation. To make matters worse, how many people died unjustly in the Korean War, which was fought in the form of a proxy war between the East and West? That's not all. Many of those who survived still experiencing the pain of separated families. Koreans who had lived until the 1950s had endured various sufferings because their motherland could not serve as a protective shield for them. As a result, I believe that the perception of, as Machiavelli said, 'Nothing precedes the survival and freedom of the motherland' is imprinted in the consciousness of Koreans today.

Second, it can be said that it is derived from the influence of Taoism.[22] Taoism, a branch of Confucianism, is another name for Neo-Confucianism, which developed during the Song Dynasty in China. Taoism was introduced to Goryeo under the name of Neo-Confucianism during the reign of King Chungnyeol at the end of the Goryeo Dynasty, functioning as the cornerstone of Joseon's ideology and culture. As Neo-Confucianism became the basic ideology of Joseon in order to establish a system of a Confucian nation during the founding process of early Joseon, Confucian scholars in Joseon came to respect and worship Zhu Hui.

The Taoist School reinterpreted the Confucian scriptures to recognize the spirit of humanitarianism based on the benevolence of Confucius and Mencius. The Taoist school emphasized that above all else, the realistic problems of human beings and the sense of responsibility for society and the state are the original spirit of Confucianism. The key point in reality of the Taoist school was that only when an individual completes his character and then participates in politics as a gentleman can the people enjoy happiness through selfless politics, which was taught by the Confucius early on. However, since political reality does not always conform to the ideal, the Taoist school maintained a sharp and critical spirit against the reality of the time. The Taoist school internally insisted on the realization of politics based on humanitarianism, and strongly resisted against the reality contrary to this ideal, and externally displayed a spirit of loyalty to protect the country and its people when there was a danger of foreign aggression.

In particular, Zhu Hui, the founder of Taoism, made efforts to restore the sovereignty of the northern territory of the Song Dynasty, which had been lost by the Jin Dynasty. He argued that it was wrong to violate the rights of other countries, and it was also wrong to have the national rights of one's own country violated. The promotion of national identity and the protection of national rights were important tasks for Taoists. The Taoist scholars' view of the state was different from exclusive nationalism or chauvinism. They rejected nationalism based on national egoism and aggressive imperialism. They presented the ideal of peaceful coexistence that preserves the individual's self-existent characteristics and pursues harmony with the whole. They insisted on the grand cause of independence and mutual respect as the basic principle.

In the Joseon Dynasty, Neo-Confucianism became the ruling ideology of the new dynasty. In the late 16th century, as Sarim took the initiative in the political scene of Joseon, Neo-Confucian culture dominated the Joseon society. The dynasty encouraged the establishment of Confucian order by distributing ethics books such as the Samgang Haengsildo, making all people aware of Confucianism ideals. In particular, the moral guidelines of the Smagangohryun (Three Bonds and Five

Moral Disciplines in human relations) became the people's living guidelines. Gunwi-Shingang (君爲臣綱) and Gunshiin-yuui (君臣有義), which speak of the relationship between the king and his subjects in the Samgangohryun, define the relationship between the state and its individuals in modern day as well. It means that it is fundamental for individuals to serve the country, and that when the country is in danger, they must be loyal at the cost of their lives. It was an idea that Koreans from an early age listened until their ears worn out and had been imprinted in their consciousness. As a result, when Joseon suffered two foreign invasions of the Imjin and Byeongja in the mid-Joseon Dynasty and the Japanese invasion at the end of the Joseon Dynasty, many Taoist scholars presented their plans and strategies to overcome national crises. Also, the numerous cases where they gathered patriotic soldiers, fought and many were killed in the battle against the enemy tell us this. For that reason, I believe that the strong moral philosophy of Taoism imprinted in Koreans, which says we must fight against injustice and protect the nation against foreign invasions, is one of the reasons for strong patriotism among Koreans today.

Third, I believe that it is derived from the scholarly spirit.[23] Seonbi is defined in the dictionary as "an old-fashioned word of a person who has knowledge but does not hold a government post, and who cultivates learning." However, in general, Seonbi is recognized by Koreans as "an upright and strong person who constantly cultivates learning and virtue for the perfection of human character, and who has the integrity to give up personal achievement and even his life like a rubbish for a great cause." As mentioned above, the Joseon Dynasty was a long-lived country that lasted more than 500 years. People say that the main reason for its longevity was because Joseon society was a Neo-Confucianism based society. The rule by virtue, not by force, in politics, that persuades and embraces the people by clarifying justification and loyalty, and the Neo-Confucian philosophy of governance that prioritizes virtue over rule of law were the power behind the 500 years of Joseon Dynasty. Here, the royal politics of virtue refers to politics that relies on human autonomy rather than relying on compulsory law enforcement. Seonbi is a model human type set in the process of humanization promoted by the Joseon Dynasty in order to persuade the people with cause and loyalty, while embracing them. Seonbi acquired training in reasoning by studying literature, history, and philosophy as basic elements, and went through emotional training by studying poetry, writing, and painting as essential elements of culture. Seonbi was a human being in which reason and emotion were well-balanced. What should be noted here is the fact that even the king, the supreme ruler of Joseon, could not be excluded from this humanization work. These factors were the reasons for the Joseon dynasty's longevity. Therefore, in the consciousness of Koreans living in modern times, the images of Seonbi who are characterized by their upright fidelity, strong spirit that does not fear even with a knife at their throat, indomitable spirit that would risk dying for the right cause, and always awake and clean mindset, are still considered as the right human image of Koreans. It is believed that the resentments Koreans felt at the compromising behavior of high-ranking officials today are also due to this spirit of classical scholars still conscious in the heart of Koreans.

The 「Spirit of Seonbi」 refers to the scholarly spirit which the Joseon Dynasty with Confucianism as the ruling ideology, set up as an ideal human type in which reason and emotion are well harmonized over the course of more than 500 years of rise and fall. For that reason, the ancestors of Koreans who aspired to become scholars worked tirelessly to become the true ideal human recognized by themselves and others for hundreds of years in the social order based on Confucian thought. In my opinion, as a result, the spirit of people who had studied for hundreds of years in Joseon society, constantly striving to become true scholars. As a human model set by the Joseon Dynasty, the ideal human figure that Seonbi should pursue was "a person who thinks of what is right when seeing profits, sacrifices his life when the country is in danger, and keeps even old promises without forgetting".[44] The spirit of scholars who gave their lives when the country was in danger built up the force that sustained the Joseon Dynasty for 500 years. This spirit became conscious in people as patriotism, the highest value that all people should pursue, through the leaders of Joseon society, bureaucrats, and moral scholars. That's why it has become a natural and highest virtue for Koreans to sacrifice their lives to protect their country when facing difficulties.

Koreans have keenly felt the importance of the existence of their homeland as they were persecuted by numerous foreign powers for generations due to geopolitical factor. In addition, Taoist scholars who followed Neo-Confucianism in the Joseon Dynasty passed down the importance of promoting national identity and protecting national rights as an important cause. That's not all. The scholarly spirit believes that if the country

---

44) The Analects Honmun section 13 見利思義見危授命 久要不忘平生之言

is in danger, one must defend it with one's life. This is generalized and is a representation of Koreans today. It is natural that Koreans' love for their country, in other words patriotism, being displayed in combination of these three factors is world class

Koreans' respect for elders or superiors is at an uncons- cious level.

This is a Korean habit that originates from the virtue of 『Jangyouyuseo(長幼有序)45)』, one of basic ethics of Confucia- nism that was established as a guideline for people's lives in the Joseon Dynasty.

There was an incident when I went to study abroad in the United States in the early 1980s. It was a few days after I rented an apartment and moved in. On my way home from school, I met an American child on the stairs of an apartment building. We knew each other because she and my daughter, who was 7 at the time, had met several times. I don't know how she got to know my name, but she greeted me by calling my name. I was dumbfounded for a moment. I thought that "No way, how can such a young child call out the name of an

---

45) There must be turn and order between adults and children. (Younger brothers should yield to older brothers.)

adult around his father's age?" I still vividly remember the feeling I felt then, 40 years later. I was momentarily taken aback and felt absurd. However, because the child was being polite and greeted me to show that she recognized me, I regained my composure. After that incident, I used to think about it from time to time.

"A name is something that is meant to be called, but there are cases in Korea where you should not call the name… . That's how long-standing customs sometimes make people feel different, even the obvious…."

Gunwisingang (君爲臣綱) in the Samgang (三綱), the basic ethics of Confucianism, means "It is fundamental for a subject to serve his king," which implies that the powerful should be respected rather than disobeyed. Also, Buwijagang (父爲子綱) means "It is fundamental for a son to serve his father," which implies that adults should be respected. The Gunshinyueui (君臣有義)[46] in the Ohryun (五倫, Five Moral Disciplines) means "there must be loyalty between the ruler and his subjects," implying that the subjects must be loyal to the ruler at any cost. Interpreted into modern day, it means that if the country is endangered, it must be defended even at the cost of one's

---

46) 'Sujeolsaeui (守節死義)'; according to Sagi (史記, the biographical record of history), it is interpreted that the subjects must be loyal to the ruler and sacrifice their lives for loyalty

life. Bujayuchin (父子有親) means "there must be a close relationship between father and son," which implies that there must be intimate love (親愛) as one loves oneself. In addition, 「Jangyuyuseo (長幼有序)」 means "there must be order between adults and children," clearly emphasizing that there must be a hierarchy in human relationships. From this, it can be said that the basis for maintaining the basic social order of the Samgangohryun lies in the formation of hierarchical human relationships.

In the Confucian society, Koreans received teachings about the Samgangohryun since childhood from their parents or teachers for generations. Due to such influence, it seems that Koreans have a basic attitude of respect for their elders and superiors in organizations. There are still many young people who give up their seats to the elderly or seniors on the subway from time to time. It is proof that the ethics of Jangyooyuseo are deeply rooted in Koreans. It can be said that the honorifics language system of Koreans also plays a large role in maintaining the ethics of Jangyuyuseo. Furthermore, I believe that the "National Open Conscription System" has also played a large role in fostering an attitude of respect and courtesy to elders and superiors. In conclusion, Koreans' attitude of respect for elders is imprinted in their minds due to being taught for many generations, the language system they use, and social systems.

Koreans' love for children is special and devoted.

Koreans are dedicated to investing in their children. This is because there is a great expectation that if one educates their children well, they can achieve what you once wanted, and if you have successful children, you will be treated well. Parents pour out a lot of money that does not fit in their budget for children's education and marriage. Even that is not enough, parents buy a house and even provide business funds for them. The following are the results of the youth consciousness survey conducted by the Ministry of Gender Equality in Korea in the early 2010s. The survey results showed that "93% of Korean teenagers believe that parents are responsible for college tuition. 87% believe that parents are responsible for wedding expenses. 74% believe that when they get married, their parents should buy a house or provide funds for rent."

It was said that due to such perception, an increasing number of elderly people were driven out to the streets after providing business funds for their children. In 2012, there were 2,100 unpaid mortgage loans to Shinhan Bank. The bank's analysis showed that 20% of the unpaid mortgage loans were cases in which children borrowed business funds by using their parents' houses as collateral. According to the statistics of financial institutions at the time, the number of real estate loans in arrears reached 400,000 a year. Considering this, it meant that 80,000 retirees were on the verge of bankruptcy each year. As a result, many retirees said they are struggling to come up with measures to protect their retirement funds from their children. An example is the percentage of retired public servants who applied for retirement pension. It increased from 47% in 1998 to 95% in 2012. This was the result of lessons learned from cases in which senior civil servants, who received retirement benefits as a lump sum instead of pensions, failed after supporting their children's home purchases and business funds.

Most westerners leave their parents when they reach the age of 18. It provides them an opportunity of independent learning and starting their own lives. It is the providence of nature for a child to become an adult and become independent from his or her parents, and learn and assume the role of a member of society. Nevertheless, Korean culture seems to go against the providence of nature. Even when children become adults, they stay with their parents. Even after marriage, parents buy a house for them in order to move out. The never-ending love for one's child is a remnant of the undifferentiated concept between parents and children.

Where did the Koreans' extreme priority of children come from? The relationship between father and son in Korea is completely different from the general ethics of human relations in other societies. It is also influenced by Confucianism. In Confucian culture, filial piety to one's parents is encouraged to be one of the foundations of human life. From an early age, Koreans learned about Bujawigang (父爲子綱) and Bujayuchin (父子有親)[47] of Samgangohryun for many generations. Such basic life guidelines remain in the minds of Koreans living today, affecting their behaviors. Human relationships between parents and children in Western societies are based on an individualistic ethic of equality. In Korean society, human relations between parents and children are based on attributes of gratitude and duty. There is a marked difference between these two.

Korean athletes call out their parents with tears of joy after winning international competitions. The psychological motivation for this behavior is to share their pleasure with their parents. This phenomenon is a clue to show the sense of unity

---

47) It is fundamental for a son to serve his father, and there must be an intimate love between a father and son as if they were loving themselves.

between parents and children and how the joy of one's parents is the child's joy. The phenomenon in which Korean parents perceive their child's success as their own success is interpreted as vicarious satisfaction from a Western perspective. However, looking at the relationship between parents and children from the point of view of being one rather than independent entities, this is not vicarious satisfaction, but self-satisfaction.

The following is data from the Gallup Research Institute of Korea[24] that shows the relationship of identity between Korean parents and children. Regarding the question asking Korean parents about the meaning of raising children, the top two answers were "Because I want to have a successor who can pursue my wishes (32.1%)" and "It is to pass on the family line (68.2%)." Regarding the question asking Korean mothers about the meaning of raising children, their top three answers were "continuing the family line (48.3%), fulfilling her dreams (43.2%), and extending her life (34%)." Among Korea, Japan, Thailand, the United States, France, and the United Kingdom, Koreans showed the highest response rate regarding extension of their lives and family line. Korean parents also said that 91.6% of them agreed with the question about the priorities of couples and children, saying, "Even if a couple wants to divorce, it's better to just live together for the future of the children." This is significant when compared to the rates for the continuation of marriage which were 51.3% in France, 30.4% in the US, and 21.8% in the UK.

At the same time, when children were asked about the relationship between parents and children, the rate of Korean children who answered "obedience to parents (83.6%)" showed the highest response rate among the six countries. When asked about the source of self-confidence for children, Korean children showed the highest response rate of 86.5%, saying, "Because my parents have high expectations of me." According to a survey conducted on Korean teenagers[48], it was found that "the biggest concern of middle and high school students with poor grades is the disappointment of their parents."[25]

These survey results suggest that the relationship between parents and children in Korean society has an extremely strong tendency to perceive that parents and children are one. Children tend to feel the pain of their parents, and parents tend to feel the pain of their children as if it was their own. This relationship between Korean parents and children can be said to be due to the fact that their ancestors have learned the Samgangohryun as an ethical framework for many generations.

---

48) Donga Ilbo, 7 Sep. 1994

It can also be said that in Confucian society, Yehak (Courtesy) and Bohak (Geneology) also influenced Koreans' love for their children. In the late Joseon Dynasty, Yehak and Bohak instilled an importance of family in Koreans. This is what made many Koreans still have the following thoughts. "I need a child to succeed me in the family. Children should take responsibility for my family by being an extension of me in the future. Therefore, children are a part of me." This shows that such thoughts are strongly entrenched in the minds of Koreans, especially of those over the age of 70 to 80. For this reason, Koreans' love for their children is strong.

In Korea, mostly wives are responsible for household management.

Men all over the world are surprised to know that in Korea, wives manage their husband's bankbooks. In Korea, in most cases where a married couple is not a working couple, the wife manages the husband's bank account. In general, even for working couples, the wife takes care of the household management. It can be said that this originated from 「Distinction of Couple (夫婦有別)[49]」, one of the virtues of the Samgangohryun. In the Gyeongju area, the Choi family made a name for

---

49) Husband and wife are kept properly distinctive.

themselves as extremely wealthy for more than 300 years in 10 generations from 1600 until after liberation in 1945. The old saying, "the rich don't last more than three generations," is ashamed. Nevertheless, they maintained the status of millionaires for more than 300 years and 12 generations. It is said that it is difficult to find a case in the world where one family has maintained wealth for such a long time. People say that the secret to maintaining such wealth for a long time is that they have followed six basic guidelines for life from generation to generation. For me, personally, the sixth guideline caught my attention the most.

The sixth life guideline is "Daughters-in-law of the Choi family must wear cotton, not silk, clothes for three years after getting married!" During the Joseon Dynasty, the hostess had the key to the storeroom in the house. Interpreted in a modern version, the hostess was managing the bankbook. It meant that the sixth life guideline of the Choi family was "Women in charge of housekeeping should have a frugal lifestyle and a saving spirit." This is also evidence that in the Joseon Dynasty, important decisions in the family were made by the head of household, while housewives were responsible for the household management. Possession of the key to the storeroom by the hostess was also a part of distinction between husband and wife. The fact that there is still a custom in Korean society for a wife to manage her husband's bankbook suggests that the long-standing traditional perception of separation between husband and wife remains intact in Korea. It seems that it has become a natural family culture in Korean society for a wife to manage her husband's bankbook.

Koreans value trust.

Regardless of the East and the West, and past and present, people say, "Leave a great job to someone you can trust." The following is my experience as an Air Force unit commander in Korea during July 2000. It happened when the Air Force Chief of staff called me into his office after the Air Force Commander's Meeting at Gyeryongdae, where the Air Force Headquarters is located.

"General 00, anyone in your position can be the commander of the unit you are currently commanding. However, the head of the 00 weapons system project, which our military is promoting now, is not a position that anyone can lead. The project will start in earnest from the second half of this year. My staff recommend that you are the right person for the head of the project. So, return to the unit and hand over the duties of unit commander to your successor within a week. Then come right up and take over the work of the project leader!"

It was an unexpected order from the Air Force Chief of Staff, so I was momentarily taken aback. However, after finding composure and thanking him, I was allowed to take an additional week for handover and returned to the unit. On the way back to the base, A phrase from Analects[50] came to my mind. It is a phrase about the five virtues that a benevolent person should have: Gong (恭, Polite)·Gwan (寬, Generous)· Shin (信, Trust)·Min (敏, Agile)·Hye (惠, Benefit).[51] Among the five virtues, the third virtue, Shin means "If you have trust, others will entrust you with work." I thought to myself that "I have been recognized by the military which I chose to serve and dedicate my youth to, and I have at least the virtue of trust among the five virtues of benevolence!" With that thought in mind, I felt truly grateful that the Chief of Staff had recommended and appointed me as the person in charge of the large weapon system acquisition project. I also felt proud and honored. I made a firm commitment to carry out my duties in a manner worthy of my honor. With such pride and commitment,

---

50) Analects Yanghwa section 6

51) It means that if you are polite, you will not be insulted; if you are generous, you will win the support of many people; if you have trust, you will be entrusted with work; if you give grace, you can manage people.

I was fully motivated from the start to the end. The weapon system acquisition project I undertook was the largest weapons system acquisition project in Korean military history. As much as its large scale, I have resolutely dealt with unprecedented sabotage, attempts to seduce and slander me as the lead person, and partial propaganda. As a result, I am still confident that I have successfully carried out my mission to ensure national interest to its maximum and to acquire the best weapon system by keeping faith.

Although the education levels of the people improved through the educational revolution, it was a natural consequence that when jobs corresponding to one's studies were not provided, social anxiety rose due to the increase of unemployment rates. This led to political instability and eventually a military revolution when national security was at stake. This is the motive of the military revolution in Korea on May 16, 1961. Fortunately, the newly inaugurated national leader planted hopes and dreams in the minds of Koreans, who had experienced poverty, disappointment, dissatisfaction; and embarked on extensive renovations for national development. His excellent insight, cool judgment, determination, and driving force laid the foundation for building today's Korea by utilizing high-quality human resources nurtured through the national education revolution in the 1950s.

In Korea, December 5th of each year is 'Trade Day'. Korea's economic development began with a national export-led industrialization strategy in the early 1960s. And on December 5th of every year, the export performance of companies is aggregated on a yearly basis and the export tower award, depending on the export amount presented. It is a day to encourage the hard work of export companies and boost their morale. Trade Day was originally called 'Export Day'. On November 30, 1964, Korea earned 100 million dollars in exports. In commemoration of this, the government designated the day as 'Export Day' and has continued to hold the event every year. Since then, Korea has achieved export records of 10 billion dollars in 1977, 100 billion dollars in 1995, and 600 billion dollars in 2018. The annual import amount also surpassed 600 billion dollars for the first time, furthering the ranking of Korea's trade volume. In 2021, Korea's trade volume reached 1.2596 trillion dollars, moving Korea's trade volume ranking from 9th, which it had maintained since 2013, to 8th. The trade balance also remained in the black for 13 consecutive years at $29.49 billion.

As a latecomer, how difficult was it to jump into the already established world export market and create its own export market that is now the 8th largest in the world today? In the global trade war where interest is the only thing that matters, Koreans made their homeland the economic powerhouse that it is today. I think it was possible because Koreans have a habit of placing importance on trust, which is a key factor in relationships with trading partners.

I mentioned above that if there is trust, the work will be entrusted. Some of the recent cases in which Koreans received and delivered orders through international competitive bidding are presented as examples. Korean construction companies made great achievements in K-Construction during the 2000s. Korea's Samsung C&T was in charge of the overall construction of the 'Burj Khalifa in Dubai' (828m), which is currently the tallest building in the world, and it was completed in 2009. The 'Marina Bay Sands Hotel', which has become a trademark of Singapore by being built in the shape of a floating boat on the upper floors of three buildings, was constructed and completed in 2010 by Korea's Ssangyong E&C. In addition to this, more than 5 world landmarks[52] in Southeast Asia were built by Korean companies. It was possible because Korean companies have gained trust from countries around the world. Through this, Korea has made a

---

52) https://www.wikitree.co.kr/articles/228856

great contribution to the development of global architectural technology.

That's not all. In a joint venture with a Turkish company, SK E&C received an order for the Turkey Eurasia Undersea Tunnel project, connecting Europe and Asia in 2008. Construction began in January 2013 and was successfully opened in December 2016. As a result, SK E&C received the 'Major Project Award' from the International Tunnel and Underground Space Association (ITA) in 2016, and in the same year, it received the 2016 Global Best Project Award in the field of tunnels and bridges from ENR, a world-renowned construction magazine. It was the first construction company in Korea to

Figure 1. Canakkale Suspension Bridge built with Korean construction technology

receive these awards. Recognized for such technological prowess, SK E&C received an order for the Silver Town project to build two tunnels under the Thames River in London in 2019 and is under construction with the goal of opening them in 2025.

In addition to that, South Korea's DL E&C and SK Eco Plant won the world's longest 'Canakkale Suspension Bridge' construction project connecting Europe and Asia after fierce bidding competition with Japanese and Chinese companies in 2017. The construction period was shortened by a whopping 1 year and 7 months than planned and opened on Mar 18, 2022. With a total length of 3,563m, the main span[53], which is the distance between the main towers, is 2,023m, the longest among suspension bridges in the world. "It was designed at 2,023m to commemorate the year 2023, the 100th anniversary of the founding of Turkey" and was opened in 2022. Previously, the longest suspension bridge in the world was the Akashi Kaikyo Bridge in Japan, completed in 1998, with a length of 1,991 m. Suspension bridges are the bridges with the highest construction and design difficulty among marine special bridges. The reason why this Canakkale Bridge has

---

53) This is the distance between main towers, and lengthening it is the key technology.

received international attention is that it is designed with a main span exceeding demon's realm of 2 km. Such a bridge was completed with the technology of a Korean construction company. I'm really proud of it.

Figure 2. The Kazungula Bridge built by Daewoo E&C of Korea

In addition to this, Daewoo Engineering & Construction exceeded expectations amid fierce competition with Chinese and Japanese companies and won the project to construct the 'Kajungula Bridge' across the Zambezi River in the Kazungula region, where the borders of four South African countries, Botswana, Zambia, Zimbabwe and Namibia intersect. The construction began in December 2014 and was completed in May 2020. An official from Daewoo E&C said, "The construction, originally scheduled for four years, took more than five years due to poor infrastructure and the practice of graft by the locals, and almost created something out of nothing." People say that the order for the Kazungula Bridge, which was in fierce competition with China and Japan, was possible because Daewoo E&C gained a reputation due to their past construction projects in Africa. As a result of Daewoo E&C's efforts, they were able to complete 10 million hours of labor without any major accidents.

After the completion of the Kazungula Bridge, the term 'Miracle of Kazungula' is being discussed in Southern Africa. The construction of the Kazungula Bridge has been a long-coveted project of Southern African countries for 40 years. The bridge construction project began in earnest in 2014 after an agreement was reached between the four bordering countries of Zambia, Botswana, Zimbabwe, and Namibia, where two countries with good financial conditions, Botswana and Zimbabwe, would bear half of the cost. Again, Korea, China and Japan fiercely competed for the Kazungula Bridge project. The Japanese companies going preemptively took advantage of the project being initiated with international aid from the Japan International Cooperation Agency. In addition to this, through the Japan International Cooperation Agency, they included the performance of the special construction method as a strategy when participating in the bidding. Chinese companies were also determined to win orders with low construction costs. Daewoo E&C, which had no 'backing ship' and was not competitive in terms of 'cost', could only offer technological competitiveness and local construction know-how.

Daewoo E&C had proposed excellent construction quality and reasonable construction costs, given the results of five road construction projects in Botswana from 1986 to 1991. In the end, Daewoo E&C, which had no backing ship and had not so good price competitiveness, succeeded in winning the order. At the time, officer in charge of the Botswana project said "Roads built by 00 company did not last for 10 years and had defects, but roads built by Daewoo E&C have been fine for 30 years", and continued to say "Because I have a faith in Daewoo E&C's quality, I entrusted this important construction project to them." In the end, trust in technology assisted them in winning the order. The successful construction of the Kazungula Bridge, which is beautiful enough to become a landmark in the Kazungula region, is expected to increase opportunities for Korean companies in the African construction market, which had been initially monopolized by China under the name of the Belt and Road Initiative. That's because Korean companies have built the trust.

Trust means belief and obligation. One of the reasons why Koreans value fidelity originates from 「Bungwooyusin (朋友有信)」[54], one of the virtues of the Samgangohryun, which was also the life guideline of the Joseon Dynasty. The concept of Shin (信, Trust) is one of the five elements of life in Five Virtues (五常說) which humans should have. They were originally Four Virtues with In (Benevolence, 仁), Eui (Righteousness, 義), Ye (Courtesy, 禮) and Ji (Wisdom, 智) which were lectured by Mencius, but Shin (信, Trust) was added by Dongjungseo during the era of former Han Dynasty of China. The four virtues that Mencius insisted that human beings should have are literally the elements that human beings should try to have internally. Trust, on the other hand, is a virtue of a relative concept. It is a duty that one has to abide by to the other person in human relationships. No matter how much a friend is equipped with benevolence, righteousness, courtesy, and wisdom, it is meaningless if you do not trust them. Perhaps, for that reason, the five virtues were completed by adding Bungwooyusin (朋友有信), which emphasizes the need for trust between friends. Sohak, which is taught to young children in Confucianism, emphasizes trust as the following: "In work,

---

54) Confidence should be maintained between friends.

you must be careful and trustworthy, and if you speak but are not trustworthy, you are not an honest friend. Integrity, righteousness, courtesy and wisdom are the basic morals and norms that everyone must abide by, and trust and loyalty must be kept between friends like a blade." With the introduction of Confucianism, the Samgangohryun had been learned as basic ethics in Korean life for more than 2,000 years. Because Korean ancestors memorized Bungwooyusin (朋友有信) while learning the textbook 'Sohak' for hundreds of years during the Joseon Dynasty, I believe that the idea of valuing Trust has also been ingrained in the consciousness of today's Koreans. In 1998, when Russia faced a difficult period of sovereign bankruptcy, most foreign companies scrambled to leave Russia. However, Korean companies that had entered Russia at the time were the only foreign companies to remain in Russia and share difficulties with them, and this also proves that Koreans value trust.

Koreans still maintain many customs of Confucianism.

Koreans still follow Confucian customs for important family affairs.

As of 2015, there are 13.4 million Christians in Korea, which is close to 28% of the total population. Nevertheless, it can be seen that many Koreans still follow Confucian procedures for important personal and family events such as weddings,[55] funerals,[56] and ancestral rites.[57] Of course, due to the influence of Christianity, the form of commemoration for the deceased has changed in the funeral or ancestral rites, but most of the procedures of the ceremonies still follow Confucian procedures.

For Koreans, the perception of marriage is based on Confucianism. Koreans recognize marriage as an occasion to prove that they have reached adulthood in society, are ready to create a family, the smallest unit of society and a starting point for prospering offspring. The wedding norms and procedures that were simplified and settled in four stages based on the Confucian clan rules[58] in the Joseon Dynasty are still being selectively implemented. When both families decide to get married, the groom's house sends Sajudanja (a letter to the family of the bride with the groom's horoscope data) and a marriage proposal as a sign of engagement. The bride's family then sends Yeongildanja (a letter with a date selection) and a

---

55) Ceremonial procedure that expresses the meaning of marriage
56) All the rites performed during the mourning for the deceased
57) The rite of burying or cremating a dead body
58) The family system based on patrilineal succession in the Zhou Dynasty of China

wedding approval letter in return. Next, the groom's family puts a gift in a box and sends it to the bride's family to confirm the establishment of the marriage. After the wedding ceremony, a pyebaek offering is performed to signify that the bride will leave her parents' home and be incorporated into her husband's family. When the newlyweds return from their honeymoon, they visit the bride's parents and the wedding is brought to an end.

Funeral procedures are also simplified to conform to the modern society from the past Confucian procedures based on the ancestral rites of Zhu Xi. After death, Seup (襲)[59] and Yeom (殮)[60] are performed for the deceased. Balinjae (Yunggyulsik, Funeral rites) are held, which are the last rites in order for the body to leave the funeral home, which is establishing a cemetery and bury the dead on the ground. Two days after the burial, the first ancestral rite, Samwooje (三虞祭), is held at the cemetery. The dead are enshrined in the household shrine and do the Talsang (End of Mourning). The funeral ceremony ends with Talsang.

Confucian ancestral rites and memorial rites held for the ancestors, which began during the Joseon Dynasty, are still

---

59) Bathing the corpse and putting on the shroud
60) Wrapping a corpse with a linen cloth for entry into the coffin

practiced a lot in Korean society. Among the rites specified in the Zhu Xi Family Ceremony and traditional family rites, the ancestral rites that are being performed even now include Shije (時祭),[61] Gije (忌祭)[62] and holiday rites.[63] Ancestral rites table setting and procedures are still conducted according to Confucian customs. I will introduce an ironic case of Confucian ancestral rites still practiced in Korean society. As a way to express respect to grandparents, parents, and corresponding adults on important occasions, Koreans bow once to those still alive and twice for the deceased at funerals, ancestral rites, and graves. In Korean Christianity, bowing at rites and funerals is interpreted as idolatry and is forbidden. Therefore, during the funeral and ancestral rites processes, Christians hold worship services instead of bowing, but still follow Confucian procedures such as YeomSeup, Balin, Samuje, Talsang, and rites on death days. How ironic is this? This is why Christian funeral procedures are necessary.

---

61) A rite held in the middle of the four seasons for the ancestors of the 5th generation or more, starting with the renown ancestor of the clan or the ancestor of settlement, by members of the clan in a village (currently only held in autumn)
62) An ancestral rite held for the ancestors of the 4th generation or younger on the day of their death
63) On New Year's Day and Chuseok, a ancestral rite held at the eldest grandson's house for upto the 4th-generation ancestor of that family

Koreans still have a strong sense of ancestor worship.

The primary goal of Confucian education is to teach bene-volence. Benevolence is a concept that originates from filial piety to one's parents and inevitably spreads to all mankind when one is polite to others. Filial piety to parents is based on ancestor worship. There are many articles about ancestor worship in the Analects such as "Confucius never ate a full meal when he ate alongside the mourners. When Confucius performed the ancestral rites, it was as if the ancestors were present. He said that " if I do not truly participate in the rite, it is the same as not holding the rite. If you perform memorial rite for your parents carefully and honor your distant ancestors with sincerity, the virtues of the people will become pure."[64]

These writings show that filial piety to one's parents is the basis of all words and actions in a person's life. And from the Confucian perspective, which regards funeral rites as the root of courtesy, when funeral rites are held, they must be performed as if ancestors were in front of them, with sincerity

---

64) The Analects, Sulee section 9, Palil section 12, Hakee section 9

and respect. It is because they believe that filial piety is revealed at funeral rites. One must serve his/her living parents as well as deceased parents and ancestors with sincerity. It means that if people respect filial piety, the virtues and customs of the people will naturally become pure.

As such, Confucianism strongly supports ancestor worship as the root of filial piety. Ancestor worship inevitably involves worshiping the spirits of ancestors. Therefore, it recognizes as a premise that there is a soul after death or a world after death. It can be argued that Confucianism, as long as it emphasizes ancestor worship, also has the character of a religion. This is a reasonable logic. However, if you know the difference between ancestor worship and worshipping of the dead, you can tell them apart. According to Max Weber,[26] worship of the dead has a strong connection to the afterlife of the dead, which is typically displayed in ancient Egypt. The belief in the afterlife is strong. On the other hand, ancestor worship is centered on the interest in reality. A case in point is the tradition of finding good burial locations for ancestors within the funeral rites of Confucianism. This is because of the theory of divination based on topography that if the ancestors' burial locations are good, then their descendants will prosper in the future. After all, the central idea is the secular concern that the spirits of the ancestors protect the descendants of the present world. It does not pay much attention to the existence of the ancestral spirits, which is the core of ancestor worship, or the composition of the afterlife.

In Confucianism, ancestral rites, which are ceremonies to honor the spirits of deceased ancestors, are highly valued. This is because it acknowledged the educational effect to cultivate the idea of respecting god and worshipping ancestors. The ancestral rites had a great political effect that brought about solidarity between families and relatives, and furthermore, the maintenance of national order. It is believed that Confucius, who maintained an atheistic position, respected the rites because of these effects. As a basis for this, a Confucius episode in the Analects, "If you strive for the duty of a human being and respect the gods but do not approach them, you can be considered wise,"[65] can be interpreted as it meant that keeping at a certain distance from God is a valid attitude of an intellect. Also, when Confucius' illness was serious, the disciple said, "I prayed to the gods of heaven and earth for Confucius," then Confucius replied "My such prayers are old."[66] From what Confucius said, "as long as you keep your morals, you

---

65) The Analects, Ongya 20
66) The Analects, Sulee section 34

don't need to pray to God," it can be seen that Confucius was atheistic. According to the long-standing tradition of Confucian society, Koreans still hold ancestral rites with relatives on New Year's Day, Chuseok, cold food day, seasonal memorial days, and the days of passing. Koreans, who have been affected by such influences for generations, still have a strong sense of ancestor worship along with the affectionate sentiment of their hometown as an extension of their filial piety toward their parents.

The patriarchal family system, the eldest son-oriented inheritance, and the concept of parental support by the eldest son still remain.[27]

The family system refers to systems related to inheritance, division of family, and adoption to continue the family lineage. The current inheritance system for Koreans has changed since 1990 from the concept of head of a family and the preferential system for sons. Inheritance ration of 1.5 for spouses and 1 for each child, regardless of gender, is legalized for equal inheritance. Nevertheless, the influence of the son-oriented inheritance system to succeed the family through the father line, still remains. Some Koreans still maintain the preference for the eldest son from the first wife. The family system of

Koreans was exclusively based on a patrilineal succession. Historically, Korean society changed to a patrilineal society centered on the eldest son only in the 18th century. According to records, until the early Goryeo period, there were many small families consisting of a married couples or couples living with elderly parents or parents-in law. After the mid-Goryeo period, family composition began to grow with two or more married couples and gradually changed to a larger family structure. In the Joseon Dynasty, the composition of large families was the norm. The change to the extended family system was due to two reasons. One was to fulfill filial piety toward parents, one of the Confucian virtues and the other was to effectively carry out labor-intensive farming work. This was because each household needed as much laborers as possible for farming.

According to records, inheritance in the Goryeo Dynasty was common in that all property was divided equally between sons and daughters, regardless of whether they were married or not. At that time, the family system was maintained in the form of kinship in which the father's, mother's, and wife's families were organically combined. As a result, the mindset of discrimination against daughters or preferential treatment to eldest sons had not yet been formed. Equal inheritance for each child was a norm. At that time, also the form of marriage in which a man married into a woman's house[67] had an effect on the establishment of equal inheritance. Under the influence of equal inheritance, the duties of ancestral rites were also divided equally among the children. In this case, property was thoroughly managed and recorded for each share. This equal inheritance continued until the 16th century into the middle of the Joseon Dynasty.

After the latter half of the 16th century, the patriarchal family system[68] was established by Sarim. As Hyangyak took the roots in rural villages, Confucian culture made its way throughout provinces. As a result, from the middle of the 17th century, gender discrimination and eldest son preference gradually began to appear. In the 18th century, equal inheritance almost disappeared, and the inheritance system was established in which sons, especially the eldest son, were given preferential treatment. The son-in-laws were excluded from the ancestral rites and the woman's property brought

---

67) Marriage customs of Goguryeo where a man moved into his wife house for a certain period of time after marriage and then returned to the man's house later; system of taking son-in-law into the family

68) Confucian family system based on the patriarchal system, which includes a patriarchal kinship system, no same-sex marriage, no adoption of kids with different surnames, inheritance of the eldest son, and a large family system of differential inheritance of children

with her when she married was also regarded as her husband's property. As the inheritance system changed, in the 18th century, the succession of ancestral rites was settled as the eldest son's sole responsibility. As the inheritance system changed to patrilineal kinship, the adoption system, albeit limited, between patrilineal kinship, developed. As for the family type, the paternal lineage family was formed in earnest.

Equal inheritance between men and women has the effect of distributing the legacy of their ancestors. Internally within family, it prevented the gap of wealth between children, but on the other hand, externally, it inevitably resulted in a weakening of the strength of family and kinship compared to other families. As the population increased in the late Joseon Dynasty, such a phenomenon intensified. In the Confucian culture, the power of the family is as important as its succession of the family. Because of this, an inheritance system centered on the eldest son emerged to maintain family power. After the late Joseon Dynasty, inheritance was given exclusively to the eldest son. Depending on the family's wealth, the gap of wealth also appeared between children, especially the eldest son who inherited everything from wealthy parents. Therefore, the responsibility for serving the parents and performing ancestral rites by the eldest son also became a norm.

During the Goryeo Dynasty, filial piety to one's parents was one of the government's recommendations. In the Joseon Dynasty, as Confucian culture became wide-spread, it sublimated into one of the social ethics. In the late Joseon Dynasty, as the patriarchal family developed, filial piety became a social ideology.[69] Joseon society is also called a family-oriented society because filial piety as a family principle has developed into a social ideology. In today's Korean society, equal inheritance to all children is legislated. Nevertheless, in many Korean families today, the father-centered family system, the eldest son-centered inheritance, and the concept of parental support by the eldest son still remain due to the influence of old Confucian culture.

Koreans have a strong tendency to help each other among neighbors.

Most Koreans have a good habit of helping neighbors in need. There is also a strong awareness of mutual aid by actively helping neighbors and relatives in their work. Relatives, friends, and neighbors all work together to help each other in major occasions of sorrow and congratulations, such as a neighbor's wedding or funeral. In particular, they have a

---

69) Fundamental thinking underlying human behavior, politics and society

strong habit of helping people who need help, such as people who have suffered a disaster, people who are sick, or people who have just moved in. They help each other willingly for ceremonial occasions of neighbors and relatives. Where did these good habits and tendencies of Koreans come from?

People who have lived together for a long time, gathered in one place and rarely visited by strangers, get to know each other well even if they are not related. There is such a thing as "neighbor cousins". Living next door to each other for an extended period of time, they became like cousins. In the climate of the Korean Peninsula with four distinctive seasons, farming must be done according to the season in order to get a proper harvest. Farming required intense physical labor, and the amount of work one person could handle was limited. Also, the Korean Peninsula is a barren soil, and droughts and floods occur frequently. Such disasters were not something one can handle alone. Neighbors helping each other was absolutely necessary. Koreans have lived in an agricultural society for thousands of years from generation to generation in such a living environment that requires others' help. For that reason, it is my view that Koreans naturally formed the habit and tendency to help those in need and help their neighbors.

Due to such natural environmental factors, it naturally took root as a moral norm in Joseon society after the late 16th century that people should live while helping each other. As the basic ethics that must be observed in the Confucian society of rural villages, Hyangyak article 4, which says "Good things should be shared and encouraged, bad things should be regulated and prevented, good customs should be exchanged with each other, and relief should be given to each other in times of trouble and disaster", became the life guidelines of the people. Since then, the content of Article 4 of Hyangyak, which is based on the concept of mutual aid, has permeated into Joseon society for hundreds of years and became a consciousness among members. As a result, it is the logic that the good habits of Koreans, who do not spare help when there is someone in need around them, and who have a strong tendency to help each other in the sad or happy times of neighbors and relatives, remain in today's Korean society.

In summary, the living environment of the Korean Peninsula, where mutual aid is absolutely required, naturally led to the inclusion of "mutual aid" in Hyangyak, the norm for rural life in the Joseon Dynasty, and it has been handed down until now.

Koreans treat guests (foreigners) well.

This is what I experienced while studying in the US in the 1980s. From an American perspective, what I went through could be natural. However, as a Korean, it was quite embarrassing for me. Here's what happened. In September 1981, I attended 00 master's course at the 00 graduate school located in California, as a Korean government scholarship student. Due to the area where the school is located being a resort area, I could not find a place to live for quite a while, so I had to live in a motel with my family for three months while attending the school. Maybe for that reason, the 00 graduate school I went to had good dormitory facilities for students. However, foreign students like me were not eligible to live in the dormitory, so I could not even apply for it. On the contrary, most universities in Korea operate separate dormitories exclusively for foreign students. It is a consideration for foreign students, so they can easily adapt to life in Korea. That is why I was perplexed. Seeing all those dormitory facilities being exclusively used by its own citizens, I wondered "Is this country truly an advanced country?" It was because I thought that developed countries should be considerate of the people from less fortunate countries. After studying abroad in the United States for 2 years and 6 months, I stopped by the laboratory to thank my academic adviser before returning home.

"You've worked hard! You are now leaving with many good impressions and memories of our America, right?"

"Professor, thank you very much for your kind guidance. But when I go back to my country, I don't think I'll have good impressions or affection toward the United States. Sorry."

"What do you mean? What made you that way?"

"Do you know what the difference between Korea and America is? Foreigners who have visited Korea come to like Korea and want to visit again. However, from what I know, I have heard that many people who have been to the United States become anti-American. Maybe it's because of the attitude and social system of people who are in the position of the strong and not considerate of the weak at all?"

I have vivid memories of the professor, who once cared for me, who became very frustrated with my stubborn attitude.

A cultural characteristic of Koreans is that they are kind to guests, especially foreign guests visiting Korea. Most foreigners who have lived in Korea say they miss Korea when returning to their home country. Famous celebrities who have been to Korea say they really want to come back someday, and some even actively promote Korea. From what reason?

Koreans never think of themselves as being above others. As a result, I have never heard or seen foreigners being ignored or looked down on. I think, as the founding ideology of Hongik Ingan represents, that since Koreans settled on the Korean Peninsula thousands of years ago and formed an agricultural society, and lived helping each other from generation to generation, it is natural for them to be kind to the others. For such reasons, Koreans are ingrained to be considerate of unfamiliar people who have come to visit our land since ancient times with an attitude of being others' shoes (易地思之).

There is a record about Hamel, a Dutchman, who drifted to Joseon as Europeans advanced to the East after the 15th century. He drifted to Jeju Island with his party and was transported to Hanyang, where he was called to King Hyojong at the time. It is said that Hyojong showed curiosity and instructed him to play some Dutch customs. The nobles of Hanyang at the time were also very interested in Hamel's party and their culture. So, Hamel and his party received considerable hospitality after being transferred to Hanyang. It is recorded that he received a hopae, the Joseon identification card, through Joseon localization education, and wore a hanbok made of fabric bestowed by the king.[28] According to the report "Fresh Country Joseon," written by German Gente in 1901, at that time, Koreans had an unbearable interest and curiosity about Westerners. However, it is recorded that such curiosity stemmed from goodwill to a certain extent, and it was never intended to harm or upset people, so it did not interfere with his trip at all.

From ancient times, it is said that the ancestors of Koreans fed their families and strangers as long as there was a little bit of leftover rice. It was to the point that it was taken for granted that when guests came over for lunch or dinner, even if they were strangers, they were to be served. They seem to have regarded entertaining guests as a duty. Such habits still remain today, as Koreans are not negligent in hospitality and are generous. It seems that Koreans naturally have a good habit of not neglecting to entertain guests who have come to visit them. There is a common sayings among Koreans, "Hardship awaits once you leave home!" For that reason, it seems that Koreans never neglect the guests who visit them, perhaps out of consideration for the situation of the guests who have left home and are going through hardships. As a result, most people who have visited Korea have left with a good impression of Koreans. Then, where did these good habits and tendencies of Koreans come from?

Due to the geopolitical influence of the Korean Peninsula,

located at the eastern end of Asian continent and surrounded by the Japanese archipelago, in the past, most foreigners visiting the Korean Peninsula were just Chinese and Japanese. In addition, Koreans became interested and curious about strangers who suddenly appeared as they lived their entire lives in an extremely limited area of about 5 miles around due to the nature of the agricultural environment. That interest and curiosity would have increased when Westerners who looked completely different from Asian counterparts appeared. I believe that the living guidelines of Article 4 of Hyangyak that says 'people in need should help each other' had been ingrained in people's mind and it is the reason why Koreans are kind to foreign guests who visit Korea today.

Koreans heavily depend on strong people, but they don't really appreciate their help.

One of the characteristics of Koreans felt by foreigners in the early 20th century was that they had a lot of dependence and little gratitude. This is in line with the characteristics of most Koreans today, who are heavily dependent on the strong, and like free things, but lack gratitude for help they received. The dependency referred here means to selfishly trying to solve the work related to oneself by borrowing the hands of a third party. If the dependency is abused, it can turn into bribery. Even in court decisions, many Koreans think that if they find and ask a favor from the judge or prosecutor in connection, they can get a favorable decision. Such thoughts are imprinted in them. If the person they are looking for is not reachable, Koreans search for a third party who can reach him/her and ask for a favor. Whatever it takes, they try to achieve what they want. The consciousness of 「無錢有罪·有錢無罪」[70] nestled in the hearts of Koreans is proof of that. Where did this Korean culture of solicitation come from? There are many reasons, but a few examples are listed below.

As mentioned earlier, the population of Joseon increased from less than 1 million in the middle of the 15th century during the reign of King Sejong to over 10 million in the early 20th century at the end of the Korean Empire. Since more than 70% of the Korean Peninsula, where people lived on a mountainous area where productive land was limited to a few areas. As the population increased on limited land, the competition for survival inevitably intensified.

In Joseon society, it was said that a comfortable life for the rest of one's life was guaranteed with just 3 years in office as a

---

70) If you have money, you become innocent even though you have sin, and if you do not have money, you become guilty even if you are not guilty.

magistrate of a county. If you become a government official, you could succeed and earn money. This was possible because bureaucrats were able to fill their personal fortunes by abusing their authority. It is a typical bureaucratic culture that appears in countries where Confucianism is the basis of government. As the population in Joseon increased, competition for survival intensified, and exploitation by officials became more cunning. Most of the people called Yangban had no choice but to become government officials or attach themselves to the government in order to gain practical benefits. What would happen when more and more people aspired to a limited management position? People would become more willing to use any means and methods in order to be appointed to the position. As such social conditions continued, all sorts of conspiracies and evil schemes were crafted.

During the Joseon Dynasty, there was a system to select the necessary talents through recommendation. It was also evaluated as a system that caused the factional strife that impoverished Joseon Dynasty. Partisan strife in Joseon originated from Jeonrang (a government position of the 5th rank), which had the right to recommend a bureaucrat. In order to become a government official by recommendation in Joseon, one had to be recommended by Jeonrang. In addition to this, a person who became a bureaucrat by recommendation rather than one's ability needed someone who would recommend him to be promoted again. It was natural that most of the people who had a relationship with and had been recommended by the Jeonrang were supposed to gather around him. It was a natural consequence for them to try to expand the influence centered around him. For that reason, factions were formed in the Joseon's bureaucratic society. The more incompetent a person was, the more they tried to form factions by rallying forces. It was to overcome the limits of one's ability with the power of the faction to which he belonged. After seizing power with the help of the faction, it became necessary to counter opposing forces. Next, in order to maintain power, they became immersed in their faction's interests and their original missions or tasks were no longer relevant.

Clan politics, where people did everything by themselves and for themselves, continued for hundreds of years after the middle of the Joseon Dynasty. Even in such a situation, people aspired to become bureaucrats. Even so, the appointed government officials had been degraded as having been appointed and promoted by solicitation rather than ability. As a result, the idea that you can become a bureaucrat as long as you have someone who supports you has become apparent to people's minds. What does this mean? Efforts to develop one's ability to achieve one's desired goal were not so important. It means that the effort to get the support of the powerful person who can help to achieve the goal was more impactful. The way of thinking to solve one's important problems by relying on a third party has been handed down from ancestors who lived in Joseon for hundreds of years. It is my view that it has been hardened in the consciousness of and is still partially expressed as a characteristic of Koreans today.

On the same regard, Koreans today are seen as liking freebies and lacking gratitude. When there is something to ask help for or to solicit a third person with influence, they call and visit frequently enough to be annoying. However, once they've achieved that goal, they don't express gratitude for your efforts. Of course, they rarely communicate, with almost no news from each other. This is a natural phenomenon in a society where the solicitation culture is common. A person who makes a request pays a bribe in exchange for the favor. The one who received the request granted what was asked for in return for the bribe. So, they think there is nothing more to be thankful for. It is natural not to have a sense of appreciation by the Joseon people who had such an idea. Seriously, there is even a proverb that says, "Your mind when you go to the toilet is different from your mind when you leave the toilet." In addition, the life guideline of Hyangyak, 'People must help each other in times of crisis', can also be said to have played a part in making Koreans lack a sense of gratitude. This is because the guideline of Hyangyak stipulates that it is a natural duty for a person with ability to help someone who is facing difficulties.

Koreans like to meddle in other people's affairs and are good at disparaging others.

Confucianism, represented by the teachings of Confucius, is to make people have the character of In (仁, Benevolence) which means love for humanity. As mentioned above, benevolence is a concept that originates from filial piety to one's parents and when one abides by filial piety, brotherhood, loyalty, trust, courtesy, righteousness, integrity, and having a sense of shame, it inevitably spreads to all mankind. In addition, the purpose of personal learning at the Confucian perspective is to grow into a good man equipped with benevolence (仁) and become a gentleman who can cultivate themselves, their family, and rule the nation and the world. This is the positive aspect of Confucianism.

The Analects contain the core values of Confucianism. In

general, it suggests to people the right way to live. However, there are many pieces expressed in the form of 'how should the words and actions of scholars, gentlemen, virtuous men, and saints be, and how relatively petty persons behave.' For example, 'A gentleman thinks of virtue, but a petty man thinks of the land. A gentleman thinks of the law, but a petty man thinks of preferential treatment. A gentleman has many friends and does not belong to one side, but a petty man has a few friends and takes sides. A gentleman helps others achieve their goals, and correct others' ill intents so that they cannot be fulfilled, but a petty man does the opposite!' And it differentiates friends into 'those who are not as good as me, beneficial friends and harmful friends, those who only have knowledge, those who like it, those who enjoy it, etc.'[71] Role models with great personalities are also differentiated into saints, virtuous men, gentlemen, good men, and scholars. As a result, approaching from the negative aspect of Confucianism, the differentiation of people in the Analects by Confucius unconsciously evaluates and classifies the other person in human relationships and induces them to discrimination. For that reason, Confucian scholars have the habit of evaluating

---

71) The Analects Yiin section 11, Wijeong section 14, Anyeon section 16, Hak-i section 8, Gye-ssi section 4

and classifying people they deal with unconsciously, finding it natural to recognize the faults of the other person.

Hyangyak was a standard of living in rural villages in Joseon society. It was a promise between people in rural villages to keep the Confucian ethics of human relations. It was said that the Hyangyak was slightly different depending on the region. However, the four ethics of encouraging each other to do good things, correcting each other for wrongs, encouraging each other to participate in good customs, and helping each other in difficult situations were considered to be common. Confucian human relations ethics were enacted at the national level as the living standards of the people. The moral norms necessary to maintain human relationships had developed into ideologies of life. Through this process, Hyangyak's principles of living were imprinted on Koreans' psychology. In an agricultural society, mutual aid is absolutely required due to the nature of farming. The purpose of Hyangyak was to organize a voluntary cooperative body centered on the people in the living environment of the Korean Peninsula, and to reform the rural villages through practices of Confucian values. This is positive aspect of Hyangyak.

Like both sides of a coin, if anything has a positive function, it has a negative function as well. Contents of the 4th Article of Hyangyak state, "We should encourage each other for good things, correct each other for wrongs, encourage each other for good customs, and help each other in difficult matters", which had a dysfunction of inducing people to interfere with the words and actions of others. In a modern concept, article 4 of Hyangyak should be carefully recommended even to very close relatives and friends because the content of Hyangyak, a guide to life with the Confucian teachings and rural regulations, had been conscious of Korean ancestors for hundreds of years. Koreans today, as a dysfunction of Hyangyak, like to meddle in other people's affairs and are good at disparaging others.

There is also a bad habit of swearing behind others' back. The teachings of Confucianism, which dominated Korean thought, and the rules of Hyangyak, which dominated Korean ancestors for more than 300 years, are one of the phenomena that remain handed down in Koreans' lifestyle and human relationships to this day.

Koreans are socially relational.

Many Koreans are relational in dealing with people in society, so they value their roles and strive to be faithful to their duty and truth. People say that Korean society has relational characteristics that are different from individualism or collectivism. This means that Koreans tend to engage in behaviors that are more focused on relationships with others than on individual or group goals. They prioritize the interests of those with whom they are related to over justice, fairness, and efficiency of their group.[29] Perhaps the factionalism that puts more emphasis on factional interests than greater cause is also related to this.

Western Christian society presupposes the idea that all people are equal and that only the Absolute can save people from their sins and that only the Absolute can evaluate their life. No one who is only a creature of the Absolute can help me in my life. They define one's life as consisting only of one's relationship with the Absolute. That is why Western social relations are individualistic. They stick to principles and value the pursuit of honesty.[30]

On the other hand, the basic moral norms of Confucianism, which had dominated Korean society, are established in human relationships. The interpretation that the character 'In (仁, Benevolence)' pursued by Confucianism means two people, a combination of two (二) and people (人), shows that Confucian moral perception is based on 'between people'. The Samgang-ohryun, which is the guideline for Confucian life, only shows a specific form of this human relationship. The most common relationship in Confucianism is the human relationship between me and the other man. The basic character of Confucianism is defined as "cultivating myself and governing others (修己治人)." In Confucianism, the relationship between me and others is a structural concept of reciprocity that one cannot exist without the other person. The concept of a reciprocity between me and others includes specific human relationships between people such as parents, children, neighbors, teachers, and disciples. It makes it inevitable to have a socially relational structure.

However, this Confucian human relationship considers each individual as the subject of all human relationships. Therefore, it establishes and maintains one's identity in human relation-ships, not the isolation of individualism. Individualism provides freedom from the servitude of one human being to another human being. But there is a danger of falling into egoism. It also has a danger of being closed in the individual isolation of human beings. On the other hand, when a human being becomes a subject in a relationship with other human beings, the fundamental equality of human beings can be confirmed. This could be seen as a civic spirit of Koreans that respects freedom and law, and plays an important role in keeping democracy sound.

Also, in Confucian society, it is premised on the idea that "a person can learn on his own, and become a gentleman through practice and training, the ideal human being." They think the evaluation of one's life is determined by their life style, outward words, and actions. They see that one's life is entirely dependent on the development of their personality and defined by their relationships with the people around them. Naturally, they value the relationship between people in the community and workplace members, through blood, regional, and academic ties. As a member of the social group to which one belongs, one considers the duty and trust to other members as an important value.

The social relational characteristics in Koreans is due not only to the influence of Confucianism, but also to the social and cultural environment in which Koreans lived for a long time. Since the Neolithic Age, Koreans had lived in an agricultural society, huddled together on the stable geological foundation of the Korean Peninsula. In particular, during the Joseon Dynasty, as farming technology advanced and income increased, the family developed into a large family system for labor-intensive farming, and methods of helping each other such as exchange of labor service. With this, a cooperative farming team naturally developed in each neighborhood.

After King Sejong the Great, the Samgangohryun gradually

became established as a basic ideology of people's lives. In the late 16th century, as Sarim led central politics, local autonomy was emphasized, and compliance with Hyangyak became mandatory. Hyangyak[72] provided rules to civilize rural villages and was a form of promise to keep each other autonomously within the community, living together. This served as a life guideline to be observed among the people of rural villages by applying human relationships with people around them to the human relationships stipulated by the Samgangohryun.

Hyangyak was beyond the ethical standards and people were officially punished in Joseon society if they didn't follow. It played a role similar to that of the law. Institutionally, all people in rural villages had to belong to Hyangyak. And it was maintained and governed by the executives of the Yuhyangso.[73] Through Confucian human relations ethics, it provided basic life guidelines for the people and forced them nationwide.

---

72) As a human being, you must be loyal to the country and filial to your parents. You must be faithful to your husband and respect your elders. Friends should keep fidelity, and neighbors should encourage each other to keep it. If others do not comply with this, they should be scolded and corrected. A covenant that requires to be courteous to each other and to help each other in case of disaster or difficulty.

73) Self-governing organization composed of virtuous and recognized figures (yangban) in rural villages, who involved in maintaining local regulations and administration, and assisting local head.

The moral norms necessary to maintain human relationships developed into basic ideologies in life, and were passed down in the psychology of Korean ancestors. So, Koreans have strong relational tendencies that place more emphasis on relationships with others than on individual or group goals. They try to be faithful to their role in order to improve their relationship with other people in social groups, whether it is a formal or informal, such as family, work place, local gathering, 00 club, etc. Such social characteristics and the accompanying lifestyle are still strongly displayed in Koreans today.

Habits and tendencies formed by cultural influence[31,32,33]

Koreans have lived between continent and maritime powers far more powerful than themselves on the narrow Korean Peninsula for a long time. However, without being assimilated to them, Koreans have built a distinctive culture of food, clothing, shelter and a unique cultural character.

Traces of human habitation have been found on the Korean Peninsula from 500,000 to 600,000 years ago. It is estimated that Koreans lived in the Korean Peninsula and the surrounding areas during the Bronze Age, when full-scale settlement for agriculture began. The time coincides with the origin of the

Korean people claiming to be a single race as descendants of Dangun. Among the Chinese, Koreans, and Japanese, who look almost identical in the eyes of Westerners, Koreans can distinguish Koreans.

The typical face of Koreans is estimated to have been formed in the process of migration of human ancestors from hot Africa to cold Siberia, and then to the Korean Peninsula. Typically, they have slanted eyes with no double eyelids. Their nostrils are large and the bridge of the nose is low. The lips are small and thin and are characterized by a look of strong willpower. Analyzing the faces of indigenous Koreans today, they appear in two forms: 80% of the northern races and 20% of the southern races. Northerners have dull eyebrows and no double eyelids. The lips are thin and the earlobes are small. Whereas Southerners have thick eyebrows, large eyes, and double eyelids. The bridge of the nose is distinct, and the outline of the lips is clear.

It is unknown when the faces of the southerners appeared. The time when Koreans were formed as an ethnic group, distinguished from neighboring peoples such as China and Japan, was during the Bronze Age. After that, it can be seen that there was some degree of mixing in lineage. However, it is said that there are few people in the world who have maintained the purity of their bloodlines as much as Koreans. However, it should be noted that the unity of the Korean nation is a concept established from a historical point of view, not a biological point of view. This is proven by the fact that Koreans recognize that their ancestors had their own customs and culture different from neighboring countries such as China and Japan. Leaders had emphasized national unity whenever the country was in trouble. Because of that, most Koreans think that they are a single ethnic group with a long history. This fact, also, can be a proof that the sense of unity was established by a historical point of view.

Since ancient times, Korean ancestors have spun yarn from hemp, ramie, and silkworms, and made clothes through weaving. The basics of clothing were jeogori (a Korean style jacket) and pants that were easy to move regardless of gender or social status. The bottom hem of the jeogori reached the hip and the collar opened to the left.[74] During the reign of King Gongmin of Goryeo, Mun Ik-jeom imported cotton seeds and began to produce cottons. After that, cotton wool and cotton clothes were used to keep warm in the winter. The rice that Koreans eat on a daily basis has been cultivated in the Han

---

74) It is the custom of the inland Asian horse-riding peoples who used bows a lot.

River basin since BC. In the early days, it was a precious food that only kings and nobles could eat. Grains such as millet, beans, wheat, barley, and sorghum were the staple food. As vegetables, they cultivated mugwort, mallow, radish, and cabbage. Livestock such as cows, pigs, chickens, and dogs were raised and used as side dishes. Adapting to the temperate region with clear four seasons, they developed fermented foods such as kimchi and pastes, made of soybeans, vegetables, and salt as the main ingredients, and ate protein and vitamins until winter. This is also an aspect that proves the ability of Koreans to adapt to the environment. According to Chinese records, Goguryeo people, ancestors of Koreans, enjoyed eating maekjeok (pork with Korean herbs) similar to bulgogi today. Based on this, among the foods that are synonymous with Koreans today, bulgogi is also an old traditional food for Koreans.

Then, what was the residential culture like? Most of the Han people slept on bedclothes on the bare floor of the room. Koreans install ondol (Korea underfloor heating system) on the floor of the rooms. Ondol is a Korean heating system that is so widely known that it is included in the Oxford dictionary along with kimchi. In the Goguryeo era, people installed partial goodle, early form of ondol, with a fire set in a part of the room. It was not until the Goryeo Dynasty and the early Joseon Dynasty that ondol spread nationwide. The partial goodle of Goguryeo were later transmitted to the West, Mongolia, and Japan.

It is estimated that Chinese characters were naturally introduced into the Korean Peninsula as trade with China began in the Iron Age around the 4th century B.C. In 108 B.C., Emperor Wu of Han attacked and destroyed Wiman Joseon, and installed prefectures as their tributary state. From this time, it can be assumed that China's Chinese characters and the ideas of hundred schools of thought were transmitted in earnest to the Korean Peninsula. At this time, it is believed that 「Samgang-ohryun」, which Dong Zhongshu proposed to Emperor Wu as the ruling ideology of the despotism system, was also transmitted to the Korean Peninsula. The basic ethics of Confucianism, that is the Samgangohryun, regulates the morals and behaviors that must be observed in human relationships, and gradually took their places as a national ruling ideologies to strengthen the royal authority in the Three Kingdoms.

Entering the Goryeo Dynasty, Buddhism came to be regarded as the root of cultivating individuals, and Confucianism as the root of governing the country (politics). In the Joseon Dynasty, Neo-Confucianism became established as the ruling ideology of the new dynasty. Moreover, in the late 16th century, as Sarim took the initiative in the central political arena of Joseon, Neo-Confucian culture settled in Joseon society. Through the education of Sohak (Lesser Learning), Confucian values became a part of life from a young age. They promoted Hyangyak nationwide to pursue local autonomy. In order to establish Confucian order, the dynasty actively encouraged the compilation, dissemination, and practice of ethical books such as Samganghaengsildo. This was the reason why habits and inclinations based on Confucian culture had been incorporated.

Pantheistic consciousness of Jininsa Daecheonmyung (盡人事待天命)[75] remains deep.

Religion can generally be divided into two types. One is monotheism and the other is pantheism. In Christianity and Islam, which represent monotheism, God is typically regarded as someone who exists outside the world we live in and rules the world. On the other hand, in a world dominated by pantheistic religions or ideas such as Buddhism, Hinduism, and Confucianism, God exists in the world where we live and is seen as dwelling in every single thing.

---

75) It means to fulfill one's duty and wait for a heaven's order.

In the worldview of monotheism, as specified in the Old Testament of the Bible, God, man, and nature are clearly in the relationship between the Creator and the creature. Even between humans and nature, which are the same creatures, nature is seen as a means for humans to live, just as all animals and plants on the ground are defined as human food. So, in the worldview of monotheism, there is a disconnection between God and humans, and between humans and nature.

On the other hand, one of the important characteristics of the pantheistic worldview is that God, man, and nature are in a continuous relationship and that there is no disconnection between them. In the world view of pantheism, the sky is a god and at the same time is heaven. It is nature itself. First of all, God and nature are one. The god of the sky gave birth to nature, dwells in all things, and is also inherent. In the case of human beings, this is no exception, meaning that Heaven gives birth to humans and dwells within them. What is the sky that dwells within human beings? It means human nature. Human nature is the sky that dwells within a human being.

Confucianism is based on a pantheistic world view that God dwells in humans and that humans are a part of nature. As a result, eastern thought, represented by the Confucianism, tends to capture everything in a fused form. So in the matter of the soul and the body, it believes that the human mind and body are composed of the same energy. This means that, unlike Christianity, which sees the soul and body as a confrontational relationship, it does not do so. Of course, it doesn't think both are equal either. It places a high value on the mind and looks down on the desires of the body. However, the two are not qualitatively disconnected, there is just a difference when labeled high and low in terms of value.

Therefore, there is no fundamental confrontation between good and evil in the basis of Confucian thought. According to Mencius, even people who are innately good can often do bad things. It is because of the negative conditions such as the environment. If the condition improves, they will naturally become good. Evil is not an independent principle opposed to good. It means that when good is placed in an imperfect state, it becomes evil. From another angle, evil also means imperfect goodness.

There is no essential break between the ideal and reality in the Eastern way of thinking based on Confucianism. In the Western way of thinking, ideals exist apart from reality. That is why it is called to be ideal. However, with an Eastern way of thinking, ideals are thought to be close to reality. The ideal is not something high and far away from reality. It is in a place based on a familiar reality. Furthermore, it believes that ideals are already partially included in reality and even as co-existing. Therefore, realism to Asians, who have Confucianism as their ideological background, does not mean "throw away the ideal and take the reality." It means "putting the ideal close to reality and seeking the ideal in reality."

As such, the recognition that heaven is inherent among all things as impersonal being establishes a pantheistic and continuous worldview. As a result, in the world of Confucian knowledge, the heaven, humans, and nature are viewed as in combined relationships, not separated ones. That is why the soul and body, good and evil, fantasy and reality, etc. are viewed as interdependent relationships. In this way, the dehumanization of the heaven god, who is always an object of reverence to humans, forms a pantheistic worldview. This pantheistic view of the world gave birth to the idea of heavenly nature and heavenly mandate, which are the basis of the human perspective of Asians and the ideological background of Confucianism. Heaven is in all things and dwells in all things. The heaven that dwells in human beings, one of all things, is so called human nature. And heaven is originally goodness itself. Because it entered the human inner world and became human nature, human nature itself is goodness. As a result, Mencius' Seongseonseol (Theory that man's inborn nature is good) has been inherited as an orthodox Confucian thought for a long time. Under the world view based on pantheism, it is a natural philosophy.

However, the heaven is not only internalized as human nature by dwelling in human beings. The perception that heaven still exists outside of humans in a transcendental aspect also coexists. It recognizes the concept that heaven exists outside of humans and restricts humans from the outside, that is, 「the idea of the heavenly mandate」. The original meaning of heavenly mandate is 'the command of the heavenly god'. However, as the characteristics of heaven weakened and became impersonal, the meaning of heaven's mandate naturally changed and took on the meaning of destiny. Destiny is a kind of force that externally determines the state of human existence. Because it is a power from heaven, it has a property that human power cannot do anything about. What this means is "fulfill your duty and wait for the heavenly mandate (盡人事待天命)." The only thing humans can do is to do their best. The success or failure of work is determined by destiny transcending human. The source of this saying is unknown, but from the saying in Anzi Chunqiu (晏子春秋), "I have done my greetings, so I am just waiting for heaven," it can be presumed that the idea has existed in China since ancient times. The heaven's mandate as destiny is deeply embedded in the consciousness of Asians with Confucius ideological background.

Most Koreans value their family names.

One of the peculiarities of Koreans is to place a value on family name that represents one's ancestors. For Koreans, a surname is originally a name that indicates a family member or blood relative. It means that you are a member of that family or bloodline. Originally, the surname (Sung, 姓) is a trace of a matrilineal society and refers to the place of origin of the mother. Whereas the surname (Si, 氏) meant the place where his father lived. But now, the surname (Sungsi, 姓氏) has become an indication of the father's lineage.

Koreans feel the closeness of blood ties between people with the same surname and the same place of origin. For Koreans, this consciousness of blood ties gives vitality to human life, but sometimes it causes harms too.

The first family names that appeared in Korean society were the founders of the ancient Three Kingdoms. Their surnames are recorded in Samguk Sagi and Samguk Yusa. As for foreign records, the surname of King Jinheung of Silla appeared as Kim Jinheung (金眞興) for the first time in China's literature,

Bukjeseo. Based on historical records, during the Three Kingdoms period, only a few privileged classes could have surnames according to their status. It was from the end of Silla to the beginning of Goryeo that surnames were spread throughout the country. It is said that during the first half of the 10th century, powerful families in each province came to call their surnames in order to emphasize their uniqueness. This is proven by the fact that most of the figures enshrined as founders in each family of Koreans today are from around this time. At the beginning, provincial lords used surnames freely. After Wang Geon unified the Late Three Kingdoms, he bestowed surnames to local powers or to people who cooperated with him. At this time, Tosung (surname of the region) was also distributed to the powerful families of each region to acknowledge that they were the rulers of each region. This is the background of the establishment of the place of origin system in surnames.[76]

Bonkwan (The Place of Origin) refers to the place where the founder of each family was born or the region from which a surname was derived. It is usually used with a family name and is used to indicate a range of paternal kinship. Prior to the

[76] It was the name of a registered administrative district during the Goryeo Dynasty, but later it represented the place of origin for the founder of the surname after the late Joseon Dynasty

establishment of the system of Bonkwan and surnames, although they were classified as relatives, they did not extend to family ceremonies. Entering the Joseon Dynasty, the consciousness of blood ties was strongly emphasized that the people with the same place of origin and family name were relatives forever. Along with that, it developed as a means to symbolize the class superiority and status of the paternal kinship group to which each individual belongs.

As a result, what appeared was a genealogy that records the lineage from the founder of the surname to the person at the time of compilation. In the genealogy, all careers and histories, such as individual names, official positions, and notable achievements, are recorded from the founder to each generation in order. The first genealogy to be written was the genealogy of the royal family during the reign of King Uijong of the Goryeo Dynasty. As the Confucian ideology became common in the Joseon Dynasty, genealogies began to appear in the general public as well. After the middle of the Joseon Dynasty, clans began to create genealogies to distinguish their families as well. Afterwards, those who could afford to, even if they were not prestigious, began to publish genealogies as a means to reveal their roots and decorate their families.

After the middle of the Joseon Dynasty, the yangban class

began to have genealogies. In imitation of this, middle class people also began to create genealogies by linking the materials that had been handed down orally for each clan. It was to show off as if they were from a noble family. As it expanded further, even the indigenous people of each region began to acquire genealogy as the same clan.

In the case of Japan, most of the people lived without a family name until the early 19th century. During the Meiji Restoration in the middle of the 19th century, the policy of surnames for all the people was implemented.[34] At the time, most Japanese people came up with surnames that made use of the location of their house or the characteristics of their neighborhood. As a result, various surnames such as Takata (田中, In the middle of rice paddy), nakamura (中村, In the middle of village), Matsusita (松下, Under the Pine Tree) were created. Currently, there are more than 80,000 surnames. In Japan, there are not many people with the same surname. This is because the history of the surname is less than 200 years. For that reason, Japanese people do not attach much importance to the history of a family surname or their own surname. Naturally, there is no such thing as pride or attachment to the family name.

Japan implemented the Civil Registration Act[77] in 1909 as

part of its colonial rule over Joseon. Even the people of the lower classes were given census registration with family names they wanted. It was to increase the targets of exploitation by turning Joseon's slaves into commoners. They implemented the family registration act without distinguishing one's status in the name of destroying the class system of the Korean Empire. They launched a campaign to have the surname for the entire people. At that time, about 20% of the people, who were born in the lower classes and slaves, were given surnames. Most of them wanted to acquire the surnames of landlords or noblemen in the same neighborhood rather than new ones. This is the reason why there are relatively more Kim(金)·Lee(李)·Park(朴) surnames than other surnames. At that time, the people of the lower classes chose the famous surnames Kim·Lee·Park and applied for their surnames. At that time, Japanese imperialism did not want the clan unity of Joseon Yangban surnames. This is the reason why the Japanese imperialism willingly allowed the surnames Kim·Lee·Park desired by the lower class people of Joseon. In Japan, people arbitrarily created their own surnames. On the other hand, in Joseon, even the lowly people at the time had a famous surname in Joseon that they wanted. This is an objective fact

77) Old name for family registration act

that tells us how important surnames are to Koreans. The people of the low class could have a famous surname that was largely classified as a nobleman overnight, but who would refuse it?

Today, there are about 270 Korean family names. Among them, five surnames, Kim (金), Lee (李), Park (朴), Choi (崔), and Jung (鄭), account for more than 54% of the total population.[35] It is said that there is no case in any country in the world where a specific surname exceeds 20% of the total population. However, if you look at the proportion of Korean surnames, Kim (金) accounts for 21.6% of the population, followed by Lee (李) with 14.8% and Park (朴) with 8.5%. This is the result of many people wanting to have surnames of famous nobles during the enforcement of the Civil Registration Act of Japan in 1909. This is the reason why the 1st, 2nd, and 3rd place in the composition of surnames among Koreans are disproportionally large and shows uneven distribution compared to other surnames.

With the enforcement of the Civil Registration Act, the yangbanization of the entire nation was naturally achieved. Since then, people with ancestors from the lower classes disappeared in Korea. Every Korean has become a descendant of a certain Jeongseung (Prime Ministers) or Panseo (Ministers).

This means that for Koreans, surnames have been considered very important as a kind of data that indicates one's origin. However, in light of my experience,[78] it seems that the idea of giving importance to Koreans' family names is disappearing in recent years.

Korean women keep their original surname even after marriage.

There are two things about Koreans which men all over the world are surprised with. One of them, as mentioned above, is that the wife manages her husband's bankbook. And the other is that the wife keeps her own surname even after marriage. In fact, Korea is the only country in the world where women retain their original surnames even after marriage. This fact is said to be incomprehensible to foreigners even if they wake up from sleep and think about it again. To such foreigners, Korea would appear to be an almost incurable natural paradise for women.

In Korea, when a man gets married, it is called "getting into marriage." This phrase is derived from the "Seoryubugaje (婿 留婦家制)"[79] where the groom goes to the woman's house,

---

78) The fact that in the 2010s, the number of households requesting genealogy decreased to 1/3 of copies issued in the 1970s.

holds a wedding ceremony, and lives with his parents-in-law. This "Seoryubugaje (壻留婦家制)" was inherited until the beginning of the Joseon Dynasty. This was a wedding practice that went against the patriarchal social system of Neo-Confucianism. Therefore, the Confucian scholars who led the founding of Joseon insisted on the introduction of the 「Chinyeongje (親迎制)」, in which women married into men's houses. A typical example of this is when Taejong and Sejong took the initiative in holding a wedding ceremony to welcome the Crown Princess as an example of 「Chinyeongje (親迎制)」. Despite such strong national initiatives, the 「Chinyeongje (親迎制)」 was not easily implemented. After going through the semi-「Chinyeongje (親迎制)」 where a man goes to a woman's house and sleeps for only three days, the true 「Chinyeongje (親迎制)」 settled down in the 18th century as the patriarchal order became dominant.

"Seoryubugaje (壻留婦家制)" and 「Chinyeongje (親迎制)」 are rooted in the Goguryeo wedding custom of living in the wife's house and the Chinese wedding custom of living in the

---

79) This is a past marriage custom of the Korean, which originated from the Seookje of Goguryeo recorded in China's classic <Weijidongyijeon> in 《Three Kingdoms》, in which once the marriage was confirmed, the groom built a small house near the in-law's house, and the newly weds lived there until the child grew, then they moved out to the groom's house.

husband's house, respectively. It took a long time for "Seoryubugaje", which had been maintained in the Korean peninsula for a long time, to change to 「Chinyeongje」 and settle down. The transition of wedding customs from Seoryubugaje to Chinyeongje was not limited to changing the residence of the bride and groom. This was because it was their lifestyles and many related customs had to be changed simultaneously.

The equal inheritance system for children, which lasted until the first half of the 17th century, was one of the powerful systems that sustained Seoryubugaje. Under the children's equal inheritance system, Seoryubugaje played a role in facilitating land inheritance from the wife's family. This meant that it provided the poor nobleman son-in-law an economic foundation.[36] Under such circumstances, would it have been possible for the bride to take the groom's surname? The logic is that the realistic conditions in which the groom moved into the bride's house and lived with the wife's family naturally allowed the bride to keep her surname.

In addition, the basic ethics of Confucianism, in which Samgangohryun says, "It is the duty of a wife to serve her husband, and there must be a distinction between husband and wife that should not invade each other (夫婦有別)", also had an impact. During the period from the early to the middle of the

15th century, the Gyeongguk Daejeon, the basic code of law of the Joseon Dynasty, was completed. At that time, the Korean family system was not a patriarchal form of Confucianism. It was a kinship structure in which the father's, mother's, and wife's families were organically combined until the end of the 16th century. Therefore, the children inherited equal shares and the service of ancestral rites was shared between children in sequence. The family system without discrimination among sons and daughters was maintained when the law was established. It can be said that the law was also enacted based on the Confucian ideology of separation of husband and wife. It is presumed that such a tradition has continued to the present day, and Korean wives keep their surname as even after marriage.

Koreans have a strong exclusive tendency and are closed.

Koreans seem to have a lot of pride in being a member of the "the Eastern Kingdom of Courteous Gentlemen"[80] since ancient times. 「The Eastern Kingdom of Courteous Gentlemen」

---

80) It is a word from the preface of history book, '鴻史', written by Ji Gwang-han in the mid-Joseon period (1731), and by citing the contents of '東夷列傳', which was written by Gongbin, the 7th generation descendant of Confucius, it indirectly indicated that Gongbin called Joseon an Eastern nation of courteous gentlemen.

comes from the following contents. In section 13 of the Jahan of the Analects, there is a phrase that "Confucius wanted to go and live in Gui (九夷)[81], and someone asked how he could live in such a shabby place, Confucius said that the gentlemen live there why should it be shabby?" In 『Dongyiyeoljeon (東夷列傳)』, there was also a quote[82] that said "Joseon was an excellent country and a country of courtesy to the extent that the ancestors of China should learn from it." There is also a content in 『Jewangungi』[83] that "Because it is a polite country, the Chinese people also called it a small China." In the West, Catholic clergies dominated thought during the Middle Ages. Similarly, in Confucian culture, bureaucrats studying Confu-

---

81) Ethnic groups living in the northeastern region of China, where the culture was relatively low at the time.

82) In the preface to 'Dong-yi-yeoljeon' written by Gongbin, the 7th generation of Confucius in 267 B.C., 'The country in the east is called Dongi, and nine tribes honored Dangun as their king. There is a Content that Huangje, the founder of the Chinese people, learned to read from JabuSeonin (紫府仙人), a scholar of the Joseon Dynasty, and received and returned with the Inner Imperial Letter (內皇文), and became the emperor. It also said that it is a country of courteous gentlemen, where customs are pure, food is conceded, and men and women live separately. By amplifying the contents of the Analects (13 pieces of Jahan), it also included the explanation that his grandfather Confucius also wanted to live in that country and that it was not shabby. (Source: cafe.daum.net/oonhyunsudang/OKvs/4)

83) A history book written by Yi Seung-hyu during the reign of King Chungryeol of Goryeo (1287)

cianism monopolized ideology and culture as intellectuals in the society. It is my opinion that the contents presented above became conscious in Koreans as the Analects, which can be said to be the original text of Confucianism, served as a guide for ideology and education in the Confucian society of the East.

In addition, Goguryeo also ruled over other peoples in Manchuria and Liaodong and repelled the national aggression of the Sui and Tang dynasties, which were the unified empires of China. The Sui Dynasty, which was a unified dynasty of China, was defeated in battle with Goguryeo and perished. Subsequently, even the emperor Tang Taizong was hit by an arrow and fled. Due to these historical facts, Koreans feel a certain confidence in China.

Goguryeo and Baekje introduced Confucian scriptures, such as the Thousand Character Text and the Analects of Confucianism, and advanced civilizations such as paper and ink to Japan. Because of these historical facts, Koreans have a kind of superior sense also to Japan. Unusually, Koreans, compared to other peoples surrounding the Korean Peninsula, seem to have lived their lives thinking that they are culturally superior as "the Eastern Kingdom of Courteous Gentlemen". This could also be seen in the Japanese evaluation of Koreans after the extortion of national sovereignty. They said, "Joseon people place extreme importance on courtesy nationwide. They evaluated that this is because the legend of Gija, that said Gija came to Go-Joseon and taught manners and help them escape from the barbaric state, and the fact that Hyeonjong of Tang Dynasty praised Silla diplomat for being polite, etc., reminded Joseon people of the pride that they are the people of the country of courtesy."[37] For that reason, I think there are still some Koreans who call people from neighboring countries demeaning terms[84] that show a lack of courtesy.

The traditional color of Koreans is white. According to the record,[85] the people of Buyeo, an ancient Korean nation, widely wore white clothes. People in the Joseon Dynasty also wore white clothes. At the end of the Joseon Dynasty, all members of the Righteous Army also wore white clothes. There was something that could not be missed in the travelogues of Europeans who visited Joseon around the 1900s. The first thing they mentioned about Joseon people was 'white clothes'. It was because many Joseon people wore white clothes. Probably not everyone wore white clothes, but

---

84) Orangkae (barbarians), Ttenom (swarms), Jjokbari (japs), etc.
85) China's 'Wei Zhidong' of Three Kingdoms

in their eyes, Joseon people wore white clothes in both summer and winter to the extent that it was considered a 'characteristic' of the people. Although it must have been difficult to deal with the stains on white clothes in those days when they were just washing clothes with lye in a stream, Joseon people just loved to wear white clothes. Koreans have enjoyed wearing white clothes from generation to generation and consider it to be their traditional color. Why do Koreans like to wear white clothes? The theory is that people liked white from the time of the birth of the nation and it naturally developed into a preference for white clothes across the country. In addition to this, equestrian peoples of Northeast Asia worshiped white horses, and all of the royal tombs of Goguryeo have their heads towards Mount Baekdu.[86] Baekseolgi rice cake (Snow White Cake), which Koreans enjoy eating, was the most basic sacrificial offering.

Even today, the color of Korean underwear is mostly white. For a suit, most people wear a white shirt inside. This fact alone shows that white color still occupies an important place in the lives of Koreans. White, which Koreans love, is the

---

86) Mt. Baekdu is a mountain considered sacred by the Korean people and the name of Mt. Baekdu comes from the practice which a white cow's head was sacrificed to the sky.

most perfect color among all colors. The purer it is, the more perfect it is, and when something else is added, that perfection drops. White appears when all wavelengths are reflected together in the visible light wavelength. It is a color that appears when all the color wavelength in the visible spectrum is reflected without being absorbed. White, which Koreans like, is a color that pursues perfection.

Just like the color white, Koreans have a strong tendency to be exclusive and do not want to accommodate strangers to their territory. Korea is a country where the Chinese have left due to not being able to settle down. It is a country where the Jewish community, which is said to be found in any country in the world, does not exist. The exclusive propensity of Koreans led to a hereditary dictatorship by the Communist Party, which has never happened anywhere else in the world. It also led Korea to maintain its number one position in exporting countries for adopted children for so many years. Even the head pastor in the church is making a hereditary succession. I think these characteristics, which are comparable to other ethnic groups, are due to the strong exclusiveness of Koreans just like the color white, which neither tolerates nor accepts other colors. As we will see from a different perspective later, strong exclusiveness is always accompanied by closedness.

Because exclusiveness is based on closedness, Koreans are inwardly exclusive and tend to be closed-minded.

Koreans like fermented food.

Kimchi is now a widely known food to the extent that foreigners think of "Koreans" when they think of it. Kimchi is a fermented food unique to Koreans developed by adapting to the natural environment in which Korean ancestors lived. In the Korean Peninsula, the four seasons are distinct, so you can eat a variety of vegetables for each season. However, vegetables are not produced in the winter. It is also difficult to store, requiring processing such as drying or pickling before winter. In such circumstances, kimchi is fermented by mixing vegetables with various seasonings. Koreans eat kimchi made in the fall as a source of vegetables for an extended period of time through winter into spring. The Chinese character for kimchi is "jeo (菹)," which means "pickled cabbage." It first appeared in the records of the Goryeo Dynasty.[87] It said that people in the Goryeo Dynasty ate salted radish kimchi all winter long. When they called kimchi, they called it "ji(漬)" meaning to soak in water or "jeo (菹)" meaning to pickle.

---

87) History of the Eastern Country (東國李相國集) by Lee Kyu-bo (1168 -1241)

Various types of kimchi, such as cabbage, radish, cucumber, and leaf mustard, which are salted and eaten, became popular in the Joseon Dynasty. 「Chimji(沈漬)」, which means to put vegetables in water and soak them, was transformed into 「Dimchae」, and later became today's 「Kimchi」 in the late Joseon Dynasty. In the early days of kimchi, only vegetables were salted and eaten. After that, it is speculated that spices were gradually added, such as garlic, green onion, and ginger. It is estimated that red pepper was introduced to the Korean Peninsula through Japan after the Japanese invasion of Korea in 1592. According to records, red pepper seasoning was added to kimchi in the middle of the 18th century, about 150 years after red pepper was introduced. There are many theories as to why people started eating kimchi with red pepper seasoning instead of only eating white kimchi. According to the theory of oriental medicine, spicy food is effective for colds. For that reason, red pepper powder was added to

kimchi. The history of kimchi with red pepper powder added is not yet 300 years old. Today's kimjang kimchi was derived from the systematic arrangement and dissemination of recipes as one of the relief foods at the national level near the end of the Joseon Dynasty. It was because the lives of the people were too difficult at the time due to frequent famines and exploitation by bureaucrats. It was not until the early 19th century that kimchi finally became established as one of the representative side dishes of Koreans.

In addition, one thing that cannot be left out when speaking of Koreans is "Jang (醬)." Originally, seasoning is to season food and add flavor. Jang, a Korean seasoning, even serves as a great side dish by itself. The first time that Jang appeared in the records is 『Wei Zhidongyijeon(魏志東夷傳)』 in 『The Three Kingdoms』 of China. There is a record that says, "The people of Goguryeo are good at making fermented foods." Soybean paste (fermented soybean paste, 豉)[88] appeared for the first time in 『Samguksagi(三國史記)』 「Shinmunwangpyeon (683)」. For Koreans, Jang was made by fermenting soybeans and salt, which had been abundant in the Korean Peninsula and Manchuria since ancient times. Jang has been one of the important side dishes that provide a stable supply of protein and salt to Koreans for generations. As such, Koreans developed fermented foods such as kimchi and soybean paste

88) Chinese character for Meju, 'Xi'

to adapt to the natural environment with four distinctive seasons. Through these, it was possible to consume stable and balanced nutrition throughout the four seasons. Even some Koreans say that they get irritated if they do not eat kimchi, a fermented food, for several days.

Koreans tend not yet to believe in laws and systems.

In any country with a backward society, bureaucrats' sense of privilege, disregard for laws and systems, corruption, solicitation, and a culture of facilitation payments exist. In such a society, bureaucrats, who can be called the ruling class, do not follow the laws and systems that they should abide by in their positions. Rather, they use laws and systems to maintain wealth or power. People do not trust laws and institutions if they are not impartially enforced. If you don't trust it, you think of it lightly. The feeling of having to abide by weakens. Laws and institutions are a kind of promise between people in a society where people live together. To achieve what society aims for, people must keep the promises that they made. It goes without saying that trust in a promise is greatly damaged when it is not kept. Korean society still values Confucian ethics, so if you were forced to deny the law or system in order to keep your duty as a human being, you would receive support from people to some extent. Now, Korea is also in the stage of becoming a modern society that prioritizes the laws and systems they have set as promises. However, there is still a strong tendency among Koreans not to trust in laws and institutions. Where does this originate from?

Most of all, it is the view that it is because 「Noblesse Oblige」[89] is not being fulfilled. This is because those in the ruling class show off and abuse their authority rather than taking the lead and fulfilling their duties. From generation to generation, Koreans have seen the people of the ruling class who consider themselves an exception and enjoy the power granted to them before complying with any systems or procedures. Perhaps for this reason, it seems that Koreans still have a sense that it is more effective to know a person in power than to follow a system or procedure. As a result of the remnants of such consciousness, some Koreans still try to show off the power when they seize something small. The above-mentioned "one

---

89) This is a compound word of 'the crest of a chicken and the yolk of an egg', which expresses that a chicken's mission is not to boast of its crest, but to lay eggs. It means that in order for people in the social leadership to be treated fairly, they must fulfill their duties (oblige) as much as the honor (noblesse) they enjoy.

law for the rich and another for the poor" speaks for this. Every time the new government comes into office, it cries out for a policy of harmony, but isn't the selection of talent based on blood ties, school ties, and regional ties openly practiced? In the past 00 government, the phrase "Mansahyungtong (萬事兄通, Everything goes well)"[90] was used in Korean society in a self-snearing manner. I think this is a word that candidly expresses the current consciousness structure and level of Koreans. There was a joke that even in hospitals with well-established normal medical procedures, one needs to know a hospital janitor to get proper treatment. That's why many Koreans still don't believe in normal laws, systems, and procedures.

There is a Korean proverb that goes, "Only when the upper water is clear, the lower water is clear." It is a saying that expresses the desire for the people of the social leadership to set the right example. The proverb came about because people in the social leadership have not been doing so for a long time, even though the responsibility to follow procedures in their position is a priority. Most of the Yangbans who represented

---

90) Originally, "Mansahyungtong (萬事亨通) means that everything goes well as intended, but the letter 亨 (hyung, prosperous) was changed to 兄 (hyung, elder brother) to indicate that everything will be done through the president's elder brother.

the leadership of the Joseon Dynasty in the past had a consciousness that they were exempted from laws and systems, and only the common people should abide by them. It seems that such a consciousness is still fixed in some Koreans. The evidence of this is that evasion of military service, solicitation, bribery, and traffic in government positions or jobs by celebrities and upper-class people that still remain throughout Korean society today.

President Kennedy of the United States was not physically strong enough at the time to enlist in the military. As a result, he failed the army and navy officer candidate physical exams one after another. He sent a mournful letter to his billionaire father asking for help, so he could join the military. His father, who received his letter, moved political and military connections and he later was commissioned as a naval officer. Kennedy was so eager to enlist because he wanted to do something big for the future of his country. He thought that if he fell out of the ranks of the people who participated in World War II, it would be socially impossible for him to hold a major public office in the country in the future. For that reason, Kennedy, who became a naval officer, was seriously injured in a battle in the South Pacific. Since then, he had to face the pain by taking turns using painkillers and stimulants for the rest of his life. The case of President Truman is similar. He couldn't join the military because he was severely short-sighted without glasses. Nevertheless, he was able to cross the French front during World War I as an artillery captain. This was because he memorized the eye test chart and passed the physical examination.

About 20% of Britain's nobility under the age of 50 were killed in World War I. The rate of deaths from aristocrats and graduates of prestigious universities was several times higher than that of workers and farmers. On the other hand, what about Japan, which created the myth of seppuku suicide and kamikaze commandos at the end of World War II? The death ratio of Japanese aristocrats and graduates of the Imperial University was incomparably lower than the ratio of British aristocrats and Oxford and Cambridge graduates during World Wars I and II. Japanese historians who discovered these statistics after the war said that Japan could never win World War II.

Then, what about Korea? There have been reports in the media of a singer who was arrested for having four teeth pulled out to avoid military service, a celebrity who got the physical exam decision for a public service job after dislocating his shoulder, and a sports player who purposely hurt himself. Even those who want to be loved by the public and stand on the stage of glory do not hesitate to destroy their bodies in order to avoid military service. There is no case where the upper stream is cloudy because the lower stream is not clear. If so, who did these celebrities and sports stars imitate and considered this deviance to be 'permissible'? The cause can be inferred by looking at how noblemen served in the military during the Joseon Dynasty.

In Joseon, people were largely divided into yangin and commoners. Yangin was able to advance to public office instead of providing labors and paying tax to the state. Commoners were not allowed to hold government posts for not providing labor and not paying the taxes. The military service system in the early Joseon Dynasty was the 「Yangin Gaebyeongje(良人皆兵制)」.[91] According to Joseon's 「Yangin Gaebyeongje(良人皆兵制)」, in principle, about two supporters are organized for one regular soldier. It was a system in which supporters were to help livelihoods of the families of regular soldiers. Supporters did not serve in military, but instead supported the regular soldiers by paying the military cost of about 2 rolls of cotton cloth a year. It is obvious that anyone

---

91) Compulsory conscription for all men between the ages of 16 and 60, excluding current or former officials who have reached the age of 70, merchants and workers, and slaves.

with money would have preferred to be supporters rather than being regular soldiers. It is easy to guess that Yangin, who had better living conditions, would have chosen the military service of supporters by spending money. This means that it was a system in which powerless poor farmers were in charge of the national defense mission at which the country's survival depended. In addition to these institutional deficiencies, as Joseon stabilized, the Bangkunsupoje[92] was implemented nationwide. Furthermore, it was legalized by Gunjuksupoje[93] during the reign of King Jungjong. The conscription system of unity of the military-farming was changed to the mercenary system. This is the reason why Joseon's regular army had no choice but to collapse without resistance during the Imjin· Jeongyu War and Byeongja· Jeongmyo Horan.

In Joseon, the military service was exempted for yangban, who were treated the best by the state and talked about the major issues for the survival of the state. This was one of the fundamental problems of the Joseon military conscription

---

92) It was originally illegal as a system in which government offices received payments in exchange for the military exemption from the subjects of conscript, but it was expanded and implemented nationwide as it helped to enrich the financial situation of the relevant government office.

93) It is a military service system in which the state receives money in return for exempting its citizens from military service, and uses the money to buy soldiers to protect the country.

system. Normally, those who acted as masters of the state were not personally responsible for national defense. How could national defense not be neglected? Originally, the Gyeongguk Daejeon, which was the foundation of Joseon's national law, stipulated that all the Yangin were required to serve in the military. In the case of yangban, the performance of official duties by incumbent officials and the studying of Confucianism at Sungkyunkwan and Hyanggyo were regarded as their direct or indirect military service. According to the Gyeongguk Daejeon, except for this exception, all yangban, including former government officials of the third rank or lower, must, in principle, bear military service. There seems to be no flaw in the legal system. However, it was a condition where those with power or money could naturally avoid military service without any guilt. This is because the military service exemption clause was ambiguous and there were many loopholes in the system. Therefore, most people in the ruling class enjoyed their rights as owners of the state during peaceful times, but when a crisis occurred in the country, they abandoned their duties as owners and were the first to flee. Those who lived under the rule of such people are the ancestors of today's Koreans. As a result of that influence, it is believed that the idea of "anti-noblesse oblige"[94] is still flowing in the blood of Koreans.

In Korea, people who evaded military service in their 20s come forward to pursue politics just because they have earned some money. During the time of their friends' military service, because they joined the society earlier and succeeded in career, now they want to be high ranking government officials. They are shameless and have remorse for their past foul plays. What is clear is that a person who shied away from duty to the state in his early twenties cannot be said to have matured as a person just because he is older or because he has attained a high position in society. Generally, people who were bad in their 20s become worse in their 50s and when he turns 60s, he becomes a very bad person. So, people who abnormally evaded military service in Korean society should never be allowed to participate in the political arena. Such people should not be selected as high officials. Otherwise, the idea of ⌜anti-noblesse oblige⌟ will not disappear from Koreans.

---

94) Opposite to noblesse oblige, the idea that people at the top of society do not fulfill their duties because they rule the country.

Characteristics formed by the combination of various factors

Previously, I presented the environmental influence of the Korean Peninsula, home of Korean life, the historical influence that Korean ancestors had to experience for generations, the influence of ideology and religions that dominated Korean ancestors' consciousness and real life, and the characteristics such as habits, inclinations and lifestyles that are displayed by most of Koreans. However, a person's personality and the behaviors induced by it are very complex and originate from various reasons. After classifying the influential factors determined to have influenced the formation of Korean personality, the characteristics determined to be formed by the corresponding influential factors were identified and presented. However, there may be characteristics that are not distinguished by any single influential factor, but are formed by combining several factors in a complex way. For that reason, in this chapter, the characteristics of Koreans, which are judged to be formed by the combination of various influential factors, and the resulting lifestyle and behavioral patterns were derived and presented.

Koreans' passion for education is world-class.

It was mentioned earlier that becoming a government official in a country with Confucianism as the ruling ideology would give him power and wealth, and he could wield his reputation for many generations. In the case of commoners during the Joseon Dynasty, in addition to this, they gained the status of yangban. He and his descendants were able to escape military service and they could escape exploitation from the nobles and their petty officials. As a result, becoming a bureaucrat was an object of envy. For that reason, intellectuals as well as commoners eagerly hoped to become officials.

In order to become a bureaucrat in the Joseon Dynasty, people had to go through the national civil examination after being educated at an educational institution, making the education system developed in line with the national civil examination in mind. At that time, those who wanted to be educated usually received their elementary education at Seodang built by a local Confucian scholar. Next, they went on to 4 regional Hakdang in Seoul or a local Hyanggyo, which correspond to a secondary educational institution. Students of the 4 regional Hakdang or Hyanggyo could apply for the Sogwa (Saengjingwa, exam for low ranking officials).

Successful applicants became Saengwon or Jinsa. And he obtained the qualifications to enter Sungkyunkwan, which corresponds to today's university. Students from Saengwon or Jinsa who attended Sungkyunkwan applied for the liberal arts exam, which is Daegwa. Even if they did not attend Sungkyunkwan, Saengwon and Jinsa could apply for Daegwa. After such a long period of education, one had to pass the liberal arts exam to become a government official.

During the Joseon Dynasty, most of the Yangin were in a difficult situation because they did not have enough money to prepare for the exam. However, the opportunity to get an education and become a bureaucrat was given to them. The opportunity given to Yangin was enough to make them determined despite how difficult it was. There is a proverb that says, "A dragon coming out of a stream." It is a metaphor regarding a farmer in the countryside who passed the state exam by studying night and day. There were cases like that, although rare, in the Joseon Dynasty. So passing the national examination and becoming a government official have been an object of envy for Korean ancestors. Yangin in Joseon had to take charge of all compulsory labor for the dynasty just because they were not yangban. They were even exploited by yangban and officials. In order to escape from such unfair treatment, they all the more hoped to become bureaucrats. Even if they made a living by farming, they wanted their children to avoid the unfair treatment they had received by making their children into bureaucrats. This is why they tried to educate their children at any cost. It was an environment where they had no choice but to dream of becoming a government official by passing the national examination.

If they couldn't become government officials, they wanted to become Yangban as the next best thing. It was to receive preferential treatment as a yangban, such as military service exemption. After the mid-Joseon period, people acquired the status of yangban as a part of Nabsokchaek,[95] or by purchasing or forging genealogical records with financial resources. In order to live as a yangban, they had to know the basics of funeral rites. In order to hold the memorial rite in accordance with the proper formality, they had to receive at least Seodang education and be able to read. Under such conditions, they had no choice but to participate in the world of education.

At the end of the 19th century, Joseon's national fortunes faced a turning point like a candle in the wind. In the face of

---

95) A policy of Joseon Dynasty that gave a government post or elevated the status of people who donated grain to the country to overcome financial difficulties and help the poor.

Japanese invasion, Joseon's pioneers recognized that education was important to develop national strength. Therefore, as a part of the national movements, the education movement was actively promoted. In 1894, a modern education system was established through the Gabo Reform of Kim Hong-jip. A ⌜Protocol of Education for National Build-up⌟ was published stating that "the wealth and strength of a nation lies in education." Based on the spirit of education for national build-up, various types of government schools were established, including elementary schools, middle schools, teaching schools, and foreign language schools. During this time, missionaries also established private Christian schools such as Baejae Hakdang, Ewha Hakdang, and Jungshin Girls' School.

After the Eulsa Treaty, nationalists launched a patriotic enlightenment movement with the goal of restoring national sovereignty. They argued that modern education based on nationalism is the foundation and essence of the national movement. Under the slogan, "Learning is power," which is still imprinted on the minds of Koreans, many private schools such as Daeseong School, Osan School, and Boseong School were established. It is the result of the idea that "the path to a prosperous country and strong military is only for the people to learn and be smart". This was thoroughly imprinted on those who were called pioneers at the time. At the time, they believed that the reason Joseon collapsed was because of ignorance and lack of knowledge on the world. They were keenly aware of the need for education.

Under Japanese colonial rule, the goal of education for Koreans was, in a word, obscurantism. Under Japanese colonial rule, the elementary school enrollment rate of Koreans was only 1/6 of that of Japanese. In higher education institutions, this became even worse. The national leaders organized the Chosun Education Association. Nurturing talents by establishing a higher education institution was the most urgent task, and hastened to establish universities. When the Japanese Government-General ignored the request for the establishment of universities, a campaign was launched to establish a private university with the hands of Koreans. In response, the Japanese Empire established Gyeongseong Imperial University. It was a measure taken to put down the passion for higher education nationwide that was boiling in the minds of Joseon people at the time.

At that time, public elementary schools had limited capacity and were expensive. It was difficult for workers, farmers, and the urban poor to get education opportunities. As the number of illiterate people increased due to lack of access to education, leaders launched a campaign to eradicate illiteracy. In the 1920s, night schools for Korean were established nationwide. They taught Hangeul and educated children in Korean. In order to suppress this, Japanese imperialists established 「One District, One School Policy」. Only one elementary public school was established in each district. The number of students accommodated here was only one-fifth of the number of eligible children who could go to school. For that reason, 16 million people, or 80% of the 20 million people at the time, were illiterate. As the literacy rate increased, the media eventually took the lead in the campaign to eradicate illiteracy. Under the slogan of "Knowledge is power, Learn to live", news outlets such as the Chosun Ilbo had students at middle school or above to go back to their hometowns during the vacation to conduct an illiteracy eradication campaign. Thanks to the efforts of these pioneers, the thought that "education is the only way to survive" became prevalent.

Still, for Koreans, the lesson that "knowledge is power, learn to live" is revived to overcome difficult situations. It is because such thought had been ingrained in them. The more difficult the situation is, the stronger the desire. After liberation, Koreans lived a very difficult life until the early 1960s on land that was in complete ruins due to the Korean

War. It was such a difficult time to the extent that people with diseases from starvation were everywhere, especially during spring cessation period. Even under such extremely difficult conditions, parents in Korea devoted everything to their children's education. It was an expression of their strong will not to pass on the same life as theirs to their children. They thought that their children should be given higher education at any cost. This mindset remains in today's Koreans as well, which is why the enthusiasm for education for their children is so high.

They have strong comparison psychology with others, jealousy, and competitive spirit.

In Korea, there is a proverb that goes, "If your cousin buys land, your stomach aches." If your cousin is buying a piece of land and your stomach hurts, how much will your stomach hurt if someone else buys it? Some argued that this proverb, which at first said "If your cousin buys land, you should have a stomach ache", had a positive meaning but it has been distorted. This proverb is appropriately used as an expression to say that Koreans have strong feelings of jealousy at the root of their psychology.

Comparing oneself to others is a natural human habit. We

imitate our parents from the time we are born and begin to learn their words and actions. Even in the process of learning, we compare our words and actions with others to check if our words and actions are correct. And we want to do better. For us, comparative mentality is naturally habituated in our bodies. Comparative mentality becomes a part of our lives without even realizing it. Even when people set their life goals at a young age, most of them set them by comparing themselves with others. Even when they evaluate their lives when they get old, most of them still compare themselves with others. Even when sad or painful things happen, we often find comfort in our hearts by comparing ourselves to others. Sometimes, in our hearts, we even get a sense of satisfaction with an achievement by comparing ourselves with others. In this way, most of our human desires in life are generated by comparison with others, and through comparison with others, we even feel satisfaction with the results obtained through our own efforts. If this comparative mentality has a positive effect on the motivation for self-development or achievement of life goals, it can be productive and development-oriented. However, it is not desirable if it develops into jealousy and negatively affects to the extent that competition with others becomes a goal in life.

This mentality has served as a driving force for the development of human society. On the other hand, it has also served as the root cause of social evil in human society. It seems that such comparison, envy, and competition are exceptionally strong in Koreans. I believe that the unique jealousy and competitive spirit of Koreans served as the driving force that made Korea into what it is today. Then, what caused the Koreans to have a peculiar jealousy and competitive spirit?

In an agricultural society where the arable land is fixed, if productivity does not increase as much as the increase in population, the competition for survival will inevitably intensify. Most people on the Korean Peninsula lived in an agricultural society for thousands of years. Entering the Joseon Dynasty, the population increased about 10 times in 500 years. The competition for survival to eat and live naturally intensified. For Yangin, common people, majority of people in Joseon Dynasty, one of the ways to live comfortably without farming, that they craved for, was to pass the state examination and become a bureaucrat. However, bureaucratic positions were also limited. In other words, the bureaucratic society had no choice but to intensify competition as the population increased. In Joseon, after Myeongjong (mid-16th century), the Jikjeon (land allocation) Act was abolished, and the landlord's tenant farming system based on private ownership and half-and-half shares became common. The land system in early Joseon was promoted with the goal of fostering self-employed farmers by dismantling the existing landlord system and redistributing land in proportion to the population. However, as Joseon society stabilized, land domination by yangban landowners spread,[38] farms were mainly owned by yangban landlords, and the majority of ordinary farmers gradually fell into tenant farmers.

As the number of tenant farmers increased in parallel with the population increase, farmers had to pay more tenant farming fees to rent the same size of tenant farmland. Also, those who wanted to become bureaucrats had resorted to unusual methods to be appointed. Due to the continuation of such a vicious cycle, the Korean ancestors' competition for survival became increasingly fierce, and they even resorted to various abnormal methods for survival. Thus, most of our Korean ancestors lived through tremendous ordeals to survive the competition until the early 1960s, when Korea's economic development began.

In the early 1960s, economic development began under the national export-led industrialization strategy. The most frequently used phrase in the process was "the only resource Korea has is human." It means that various resources, including natural resources, are needed for economic development, but people are the only resources in Korea. This phrase also suggests that the competition for survival is inevitable in Korean society. In a society where people are the only resources, people must play the role of other resources necessary for economic development. Because they had to perform the role of other resources, Koreans had no choice but to make efforts for continuous self-development in order to survive.

How can we measure the quality of human resources? The most common and general measure that has been used in Korea so far is the person's academic background and school of origin. This is seen by the fact that the format of resume requires academic background with the name of school before qualifications, licenses and previous jobs. Since the 1960s, as economic development has been promoted, Koreans have begun to live in an environment of fierce competition for survival to become better human resources. A desperate life in which everyone in the family struggles to get their children to enter a top-notch university! That was the way Koreans lived after the 1970s. In a society where survival is fierce, jealousy and competitive, based on comparison mindset has a large effect on members of society. How fierce must have been the competition to enter first-class universities if the government has maintained the equal education policy since the 1980s? It was to reduce the side effects of the fierce competition for university admissions. Humans are innately born with their own unique strengths. As a result, there is a difference in their abilities. Then how is equalization possible? This, too, is a by-product created to suppress jealousy and competitive mentality which have a strong negative impact on society.

As will be explained in detail later, the Saemaul movement, which began in 1970, was promoted as a campaign to increase farm household income. However, this also allowed Koreans to have a competitive spirit beyond the jealousy caused by comparison mentality with others. At that time, it instilled confidence in rural farmers that they could live well if they worked hard and cooperated with each other. Under the government initiative, the Saemaul movement began with free distribution of cements and steel bars to villages in rural areas under. It was a condition that encouraged villagers to work together in order to expand the village access roads and improve the roofs of the farmhouses. On the other hand, it adhered to a policy that government further expanded for support, when it was used according to the requirements, and discontinued, if not. The implementation of these policies had the effect of dispelling the public's distrust of the government at once. At the same time, it also had the effect of arousing positive competition between individuals and villages.

At the time, through the basic spirit of the Saemaul movement, "diligence, self-help, and cooperation", the government adhered to the principle of first supporting the villages that achieved expected results. In 1972, 16,600 villages that had high participation rates and results to the Saemaul movement received expanded support. The remaining 18,000 villages that did not perform well were not supported. At that time, the mental state of farmers was represented by frustration and lethargy, backing-down and negligence, and submission. The government's performance based support acted as an occasion to dispel the distrust of government policies at once that had been dormant in their hearts. It also gave them a sense of envy and competition with their colleagues, and it gave them a spirit of cooperation for a common goal. It provided a decisive opportunity that aroused positive motivation to work, saying, "If you work hard, you can live well." Most Koreans today have their roots in the countryside at that time. As a result, it is the opinion that most Koreans today have a strong sense of comparison, jealousy and competition with others. Most Koreans work hard and they are diligent. These are habits and inclinations evolved in Koreans in order to survive.

On the other hand, when the competition for survival intensifies, people are bound to mobilize various abnormal methods to survive at all costs. Under such circumstances, people take their abnormal behaviors for granted, thinking, "If others are paying bribes, shouldn't I pay bribe myself?" They even try to justify their own illegal actions by saying that "Others are making money regardless of means and methods, so what kind of a patriot am I to use only legitimate means and methods!"

That's not all. They do not consider their own children's abilities and only lament that their grades are worse than other people's children. Even after being denied a promotion due to lack of ability, they mourn that a colleague who is inferior to them has been promoted. Most of the thoughts of said people in such a society are based on comparison mentality with others. As such, it can be seen that the comparative mentality inherent in people becomes negative when it acts as a basis for judgment in everyday life. Due to the geopolitical environment and the significant population increase in modern times, Koreans have lived through many generations in an inevitably fierce competition for survival. In addition, comparative mentality was further fostered in the process of implementing policies at the government level after the 1960s. As a result, I believe that Koreans came to own a personality that has formed a strong habit of jealousy and a competitive spirit.

Koreans have excellent devising capabilities.[96]

As mentioned earlier, Koreans are highly adaptable to difficult environments. They are settled people based on an agricultural society. They did not fill their hunger by invading and plundering others even though their living conditions were difficult. Rather, they have adapted to the given environment while surviving on grass roots and bark, and made preparations by demonstrating their ingenuity in order to survive. I believe Korea is a wise nation with strong survival power.

Even though Korean ancestors have lived in the gap between huge continental and maritime powers, they were not biased towards either side. It has led them to develop a unique, yet superior culture of food, clothing and shelter than those of neighboring countries. This leads me to believe that Koreans have excellent devising skills.

---

96) Devising: research, design, study in depth the logic of things

Koreans are one of the few people in the world who have their own language. The ancestors of Koreans created Hangeul, their own alphabet, and have been using it to this day. Hangeul was selected as the best alphabet in the world based on rationality, scientific design, and originality at Oxford University, the world's top authority in language research. On October 1, 1997, UNESCO designated Hunminjeongeum (Hangul) as a Memory of the World. Hunminjeongeum is completely different from neighboring countries' Chinese characters and Hiragana and Kana of Japan. It is a system with the best scientific and originality proven in the world linguistic community. Koreans are the people who developed such alphabets and have excellent devising capability.

How about Admiral Yi Sun-sin's devising ability in the naval battle against Japan? Admiral Yi Sun-sin was appointed to the Jeolla Jwasusa a year before Japan, which had the world's best navy at the time, invaded. Admiral Yi Sun-sin built a Turtle Ship in addition to the U-shaped battleships equipped with a gun barrel, in preparation against quick approach and close combats by the Japanese Navy's narrow

V-shaped battleships. Using these battleships, he won 23 victories in 23 battles during Imjin and Jeongyujaeran with Japan. He is a hero of the century who defeated Japan's dual assault strategy on land and sea, rescuing Joseon from a turning point. He won the battle by neutralizing his opponent's strengths and making the most of opponent's weaknesses. The strategies and tactics he used in the battles were based on his excellent devising ability.

The following is the ingenuity of Koreans who made kimchi. In the past, Kimchi was a smelly food that only Koreans ate and was treated with wariness by Westerners. Entering the 21st century, it has been selected as one of the top five health foods in the world. This is because kimchi is rich in lactic acid bacteria, vitamins, minerals, and dietary fiber, so it has been found to be a food with excellent effects such as anti-cancer effects, suppression of inflammation, and enhancement of immunity. Now, it has become a food that attracts attention from people around the world. Other countries also have pickled vegetables. But fermented foods like kimchi are hard to find. Unlike pickled vegetables in other countries, Korean kimchi is characterized by being pickled twice. First, the vegetables are pickled with salt. They are washed and dehydrated to create conditions for good fermentation. To make

Kimchi, the second pickling are made with ginger, garlic, red pepper, chives, and other various seasonings. These days, China and Japan imitate kimchi and even put it on the global export market. Koreans have developed and eaten kimchi uniquely in the gap between the giant China and Japan, which is nearly twice as large. How can it not be said that Koreans have excellent devising skills?

The following is the devising ability that developed Ondol, a unique Korean heating system. Ondol is also called Gudeul. This system is a floor heating system that heats thick floors by burning wood and converting it into heat. In oriental medicine, it is said that "a person's upper body should be cool and the lower part of the body should be warm." Ondol is said to have been designed based on this principle of oriental medicine. The characteristic of ondol is that it reduces fuel costs by using the fire used for daily meal preparation also for heating purposes. Ondol is also a technology that Koreans developed by demonstrating their outstanding devising skills. It was their own heating system designed and developed to maintain a warm environment for a long time with the least amount of fuel consumed in the cold winter.

The following is an example of how Koreans recently showed off their excellent devising skills to the world.

Normally, a flight demonstration team consists of six aircrafts. The flight demonstration team of the Korean Air Force, 「Black Eagles」, consists of 8 supersonic aircrafts (T-50), the only one of its kind. It is a fact shared by all pilots that a flight demonstration team consisting of 8 planes rather than 6 is much more difficult, it is not just adding 2 more planes. Even so, the Black Eagles participated in the 「Waddington International Air Show (June 30-July 1, 2012)」 in England called 「World Air Show Olympics」 for the first time and won the 'Best Air Show Award'. Subsequently, at the 「RIAT Air Show (July 7-8)」 held at Fairford Air Force Base in the UK, where 40 teams from 11 countries participated, Black Eagles received the 'Excellency Award for Demonstration Flight' and the 'Popularity Award' selected by 1,397 military aviation enthusiasts sponsoring RIAT. This means that the Korean Air Force Black Eagles team was the best in the world both in name and reality as a result of winning awards after competing with world-class air show teams under unfavorable conditions such as their first overseas appearance, unfamiliar environments, and poor logistics support. That's not all. Black Eagles team participated in for the second time the RIAT Air Show from July 15th to 17th, 2022, among 38 teams from 34 countries including England and Germany, and they received the Grand Prize and Popularity Award, which they had won 10 years ago. How can I not say that this is a splendid feat?

The achievements of the Black Eagles team can be summarized in two main points. One is that the flight skills of Korean Air Force pilots are world-class. The other is that the performance of domestic T-50 aircraft is excellent. The Black Eagles announced twice to the world that the pilots of the Korean Air Force are technically talented and that the T-50 aircraft made by Koreans is a masterpiece. In particular, performance at the air show with domestically produced T-50 aircraft, which canbe considered to be a comprehensive art piece of modern science and technology, is also an example of Koreans having excellent devising skills in the field of science and technology. This can show how Koreans' outstanding devising skills were behind the scenes of today's economic growth.

Koreans are characterized by fluidity and peripheral character.

Fluidity refers the ability to adapt to a developing situation. Peripheral character refers to the quality of being flexible in order to accomplish a task, by mobilizing available methods according to circumstances and developing situations. Fluidity and peripheral characters appear as dispositional characteristics for Koreans who have lived in a narrow territory like the Korean Peninsula.

Hayeojang, a Chinese minister who came to Joseon at the end of the 19th century, is said to have told Western diplomats, "Koreans are like children who easily follow, when appeased, while showing their power subtly."[39] Even recently, such cases are often occurring in the international political arena, and seem to hurt the hearts of Koreans. Why do they look down on Koreans so much? It could be because they have the arrogance that their country is a great country that no one in the world can look down on. However, it is necessary to think about whether the behaviors of Koreans have caused others to view them in this way.

Koreans generally take a low profile when it comes to seemingly strong forces. This is a strategy that has been constituted to adapt to the times in the process of surviving against the constant pressure and aggression of big foreign powers for generations.

When referring to islanders in a demeaning way, they are often said to have island spirits. It is said that living confined to an island surrounded by the sea on all sides, can lead to having a "narrow, exclusive, and miserly" personality. Even with natural disasters such as typhoons and volcanic eruptions, or in case of foreign invasions, there is no place to escape to. In order to survive, they must cooperate with each other. So, the people of the island nation are socially group oriented and logical. On the other hand, living in their own world, they do not trust others, are intolerant and exclusive.

In the meantime, people in neighboring countries have disdained Koreans and said that they have a peninsular temperament without a backbone, which is represented by fluidity and peripheral character. The nation formed on a relatively small peninsula at a junction connecting the ocean and the continent is to be pushed around depending on the size of its power. For this reason, especially for those who have lived on a small peninsula like Korea, social characteristics represented by fluidity and peripheral character are inevitably formed for survival. The social characteristics of Koreans formed in this way are negatively viewed by people in neighboring countries as being heterogenous and having a strong tendency to follow blindly. In general, continental people are expansion-oriented whereas islanders are reduction-oriented. On the other hand, the people of the peninsula connecting the continent and the island are in the middle, so they are dismissed as having no clear identity.

The area of the Anatolian Peninsula, where Turkey is located, is 220,000 square kilometers, approximately 3.4 times the size of the Korean Peninsula. The area of the Iberian Peninsula, where Spain is located, is 2.6 times the size of the Korean Peninsula. The survival strategies of people from large peninsula countries, such as Turkey and Spain, whose national power equals or sometimes overwhelms neighboring powers with relatively large territories, and people from small peninsula countries, such as Korea, whose national power is overwhelmed by neighboring powers are inevitably different from each other. In order to survive between the maritime and continental powers, Koreans sometimes fought in solidarity. However, the difference in power was so great that if it was difficult to oppose, they resorted to the stronger side. Koreans' fluidity and peripheral character of peninsular temperament, which people in neighboring countries say are characteristics of Koreans, are a survival strategy ingrained in Koreans.

Koreans are clear-minded, weak in unity, highly individualistic, and prioritize the individual over the nation. These are what people in neighboring countries said when they speak poorly about the people of Korea. Look at them from a positive perspective. Koreans, who live on the small peninsula, inevitably feel the power of the strong flowing towards the weak side between the continental and the maritime power. In such an environment, they have not been broken or absorbed by any powerful military, ideological, or cultural forces around them until now. It is because they have been embedded with fluidity, a social tendency to cope with and wisely adapt to the real situation for a long time. The fluidity inherent in them has acted as a driving force to create new things that suit them by selecting only those that match their needs. Between Chinese characters and Japanese kana, Koreans created Hangeul, the world's best character. Fast food represented by McDonald's and Coca-Cola in the United States spread around the world in the 1960s and 1970s and took root in many countries. Nonetheless, Koreans are adapting when developing native Korean fast food from the United States' basis for McDonald's. In this way, the peninsular temperament represented by such fluidity and peripheral character has led to a flexible response to any powerful force without being broken. It is my opinion that due to such social characteristics of Koreans, Koreans retain their own human characteristics, food, clothing, and shelter culture without being subordinated to the cultures of neighboring powers.

People from neighboring countries who devalue Koreans

say that their unity is weak because they are from the peninsula. This can be said to be the result of a piecemeal evaluation of Koreans. In the late 1990s, when the IMF economic crisis occurred, Korea overcame the economic crisis in the shortest time by launching a national gold-raising campaign. Also, although Korea has been a country located on a small peninsula on the eastern edge of China for thousands of years, it has never been incorporated into Chinese territory. These are good examples of how strongly Koreans express their unity when their country is at stake.

As mentioned above, taking a binary view, some say that Koreans are peninsular people and so do not have a clear identity of their own. This also has a solution if approach it with the decimal rather than binary concept. From a decimal point of view, expansion-oriented continental people are 8 to 10, reduction-oriented island people are 1 to 3, and people in the middle of the peninsula are 4 to 7. It can be seen that the people of the peninsula also clearly have an in-between identity. The statement that the people of the peninsula do not have an identity is an argument that people of the continent or island countries use to glorify themselves and put down the people of the peninsula.

Below, I introduce various attitudes of Koreans attributed to the strong temperamental characteristics represented by their fluidity and peripheral character of Koreans.

Weak to those who seem powerful. An example of this is that, in diplomatic relations with neighboring powers, when the other party pushes strongly, they first display a weak attitude. To a person with a loud voice, they seem to be surrendering. Even in negotiations, if the opponent is strong, they take a weak stance. In front of a gang, they easily back down. They are also busy creating a faction for themselves to achieve their own goals. They try to solve the problem by using the faction.

Behaviors vary depending on circumstances and surroundings. For a long time in history, Koreans have lived against pressure and aggression between relatively strong continental powers and maritime powers. In the process, they learned that relying is more advantageous than resisting or challenging for survival. They also learned that an attitude of pretending to be obedient is necessary. Varying behavioral patterns appeared as such perceptions become habits. While resisting in unity, they appear to be divided in order to survive. For that reason, it is said that their unity is weak. Nevertheless, in the face of a national crisis, an indomitable sense of resistance is expressed. They seemed to become submissive to the invasion of a strong foreign power. However, they still managed to firmly maintain their original identity. It is the result of their varying characteristics acting as a driving force to create their own unique culture.

They take any means and methods to achieve their goal. It is an indispensable behavioral pattern and life attitude among the characteristics of Koreans. This is because of the geological and topographical environment. It is because of the peripheral character that has been embedded in the process of living while overcoming historically tough adversaries. There are many people who act honest and sincere to achieve their desired goals. Nevertheless, most Koreans, if there is something they want, try to achieve what they want by any means, whether it is something big or small. There are not-so-beautiful aspects of Korean society such as high-priced tutoring for children who cannot afford it, illegal admission by disguising one's identity or bribery, disrupting open competitive bidding through bribery or solicitation, receiving contracts illegally, expedient inheritance, raising slush funds, and more. These are unjust and dishonest means and methods that Koreans use to achieve their goals. However, these are negative aspects that exist everywhere in human society, with only a difference in degree.

Not long ago, it was reported in the media that "an average of more than 200,000 crimes such as fraud, embezzlement, and breach of trust occur every year in Korea." Comparing false accusation cases[97] between Korea with Japan, Japan indicted 9 people and Korea 1,544 people in 2007. Japan's population is 2.5 times that of Korea. Considering this, there are 427 times more perjury cases, and 542 times more false accusations. This shows that Koreans are trying to achieve their goals even by mobilizing abnormal methods. This is because fraud, embezzlement, perjury, and false accusation are crimes that are used when trying to achieve one's purpose without following the rules and procedures in place.

Try to solve own problems with other people's influence. This is also a cross-section of the life attitude of some Koreans today, who are jealous, competitive, and like to watch from sidelines. A common example is the solicitation for one's advancement. It is a way in which one seeks to be promoted by asking or soliciting from the person who has authority over personnel affairs, rather than getting promotion through one's own efforts. Many Koreans think that Korea has developed into an advanced society. However, there are still people who

---

97) False testimonies in court or cases in which a person accuses others by lying, or fabrication.

think that in order to succeed, it is necessary to have a strong "Back (Sponsor)" from behind. The fact that the government has selected and appointed people with personnel connections such as work ties, regional ties, and school ties to high government positions also played a part in further fixing such a mindset among Koreans. Most Koreans think that networking is more important than abilities related to their work in order to get a position or promotion. Even if they are not promoted due to lack of abilities, they feel that they failed because they do not have a "Back (Sponsor)". Regarding those who have been promoted, it is frowned upon that they have been promoted because they have "Back (Sponsor)" rather than ability. This creates a lack of trust among people. It is a negative trait that still remains in some Korean people today.

An example of this is the fact that after the establishment of the government, all powerful Presidents stumbled due to familial corruption. Social trust is the expectation in society that members will behave regularly, honestly, and cooperatively based on universal norms. A society with low trust must pay the cost of distrust. This is because in a society where distrust is prevalent, it is necessary to institutionally create and maintain compulsory trust to replace distrust among members of society. This is why Koreans should change their method of trying to solve their own problems by using others in order to build a trustworthy Korean society.

The tendency of herd behavioral phenomenon in public opinion is strong with pot like temper.[98] This is also a pattern of behavior that is common among Koreans. The common opinion of the masses is called public opinion. Koreans have a strong tendency to suddenly become quite even after massively supporting an opinion on an issue. There is a strong tendency of herd behavior in regards to public opinion. Koreans are innately docile and are weak when it comes to strong power. They adapt by calculating their interests according to circumstances and standing on the more powerful side. Herd behavior in public opinion is a behavioral pattern that appears due to these habits and tendencies of Koreans. Koreans have a habitual mindset that they are weak and depend on the strong. When a certain public opinion is formed and its influence is judged to be great, for everyone regardless I or you, a group forming tendency ("we" community spirit) activates. They all become an active supporter of that public opinion. The group formation tendency among Koreans makes many people quick to support public opinion in a short period

98) A phrase that compares the spirit of Koreans, easily getting up and rebelling and easily forgetting as if it had never happened, to the characteristics of a pot that boils quickly and cools down quickly.

of time. Even if public opinion is supported by many people, if it does not get attention, it can no longer be a strong power. Then, people forget that public opinion as easily as when they supported it. As such, Koreans have the habit of easily getting up and rebelling, then renouncing things easily. Regarding such an attitude, some compare it to the "characteristics of a pot that boils quickly and cools down quickly," and belittles Koreans as having a "pot like temper."

In Korea, there are influential people, but not many highly trusted social leaders. Koreans boast that they are a single ethnic group. However, there are not many trusted spiritual leaders, or adults, in Korea. Perhaps it is the influence of Confucianism, which has dominated Korean society for a long time. In Confucian society, the highest value is to become a high-ranking official, to increase their reputation, and to shine their family by making their names known to their descendants. In order to shine a light on a family, it is important to be listed in the official records of the government as a powerful person in a high official position rather than a person with knowledge or virtue. Such outward values have dominated. This is why there are few spiritual leaders who are highly trusted in Korean society. A spiritual leader is a virtuous person,[99] a knowledgeable person,[100] or a person with indomitable will,[101] who can influence people's consciousness. For that reason, there are only influential people who wield power with the protection or support of a specific regime or business world in Korean society. Koreans are weak to those who seem powerful. They try to solve their own problems with the power of others and that is why Koreans gather around influential people rather than spiritual leaders. such as virtuous people, knowledgeable people, and people with strong will. This is because only influential people are the ones who can actually provide direct support to them. Koreans prefer powerful people who can support them right now or help them in the near future rather than spiritual leaders. Such ideas dominate Koreans. The events that occurred during the presidential election process in Korea at the end of 2012 tells us this. At that time, members of the 1st opposition party supported their party's presidential candidate. However, when a public opinion poll indicated that an independent person had more chances for being elected as the President, many people shifted to that direction. It is a cross-section of mant Koreans with the influential people centered mindset.

---

99) A person with a reputation who can lead the people in the right direction when chaos or difficulties arise across the country

100) A person who has made great personal academic achievements

101) A person with a strong will to keep his or her belief in the face of a national crisis

Koreans have a strong sense of 'we' community.[40]

Among the terms that Koreans often use, there is the word 'we'. As mentioned above, it is a naturally developed consciousness because Korean society is relation oriented. In terms such as our country, our parents, our brothers, our friends, etc., the word 'our' means that we are socially connected. It implies that it is a part of me as a living community. The collective identity in which you and I are not separated is 'we'. 'We' is a socio-cognitive product that materializes when the individuals constituting 'we' include oneself and others within the framework of 'we'. Also, the term 'we' has a characteristic where the recognition of 'we' develops only when 'we' and 'they' can be separated. This exclusive nature makes a clear distinction between 'us' and 'them'. Among the members of 'we', they form a social network with each other within the framework of 'we' and feel a strong sense of solidarity. "We" is formed on the basis of materialistic attributes such as similar background and common ownership. It can also be formed based on the homogeneity of the same social relationship such as the same nationality, country, community, school, workplace, home-town, and surname. In conclusion, the 'we' that relation and group-centered Koreans value is formed based on the homo-geneity of social relationships.

When Koreans speak of 'we' as a group, members recognize each other as 'we' and their individual identities are almost ignored. The commonality or similarity of the members, which is the basis for forming the group 'we', is emphasized. However, in order to form a socially speaking 'we', it is possible when members share a clear perception of 'we' and a sense of social identity. 'Us' can be divided into 'attributed us', in which members are determined at the time of birth, regardless of their will, and 'achieved us', which are formed by their own abilities, efforts, and will. The 'we' in the Western collective concept assumes that the individuals constituting the group are autonomous, independent, and separate beings. It is the meaning of a group in which individuals do not disappear. On the other hand, the Korean 'we' is not premised on the existence of an individual. In particular, it cannot be established as a collection of individuals' uniqueness. It is the concept of 'we' of collective nature based on the commonality or similarity of members.

If Koreans include another person in the category of 'we', the resulting feelings, bonds, and responsibility for him or her are qualitatively different from the concept of 'we' used in

Western cultures under the same circumstances. If Koreans included the other person in their category of 'we', sometimes they go beyond the concept of sharing and recognize them as 'collective us' of being one, sense of unity, deindividuation, and identity. When Koreans have the idea of 'us' with the other person, they feel warmer feelings, psychological stability or comfort, and a sense of close harmony with the other person. So, when Koreans form a 'we' group with others, the boundary between oneself and others weakens in the 'we' group. A phenomenon that one's inner self also harmonizes or assimilates to the needs and characteristics of the group appears. As a result, Koreans have a strong sense of group identity that interpolates the social and normative identity of 'our' group that he/she joined rather than their own sense of identity. Koreans value their sense of identity, social status, and the role at the position of the group according to "Which 'we' group do I belong to?", rather than "Who am I?". Consistency between internal thoughts and externally expressed words and actions as an individual with a separate identity is not considered important. The suitability of behavior according to the position in the "we" group to which one belongs has a greater effect on words and actions. This is why Koreans value situational behavior and group harmonious behavior more than justification, ideology, and consistency of their own behavior.

The teachings of Confucianism, which has led Korean society for more than 2,000 years, tend to discriminate and classify people. Koreans, who have learned such teachings from generation to generation, are accustomed to dividing and classifying people. I think that the habit of dividing and classifying has become conscious, and the unique concept of 'we' has developed in Koreans to distinguish them from others and express a sense of the unity. As Korean ancestors had lived under the persecution of continental and maritime powers for a long time, they called those who persecuted them 'barbarians', distinguishing them from 'us'. 'We' means that we are civilized people who are aware of benevolence, righteousness, courtesy and knowledge, (仁義禮智) different from 'them'. Internally, due to the nature of the agricultural society, people had gathered in one place for a long time and had lived with each other. As a result, it can also be said that a sense of community called "we" naturally emerged, distinguishing it from other towns and regions. It can be also said that it developed because it was more effective to form a group called 'we' to resist the exploitation of noblemen and aristocrats in the past than resisting alone.

Putting this all together, whether it was formed naturally to maintain harmonious human relations after living in Confucian society for hundreds of years, whether it was formed to effectively resist the aggression of continental and maritime powers over a long period of time, or whether it was naturally formed to adapt to an agricultural society for a long time, Koreans have a strong sense of community called 'we'.

Looking at it from a different angle, it can be said that Koreans' sense of 'we' community is a unique characteristic that appeared as a result of a combination of Korean characteristics, such as reluctance to step forward, strong jealousy and competition, fluidity and peripheral character, and self-protection, and etc. One of the reasons for thinking so is that many Koreans create 'we' for themselves and use that in their lives. The human relationship of socially relational Koreans begins with a connection with a specially formed partner. This means that human relationships between people are governed by the connections they have already formed with each other. Typically, the connections mentioned by Koreans are blood ties, regional ties, school ties, and work ties. These connections act as a precondition for the formation of human relationships. Generally, when people meet someone, they introduce themselves. At that moment, they check whether there is a clue of natural connection between them. Depending on whether there is a connection, the other party is classified as 'we' or 'they'. It is the result of a sense of community called 'we'.

In the emotional aspect, the archetype of 'we' for Koreans is a family relationship based on affection (情). Therefore, if you express the other person as 'our 00', it means that the other person feels close like a family. For example, 'our alumni' means family-like alumni. 'Our friends' means close friends like a family. 'Our 00th meeting' means a gathering of close people like family. Koreans try to feel emotionally close to anyone once they come within the framework of "we." They may even unconsciously feel intimate. In Western societies, Korean babysitters are generally popular. Koreans express the sentiment of 'our baby' when it comes to a baby who comes to their house, even if he/she is someone else's child. So I think it's because they take care of them like their own children. 'Children over 30 living with their parents', which is also a disease in Korean society, is because both parents and children have a strong sense of 'our family', before the fact that they are grown-ups.

In dealing with people, Koreans first distinguish the other person in a dichotomous way, whether they are 'us' or 'them' and develop human relationships from there. For Koreans, when a person commits a mistake, the standard of judgment is usually 'was it us?' or 'was it someone else?'. For example, if the person who made the mistake is 'our 00', they think about what happened from the point of view of the person who did the wrong, as if it were you. They forgive, excuse, and try to cover it up. On the other hand, when the person is one of 'them', they judge from a rational point of view rather than emotional sympathy with criticism and even condemn in their heart.

In Korea, there are countless family gatherings such as end of mourning ceremony, ancestral rites, cold food gathering, seasonal memorial services, birthday, 60th birthday, 70th birthday, 88th birthday. There are also many school related gatherings such as elementary, middle and high school, university, 00 course, 00 national examination, alumni gatherings. There are many gatherings related to region and work, such as 00 society / 00 comrades / 00 hometown associations. Why are there so many gatherings related to blood, school, regional and work ties? It is the opinion that it is because of the characteristics of Koreans who want something but lack the ability, and are even more insecure to go for it alone. This is because they need someone to support them within the framework of 'us' if necessary. As a part of themselves, they need someone who can think from their point of view, advocate for them, and support them. Westerners usually spend time with their families after work or on the weekends. Koreans spend a lot of time with others after work or on weekends. During the week, there are frequent dinner parties to form close bonds with people within the category of 'us'. Weekends are also busy attending 'our 00' meetings, such as mountain climbing, travel, and sports meetings that have been maintained so far. As a result, Koreans value blood ties, regional ties, and academic ties, which are the basis of "we," more than people of any other country. In this way, Koreans live a busy life today in order to create many of their own 'we', and to maintain a strong 'we', who can stand up for and support them when needed.

Many Koreans still prioritize interests[102] over great causes.[103]

In the course of people's lives, their activities are largely governed by interests. There are only differences in the scale of the activity, but they move forward in anticipation of profit,

---

102) Profits and losses. merits and demerits
103) A grand duty to be followed as a human being

and they move backward in fear of loss. It means that people act in anticipation of the benefits that will return to them. However, the premise that humans are social animals sometimes limits personal interests and demands sacrifice for a cause. In a mature society, the grand cause is amicably observed. As Korea recently entered into the ranks of the developed world, Korean society was widely evaluated as a mature society. As a society governed by ethics, it is said to be one of the few safe societies in the world. However, many Koreans still value benefits rather than a cause. It means that the majority of people prioritize their own interests rather than the duty to abide by as members of society. They urge you to take their side before you judge right or wrong. They are trying to protect their interests before society's justice and fairness.

it's a fact that even I, a Korean writer can't understand, but it happens all the time in everyday life. Below are a few examples of prioritizing one's own interests over a minimal cause that I have personally experienced. It happened in the rural town where I stay for the weekend. A neighbor who was close to me once embezzled public funds in the neighborhood. I had been close to that neighbor ever since I moved to that neighborhood. As the news of embezzlement of public money became known, critical public opinion against him was widely spread in the neighborhood. Since we were close friends, I proposed him to reconcile with the neighbors while maintaining a minimum of face under the premise that "anyone can make mistakes." However, the neighbor's reaction was completely unexpected. He made no mention of his faults and insisted that the people in the neighborhood were framing him. He was angry at me for not taking his side. I said that I am not on either side, and wanted to live in harmony with neighbors, but he was defiant. It was a really awkward situation for me as he called me first and said that people in the neighborhood were swearing at him, so I gave him advice……

The following is a case that everyone in Korea experiences. We experience it every time we elect a political leaders who will be responsible for the future of our country, Korea, in for every 4 or 5 years. Many Koreans still choose candidates based on whether they are from the same region as them, that is, on the same side, rather than on their qualifications or abilities. I've seen that kind of behaviors for almost seventy years of my life. I thought about it as I witnessed such a situation during every election. What is the motherland to these people? Does it mean that their own side takes precedence over the bright future of their country? If you are an advanced citizen, shouldn't you prioritize candidates who will bring you a bright future before being on your own side? Let's say my child has committed a sin that deserves death. Parents will try to defend them from the point of view of their child before recognizing the fact that he has committed a mortal sin. Prioritizing profit over the cause is a habit inherent in human beings. However, this tendency is more strongly displayed in many Koreans.

Where does the Korean habit of prioritizing profit over the cause come from? Of course, there may be several reasons. Below are two examples of what I believe to be the reason. First, it is thought to be due to environmental influences. As mentioned above, because Koreans have lived in the geology and topography of old age, about 70% of Koreans display characters of elders. With this, it was said that the temperament of the elderly is similar to the temperament of the yin in Sasang-medicine. One of the characteristics of the elderly and the yin people is that they place importance on gains and losses. It is due to their perception that "Does being right or wrong feed you? Being useful in my life comes first!" People often say, "Human relationships are based on interests, and people cannot have a relationship without the medium of gains and losses." Of course that is true. However, in order to form the right human relationships, the cause that corresponds to social values should take precedence over personal interest. This is how justice and fairness can be implemented in the society in which we live. For that reason, in order to form a proper human relationship, an appropriate balance between social causes and individual interests is sometimes required. However, it is the opinion that many Koreans are more inclined towards gains and losses due to their strong temperament that appears in the elderly due to the influence of the geology and topography of their lives.

Next, it is the view that Koreans' habit of prioritizing interests over causes is also due to political and historical factors that have been passed down for generations. In the past 500 years of Joseon's history, political bureaucrats from noble families played a leading role. The characteristic of the Bungdang politics of Joseon, which developed after the 16th century led by political officials, was that they recognized the opponents at the beginning. Bungdang politics was possible because the ruling faction did not occupy all the major positions and guaranteed some positions to the opposing faction. It was similar to political parties in modern democracies. Such Bungdang politics changed through the frequent coup of Hwanguk[104] during the reign of King

Sukjong in the late 17th century. It had developed into a one-party despotism trend that did not acknowledge the opposing force. Since then, the other side was not a negotiation partner, but an object of elimination. For more than 300 years, this political situation continued. As a result, it was necessary to clearly distinguish one's side in order to oppose the other side. It was only natural to blindly follow to one's own side in order to survive regardless of the cause. As a result, it is the logic that the habit of prioritizing self-interest rather than the cause is still imprinted in the consciousness of Koreans today. It means giving priority to being on one's side rather than social causes. Today, it is the appearance of Korean party politics that prioritizes only the interests of the party in the name of a force to defeat the ruling party, even when the other party is doing the right things. How tired and annoyed are the people by watching them doing only "opposition for the sake of opposition"? Just because they are not on our side, which shares my interests, there is no sound criticism and only opposition for the sake of opposition. There seems to be no

---

104) It means that the situation or the state of affairs has changed and in modern terminology, it is similar to the dissolution of parliament or the total resignation of the cabinet. It refers to a large-scale purge related to a regime change between factions in the Joseon Dynasty and caused the collapse of political balance in the late Joseon Dynasty.

social cause anywhere. It is typical of Koreans to prioritize their own interests over the cause that has been the mindset of their ancestors for generations.

Above, I have described the habit of prioritizing interests over causes which is common to many Koreans due to environmental influences, political, and historical factors. I will continue to describe the regionalism that prioritizes interests over causes that still strongly influence Korean society.

Still, the majority of Koreans have strong regionalism based on their place of origin. Among Koreans, there are many people who are trapped in the framework of regionalism, that is, regional precedence. This is especially true for those who are rooted in the Yeongnam (Southeastern) and Honam (South-western) regions. The regionalism expressed between them is characterized by being mutually exclusive. Yes, regionalism exists in every country. Regionalism between Yeongnam and Honam people in Korea has a long historical background. It is generally accepted that it originated from the instruction of King Taejo of Goryeo a thousand years ago to not hire talented people from the Jeolla-do (Honam) region. Irrespective of whether the teachings of King Taejo of Goryeo were true or not, discrimination between Yeong and Honam continued until the Joseon Dynasty. Yi Ik, a Silhak (Practical

Learning) scholar of Joseon, praised Yeongnam and down-played Honam according to the geomantic principle. He praised Gyeongsang-do (Yeongnam) as the best place among noblemen and a warehouse of Joseon talent. On the other hand, he slandered Jeolla-do (Honam) by saying that talented and virtuous people rarely appeared. These regional prejudices and conflicts have continued in Korean society to this day. The perception that people in the Honam region have been discriminated against for more than 1,000 years since Goryeo is inherent in the consciousness of Koreans. Perhaps that is why the mutual hostility between the people of Yeongnam and Honam in Korea seems to be rooted deep in their bones. The proof is that many people even use the expression "destroying the nation" to explain the mutually exclusive feelings between the people of the two regions. The characteristic of mutually exclusive regionalism that occurred between the two regions is that when people in one region exclude people in another region, the people in the excluded region unite more to exclude the other region on their end as well. This is because they think that this is the only way to minimize their losses. "If object A exerts a force on object B, object B also exerts a force of the same magnitude on object A" is a phenomenon similar to the "law of action and reaction" in the natural world.

Mutually exclusive regionalism takes precedence over social causes and issues on which the very existence of the nation is at stake. It stipulates that only the opinions of people from the same region are good, and the opinions of people from the opposite region are unconditionally evil. This is why people lament that it is ruinous.

In the past, Seowon in the Joseon Dynasty also played a big role in intensifying regionalism among Koreans today. Among the Seowons, the state-approved academy is Saaek Seowon (賜 額書院). Saaek Seowon received a signboard with the name of the academy, slaves, and books from the state. In 1543, Ju Se-bung founded Baekundong Confucian Academy. At the insistence of Yi Hwang, the governor of Punggi at the time, it was the first of Saaek Seowon, which was bestowed with a name board and books such as the Four Books and Five Classics. With this occasion, 577 new Seowons were newly established for about 150 years from King Seonjo to King Sukjong, and 100 of them received Saaek designation. One of the reasons for this increase in Seowons is that Sarim tried to establish an academic base in their region of origin and to exercise their influence based on this background.

Seowon, which was established after the middle of the Joseon Dynasty, was a place where ancestral rites were held for Confucian sages. At that time, as the function of rural self-government was strengthened politically, it even performed the role of local self-governing organization. Since then, the Seowon has become a gathering place for the local people as a central organization of local autonomy. As a result, Seowon played a key role in making Sarim, a unit faction of regional and academic ties. As a result, Seowon became the basis of Bundang politics at the time. To Salim, the Seowon, which produced them, was a medium to show off the academic and political superiority of the Bungdang faction to which they belonged, to the other Bungdang factions formed in the background of other academic and regional ties. At that time, yangban induced people from their families to pay homage to the Seowon they attended. They also used Seowons to raise the authority of their families and to forge ties among fellow tribesmen strengthening solidarity. During the Joseon Dynasty, Saaek Seowon had the qualifications of an educational institution equal to Sungkyunkwan. Nevertheless, rather than academic achievement, it played a role in forming a group of local people for political power. At that time, it was a society where it was difficult to get promoted even if you passed the national civil exam, if you did not have someone to guide you. This was because it was a society in which only those from a certain Seowon held key political power. Seowons in the Joseon Dynasty had played a role as a medium to recognize the importance of regional ties and academic ties in the blood of Koreans for many generations of their ancestors. For that reason, it is the view that one of the key factors that led to the regionalism that puts one's own interests first, which still remains strong among many Koreans, is the Seowon.

After the founding of the Republic of Korea, the political world also played a part in driving Koreans' regionalism. Even today, it is a reality that Korean politicians are promoting regionalism for their benefit. Since the founding of the country in 1948, most Korean presidents have appointed people from their regions of origin to high-ranking positions in politics, regardless of ability. As a result, it naturally resulted in further promoting regionalism. However, they claim that they are victims of regionalism. So, they have been claiming to take the lead in eradicating regionalism. Nonetheless, after they were elected president, they did not hesitate to make personnel appointments that incited local sentiment. It can be said that having Presidents who lack a vision for national value has intensified regional feelings.[41] From a politician's point of view, it may be an inevitable measure to receive strong support from their region of origin. In other words, all Koreans are perpetrators and victims of regionalism.

As listed above, the inclination of Korean people prioritizing interests over causes due to environmental and socio-cultural influences, combined with nepotism and regionalism, still appears strongly and negatively to some people.

Most Koreans are extreme and try to judge the world only with right and wrong.

It is said that the things that Joseon people feared the most were tigers, noblemen, and the spring austerity. During the Joseon Dynasty, tigers existed on the Korean Peninsula, threatening people's lives. The exploitation of the Yangban was harsh, and the life was miserable during spring cessation period between April and May of the lunar calendar, when provisions ran out.

As mentioned earlier, the goal of most scholars in the Joseon Dynasty was to pass the state examination and become an official. The subjects of the state exam were the scriptures of Confucianism. Therefore, the main scriptures of Confucianism were degraded to the subject of the examination, not a subject of study. Also, devoting yourself to Confucianism meant studying hard for the national exam rather than character development or academic achievement. In addition to this, once having passed the state examination and becoming an official, structurally, the circumstance was that pursuing a higher position became the only goal. To bureaucrats, the rank of their positions was important. This is because the rank of the position indicated the degree of power, which was the social ideology of the time. They had little or no regard for what to do in their positions. As such, for most bureaucrats in Joseon society, obtaining power was the goal itself and the highest value they pursued.

That is the reason why mid-level officials in the state organization formed a faction only for their own gains and followed higher authority blindly for the 500-year history of the Joseon Dynasty. Such a culture became common after the mid-Joseon Dynasty. To the bureaucrats, the people were only objects of exploitation for their own survival and prosperity. The national organizational system was a pyramidal structure of exploitation with the people at the base, small thieves over them, in turn a little bigger thieves, even bigger thieves and the biggest thieves at the top. Under this pyramidal structure of exploitation, due to the nature of exploitation, most of them are just subject to exploitation except for the people of highest position. Among them, the most impacted were the common people and the lowly people who were the lowest target of exploitation. The fact that the most feared and abhorred by the people was the Yangban, proves this. This pyramid of exploitation had been passed down for hundreds of years. In Joseon society, the principles and social morality of state management collapsed due to the immorality of exploitation. People's lives became more and more impoverished, a great sense of victimization continued to build up in the hearts of many people, people naturally formed gangs to survive, and it became habit to follow strong people blindly. That was the reason why the common people did not oppose much even in the process of annexation of Joseon by Japan.[42]

Today, when the emotional tendencies of Koreans are expressed at the pan-national level, they are often referred to as attitudes of righteous soldiers. Examples include the tendency to focus on public opinion, which is common during times of national crisis or during elections. However, this militant attitude is not necessarily positive. This is because the base of the righteous army attitude is the expression of strong antipathy or hostility that comes from victim experience. The extreme sense of victimization accumulated at the bottom of people's minds divides the world in a dichotomous way. it categorizes into perpetrators and victims. The other party who is the perpetrator is wrong and evil. As a victim, I am categorized as being right and good. They consider people enemies if they side with the perpetrators and allies if they side with the victims. People who are entrenched in such a strong sense of victimization are not necessarily positive because they divide the world only into right and wrong.

In the consciousness of Koreans living today, there is still strong antipathy and hostility from the sense of victimization accumulated from generation to generation. As a result, the attitude that even a little loss is considered a big loss and can never be accepted exists. Concessions or compromises are considered damage. The content that can be seen most often in pickets, slogans, banners, and posters at demonstrations in Korean society today is "決死反對".[105] Koreans risk their lives even when they express their intent that they cannot make any concessions. How extreme is this? Whenever I see such slogans or posters, "Is 00 an issue worthy of risking my life to oppose?", and I cannot help but laugh, thinking "We Koreans give up our lives too easily."

In addition, Koreans have a strong tendency to divide world affairs into good and evil, right and wrong, and me and my opponent (enemy) in a dichotomous way. As mentioned

---

105) Opposition to death: means to oppose with the determination to die

above, a typical example of this is the results of the elections that are divided into East and West in the elections for the President and members of the National Assembly. Whatever the people of the eastern region support, the people of the western region support a candidate who opposes them, regardless of their qualifications or abilities. Then, where does the extreme sense of victimization of Koreans come from? It is due to the sense of victimization that had been accumulated in the minds of our ancestors for a long time.

Koreans had to suffer a lot of injustices as the weak in society for generations. Let's examine cases of the injustice from recent times to the Joseon Dynasty; the resentment of those who were oppressed by the military regime in the 1970s and 1980s because they denied their regime or became an obstacle to implementing their policies, during the Korean War, in the process of advancing and retreating between the South and North Korean troops, the extreme treatments they had to suffer from the regime they did not support, the bone-chilling damages by the guilt-by-association system[106]

---

106) As a disadvantageous treatment inflicted by the government on relatives of the those who were ideological offenders, collaborators, and defectors to North Korea, and it was a system in which immediate relatives, spouses, and relatives were excluded from public office through unofficial ideology verification policy until 2005.

that their descendants suffered because they supported the North Korean regime during the war, the national level of contempt and resentment accumulated under Japanese rule, the resentment of the unfair treatment suffered by the common people and the lowly in the Joseon Dynasty, the resentment of inherent discriminatory social system for descendants of concubines, the resentment of the tenant farmers for the exploitation of the landlords, resentment at the damage caused by regional discrimination. All Koreans today can be said to be victims in one or several of those injustices. Who in Korea can escape this resentment? It is the view that the consciousness of almost all Koreans is embedded with the sense of victimization accumulated by perpetrators from generation to generation, including themselves. These are the background of accumulated strong antipathy and hostility. As a result, Koreans tend to be emotional and extreme before being rational. It divides the world only into right and wrong, victims and perpetrators. Koreans have a strong tendency to distinguish between me (right) and the other person (wrong).

Koreans even evaluate the former presidents of Korea who are widely respected by the world, as being only right or wrong (O, X). This is one of the typical examples of Koreans committing a folly in the grip of an extreme sense of victimization. They are committing the mistake of undermining the great achievements by highlighting only small faults. Among the former presidents of the Republic of Korea, former Presidents Rhee Seungman and Park Chung-hee were clearly dictators, just like shadow darkens when light is bright. They also made mistakes and people suffered under their rule. However, they built the foundation for an advanced Republic of Korea that foreigners envy and use as a model for development. These are the people who played a decisive role in making Korea what it is today and are the people who are praised as great politicians and leaders around the world. However, there is still not a single statue commemorating them properly in Korea. It won't be easy as long as there are families who have suffered under their rule. What about former President Roh Moo-hyun? Some believes that he lacked somewhat the experience and discernment required to carry out the presidency commensurate with Korea's economic scale. The failure to manage the surrounding people also led to the result of disappointing the public's expectations. But he tried to fight the vested interest. Although he did not succeed, he conveyed a message to the people that even those who have nothing can achieve their dreams. Still, conservatives in South Korea do not give him high praise.

What about the "pro-Japanese" issue? It is also one of the examples of making mistakes due to being caught up in an extreme sense of victimization. Even the patriots who gave everything for independence are often accused of being pro-Japanese by the dichotomous assessment standards. Let's take a look at the case of Yun Chi-ho, whom some consider to be pro-Japanese. He was convinced that education and enlightenment were essential in the preparation for independence. For this, he led the patriotic enlightenment movement using the conveniences provided by the Japanese Empire. Like him, many intellectuals at the time cooperated with Japan. Among them, there were patriots who cooperated because they believed that this was for the sake of their country rather than pursuing only their own achievement. Still, can it be said that it is reasonable to be classified as pro-Japanese and belittled because they cooperated?

In human life, for each affair, if there is a right, then there is a wrong. People become perpetrators and victims without realizing it. Nevertheless, Koreans have a strong tendency to judge complex human social issues only with the dichotomous thinking. I believe that it is because of the extreme sense of victimization accumulated in their minds.

The ideological tendency of Koreans is clear, either left or right, mostly related to family history, and is extreme.

Historically, many Koreans suffered unjust lives and shed blood as they went through the chaos after liberation, the Korean War, and the process of industrialization and democratization. Sometimes, even children were victimized and had to suffer. For that reason, it is common that the ideological tendencies of Koreans are mostly determined by family history. This is expressed emotionally and aggressively rather than rationally. It is clear and extreme due to the victim's awareness of the lack of fairness. This tendency does not change easily.

On November 23, 2010, from 2:34 pm to 2:45 pm, North Korea fired about 150 rounds of long range artillery at Yeonpyeong Island in South Korea. It was an obvious artillery provocation by North Korea. Regarding this, Koreans also displayed an absurd division of national opinion. After liberation from Japanese colonial rule, Korean society went through the process of division into north and south, the Korean War, industrialization, and democratization. The violence of the times divided the lives of many people into two different sides (enemy and friend). Dichotomously separated, trampled and shed blood. Furthermore, the guilt-by-association system had devastated even the lives of their families and close relatives. It is true that many of today's figures who deny the legitimacy of the Republic of Korea have painful family histories of suffering and discrimination from rightists in the past. Also, there are Koreans whose families were massacred by the leftist, and were the relatives of soldiers, policemen and veterans of the war. For that reason, many Koreans' ideological tendencies were not chosen because they believed in that ideology or because it was right. There are characteristics that were formed as a reaction against painful experiences and damages in family history. The unfair and resentful treatments they personally experienced remain in their hearts. Then, it is expressed in an extreme fashion and does not change easily. In this way, the sense of victimization that came from experiences of family history explodes emotionally. North Korea's shelling of South Korean territory caused a national disaster, but some even claimed that the South Korean government was to blame. The emotional side of victimization led people to make irrational statements, without any hesitation, in defense North Korea. It is true that in the current

Korean society, to some people, a strong sense of extreme victimization that has been handed down still remains. To them, the rational judgment is not important in matters related to the entity that they think has harmed them. They only express emotional aggression. For this reason, even if Yeonpyeong Island, a South Korean territory, was bombarded by the major enemy, division of national opinion occurred.

On the political level, the right and the left are complementary. The National Assembly convened immediately after the French Revolution in 1789 which separated them politically. From the chairperson's seat, the royalists (conservatives) sat on the right and the republicans (radicals) sat on the left. Since then, it has become customary to divide conservative and moderate forces into the right, and radical and extremist forces into the left. Politically, the right wing refers to a person or group that is conservative and has capitalist ideas or tendencies. A leftist is a person that is progressive or innovative, having socialist ideas or tendencies. The distinction between right and left is not an absolute concept, but a relative one. In Korea, it seems that the right wing has been recognized as a believer in the liberal democratic system, and the left wing as a believer in the socialist or communist system. As the Soviet Union and

Eastern Europe collapsed and China accepted the use of a market economy, communist (leftist) ideology became a failed attempt. Nonetheless, there are people in the world who are sympathetic to the ideology, arguments, and values of the left. This is because the universal human rights or social values of freedom and equality pursued by the left are persuasive in their own way. In that context, the left and the right are both conflicting and complementary. So, it can be said that they are both necessary ideologies to realize a sound and open society.

Korea is a liberal democratic country. In liberal democracy, justice is maintained in human society. The free and democratic basic order that guarantees freedom and equal opportunity is considered as a universal value. The state is managed by liberal democratic values and market economy. Equal opportunities and the demonstration of competences are guaranteed in all areas of politics, economy, society, and culture under the basic free and democratic order. The values of fulfilling these responsibilities and duties entailed from freedom and rights are emphasized.

In advanced democracies, political forces are generally divided into conservative camps and progressive camps. The camp that considers freedom as a higher value is called the conservative camp, and the camp that strives for equality is called the progressive camp. In a liberal democratic country based on a market economy, it is a society where the demonstration of individual competences is guaranteed, so the rich and poor people naturally arise. Then, the accumulation of wealth by the rich and the lack of fortune by the poor is repeated continuously by the virtuous and vicious cycles of the free market economy. Society is bisected into a few rich members and many poor ones as well. The gap between the rich and poor in a divided society gets worse. The greater the gap between the rich and the poor, the greater the sense of incongruity, and the more anxious society becomes. If that happens, the position of the rich will no longer be guaranteed. That is the basic flaw of liberal democracy and that's why the leftist values are needed.

Therefore, in order to become an advanced democratic society, it is necessary to make efforts to create an equal society where freedom is guaranteed. We need conservatives who pursue freedom as a fundamental value, but we also need progressives who strive for equality. For that reason, conservatives and progressives should complement each other rather than be in conflict with each other. Only then can a truly just and open society be built.

The ideological confrontation between conservatives (right)

and progressives (left) in Korean society is unique. Progressive people in Korea do not have any clear leftist philosophy or ideology. They appear as being dragged by the "pro-North Korea forces" who only dream of a communist violent revolution that had failed. In Korea, the forces claiming to be progressive show behaviors that cannot be understood by not only conservative values but also progressive values. They are ignoring the universal human rights of North Koreans and their defectors, which can be considered to be a basic value of progressiveness. They praise the succession of power over three generations in North Korea and speak in defense of North Korea's nuclear weapons development. They do not respect or pursue any basic values of their own affiliation. They are only participating in way that praise and represent the North Korean communist hereditary regime. In order to establish a truly open society in Korea, genuine progressive forces are needed to keep the conservative forces in check. However, it is unfortunate that the attribute of progressive people in Korea cannot be said to be seen as the progressive left that is truly necessary for an open advanced society. Unfortunately, many people believe that most of leftist Koreans are just extreme followers of the North Korean regime, wearing the guise of progressives because of family resentment rather than progressive ideology.

The opinion that Koreans' ideological tendencies are related to family history is based on the following facts. During the Korean War on June 25, approximately 760,000 civilians were killed, missing, or captured. Many of them are those who were unfairly executed by the North Korean army during the occupation period, those who were abducted by North Korea, and those who are missing but presumed to be dead. On the other hand, there are some people who were killed in retaliation by the South Korean army for supporting the communist regime during the occupation by the North Korean army. About 1/3 of the civilian massacres, missing persons, and prisoners of war were presumed to be suffered in retaliation for siding with the communist regime, making the number approximately 253,000. Their families suffered from guilt-by-association after the war. Until the early 2000s, they had been officially restricted from living as normal Korean citizens, such as entering public offices and traveling abroad. If the population of Korea at the time of the Korean War is estimated to be 20 million people, about 1 million to 1.5 million people (approximately 5 to 7.5%) were subject to guilt-by-association based on 4 to 6 family members per person (including close relatives). All the people subjected to the guilt-by-association were not treated the same. However, most of them have suffered unfair treatments simply due to family history without committing any crimes. For that reason, they take the side of the North Korea not because they like its regime, but because they hate the South Korean regime. The results of a public opinion poll on security awareness of Koreans[43] back this up. The following are the average values of public opinion polls from 2006 to 2011 on the contents corresponding to the claim of pro-North Korean forces in South Korea. For those questions related to the USFK which have been the key deterrence to North Korean aggression, 6.25% of Koreans agreed with "USFK is not important", 8.25% chose "Withdraw USFK as soon as possible", and 7.5% said "There is no need for ROK-US joint drills." The ratio of those who have suffered from guilt by association is similar to the ratio of those in favor of the pro-North Korean assertions. These facts prove that Koreans' ideological tendencies are rooted in family history.

After the Korean War, South Korea had developed an anti-communism state policy against the threat of the communist regime in North Korea. In the process, words and actions that went against national policy or direction were viewed as pro-North Korea propaganda. Many unfair sacrifices were also produced by such standardized violence of the times and they too can be said to be victims. As such, the left and right ideological tendencies of Koreans are unfortunately dichotomous and extreme, as most of them stem from unfair family history.

Koreans place more importance on the motives or feelings that evoke words and actions than the outward expression of words and actions.

Among familiar words to Koreans, there is a saying "How desperate they must be···, the hunger, makes any man a criminal···" This is a proverb used to defend the inevitability of a person committing a crime or doing something ethically unacceptable. Koreans had suffered as people of the weak country in the middle of the continent and maritime power for generations. Most of them also lived as subjects to their exploitation while paying taxes under the rule of despots and other privileged classes. In the process of living in the position of the weak, inevitable situations may arise in which they have no choice but to break the law or behave ethically unacceptable. Most Koreans have lived in empathy with such living environments and unfortunate conditions for a long time like their ancestors. As a result, even today, they sympathize with the words and deeds of a person who has been forced to break the law or act unethically in order to survive or to protect his/her family, by saying "How desperate they must be to do that?"

In Western society, each person is regarded as an independent being in society, and individuality and independence are regarded as important virtues. Because they value each person's behaviors or actions, each individual must be held accountable for his/her own actions. In the West, rules or standards are specific and are used as a criterion for judging the results of behaviors. On the other hand, in Korean society, each person's role as a member of society is more valued. It encourages the ethical responsibility of each person to fulfill their duty in their place or social position. In other words, rather than observing specific rules or standards of behavior, it is more important to act in accordance with the person's position or social status in a specific environment. They evaluate situation-dependent behavior with the ethical standards based on human interrelationship values. For that reason, the rules or standards of behaviors are generally not specific enough.

This originates from the difference between values of Westerners based on Christianism and Korean values based on

Buddhism and Confucianism. In Christian and Muslim societies, people, as creatures of the Creator, must believe in the Creator and act according to the Creator's commandments. They emphasize specific words and behaviors rather than thoughts in their mind. A common example of this is making a pledge of "I do (believe in God!)" during the Christian baptism ceremony. It also corresponds to the wedding vows from the bride and groom at a wedding. In the Christian worldview, it is said that everything, from being born to living today, is according to the Creator's plan. One's will is also important. However, the will only refers to asking the Creator questions within the scope of the commandments. As mere creatures of the Creator, the value lies in believing in him and acting in accordance with his commandments. So, Westerners place more importance on what the other person did to them rather than what kind of thoughts or feelings the other person had towards them. They discuss a person's character, responsibility, and humanity based on their outward and observable behaviors. Inner thoughts or feelings that are not expressed are not considered as important when discussing issues of responsibility or personality.

As mentioned earlier, in the world of pantheistic Buddhism and Confucianism, it is assumed that God exists in the world and dwells in all things. The basic idea of Buddhism says that you can become a Buddha if you recognize the mercy of Buddha inherent in you through cultivation. The basic idea of Confucianism is to preserve and cultivate one's innate nature, that is, goodness, through the discipline and training of the mind that triggers one's words and actions, and to pursue a sage who is considered to be perfect. The Avatamsaka Sutra's thought of "All is what comes from the mind"[107] is said to be an expression that implies all the contents of Buddhist scriptures. The concept of Jongshimsoyok Bulyugu (從心所欲 不踰矩)[108] in the Analects also refers to the stage of becoming a mature human being pursued in Confucianism. All of these are saying that the heart is at the center of a person's words and behaviors. This means that the mind that caused the words and behaviors is the key rather than outward words and behaviors.

From generation to generation, Koreans have been influenced by the ideology that views words and behaviors as the results of the mind. Therefore, rather than outward words and behaviors, the motive or feelings that caused such words and behaviors are more important. "What caused them to

---

107) Everything comes from what the mind creates.
108) Even if he does what his heart wanted, he does not go against the norm.

behave like that?" is the question at hand. So, if the motive behind the action is to survive or to protect one's family, people become generous, sympathetic, and forgive. As such, Koreans have a strong tendency to view external behavior as a clue or by-product of the expression of the mind.

Koreans are hot-tempered and enjoy excitement, but are vulnerable to feelings of helplessness and victimization.

"Korean" refers to the people who live in the "Korean Peninsula" protruding south from the coast of Manchuria, which is located in the eastern part of the Asia. It is said that people who have lived in the peninsula have an emotional and hot-tempered peninsular temperament. Having lived for generations on the peninsula, it is the result of their unique temperament formed by the geopolitical environment. Let's take a look at the characteristics of people who live on the peninsula. Spaniards are passionate and laid-back. It is said that they like to dance and have fun.[44] Italians are passionate and hot-tempered. They value family and lineage and enjoy singing and entertainment. It is also said that they get easily excited due to hot tempered characteristics.[45]

Then what about Korean people? It is said that Koreans are hot-tempered, easily heats up and cools down quickly, and enjoy excitement.[46] It is believed that the temperamental characteristics of the above-mentioned "peninsula people" originated from these facts. Influenced by the geopolitical environment, peninsular people are passionate and enjoy the excitement. In addition, it can be seen that they have similar temperamental characteristics to each other, as seen through their hot temperament.

In 2020, 13,195 Koreans committed suicide, recording a suicide rate of 25.7 (number of suicides per 100,000 people). Although the suicide rate decreased by 4.4% compared to the previous year, it became the record of the highest suicide rate maintained since 2003 among OECD countries. It once again recorded the disgrace of being the country with the highest suicide rate in the world. The 2020 record is also more than double the suicide rate of 10.9 across 38 OECD countries.[47] Suicide is considered dishonorable in Korea. Therefore, even if a person actually commits suicide, when reporting a death, those related to the deceased are reluctant to mark it as a "suicide." Considering this, the actual suicide rate is estimated to be much higher than this.

Where does the high suicide rate of Koreans come from? In

the past, in the 1970s and 1980s, I often heard the saying, "Koreans are the people with a lot of Han (恨, bitter feelings)." 「Arirang, 150 years, Miari Pass, Chilgapsan, etc.」 are representative folksongs of the Korean people. 「Hanjungrok, Janghwahongryeonjeon, Honggildong Jeon, Cheongsan Byeolgok, Samogok, etc.」 are classics that have been popular among Koreans. These classics contain a lot of resentment, and I think that is why Koreans like them. Koreans tend to have high emotional ups and downs. They tend to get angry at the slightest difference of opinion. When they suddenly explode in 'rage', they would even run through fire and water. They don't try to compromise or complain. Rather than overcoming the mental pressure they feel, they are more likely to give up. Due to such a temperament, it is believed that is why Koreans have a high suicide rate. I believe that the reason why the suicide rate is relatively high among Koreans is that they have a lot of resentment accumulated from their ancestors in addition to their inherent peninsula temperament. Although it is a peninsula country like Korea, the suicide rate of Turkey (4.4 people), Italy (5 people), and Spain (7 people) is much lower than the average suicide rate of OECD countries. This contrasting situation is said to be due to the Han (grudges) accumulated in Korean minds.

Suicide is the act of taking one's own life by one's own will. It is an act of self-destruction. Looking at it from a microscopic point of view asking "how depressing the situation must have been for someone to commit a suicide?", they might have a clear reason why they chose to do so. However, from a macroscopic point of view, it points out that all kinds of pathological phenomena of modern society, such as materialism, family disintegration, violent Internet culture, academic elitism, and lookism, are the root causes. If pathological phenomenon in modern society is the cause of suicide, can it be said that only Korea has such a high suicide rate? I don't believe so. Then, why do so many Koreans choose the road leading to suicide? Recently, a British press also covered an article titled "Korea's suicide rate, the highest among OECD countries." Compared to people from other countries, there is no other reason to commit suicide that is unique to Koreans. The article pointed out that it is strange that so many people in Korea are having a hard time. If there is no special reason to point out in regards to the environment, I think the reason is because of human characteristics.

Referring to past records, it can be seen that the high suicide rate of Koreans is due to the human characteristics of Koreans. It is recorded in Hankookji (韓國志)[109], published in 1905, that Koreans value their lives lightly, choosing actions such as hanging or drowning when they suffer severe mental pain. Records say that they easily choose suicide in the face of trivial and insignificant discomfort, insults, and circumstances that are completely unworthy of concern. This is almost unbelievable to people from other countries. According to the Mokpo Newspaper on June 17, 1923, 134 Japanese committed suicides in comparison to 1,256 Koreans in 1922, almost reaching 9.4 times the level in comparison.[48]

If you analyze the personalities of people who commit suicide, most of them are people with extreme emotional ups and downs. Even when they are in a good mood, they easily express strong displeasure over trivial matters. They are people who are prone to anger or frustration. Due to the fact that Korea's suicide rate is the highest among OECD countries, one can assume that Koreans have high emotional ups and downs, which can lead them to easily make extreme choices.

People feel resentment when they are scorned or insulted by others, and they feel resentment when they are treated unjustly or unfairly. Then people get angry. It is said that anger is

109) It is a booklet researched by Imperial Russia in 1900 for the expansion policy at the end of the Joseon Dynasty and it was first translated and published by Japan's Forestry Bureau in 1905.

released when resentments and unfair feelings explode. But what would happen if a person was so resentful, but held back their anger because they couldn't get angry, shouldn't get angry, or that the situation prevented him to get angry? If such a situation lasts for a long time, unresolved emotions remain in the heart. The Chinese character of Han (恨, grudge) is consist of the mind (心) and being still (艮). Han is a feeling of victimization that causes internal conflicts, dissatisfaction, resentment caused by external influences, the anger of having to endure resentment, and the feeling of helplessness that cannot be expressed, forming a lump in the mind.

It is said that the Han (恨) is inherent in Koreans. Some expressed it as the fundamental mentality of Koreans, the spirit of Korean culture, and even a collective representation of Koreans. It is a trait that is imprinted in the DNA of Koreans. It is an emotion not found in the consciousness of the people of Turkey, Spain, and Italy, who are peninsular countries like Korea, but have had experiences in conquering and ruling neighboring countries based on their roles as a transportation, economic, and cultural hub for continental and maritime countries, and sometimes based on strong national power. Koreans had to suffer from poverty for many generations due to the population increases, exploitation and in part a limited amount of farmland on a small peninsula. Externally, because of a relatively small peninsula as its territory, it was inevitably subject to more aggression from neighboring powers compared to other peninsula countries. As a result, Koreans had no choice but to live in poverty-stricken conditions and a sense of victimization accumulated in their hearts for generations. With numerous invasions by neighboring countries, they had lived in grudges due to experiencing all sorts of humiliation. Due to this, resentment and Han piled up without being expressed. The feelings of anger and Han (恨) have been passed down from generation to generation and accumulated in their hearts.

In the past, when Koreans faced particularly unfair situations, they took comfort in releasing resentment in their hearts through anger releasing dances or shamanism practices, rather than expressing hostility toward the other party. Through active emotional activities that arouse feelings of joy or pleasure, such as singing or dancing, they soothed their lumps of resentment and sadness. It has become a habit and even now, Koreans thoroughly enjoy singing and dancing. But what will happen if they leave the accumulated resentment in their heart unresolved? It will naturally build up in their minds.

Let me explain this in detail. Let's say that a person has not been able to resolve or radiate anger and resentment in their life. What will happen? As mentioned above, it will harden into the form of grudge and accumulate in the heart. If the same grudge has been accumulated in that person in addition to their ancestors', it will grow. Then, what will happen if the same emotion of anger and resentment arises in everyday life? Naturally, it will be aggravated with the emotional grudges piled up at the bottom of their heart. And, when the aggravated emotions exacerbate and explode beyond the level of self-control, extreme choices such as self-torture or suicide are made. It is the logic that Koreans have a relatively low threshold of victim mentality, resentment, and helplessness that can be overcome because Han, which has been accumulated and passed down for generations, is located at the bottom of their hearts. An example is provided below for better understanding.

Assuming the sense of victimization or resentment that general people can overcome is 100, for Koreans, the sense of victimization or resentment that has been accumulated through their ancestors accounts for about 40 to 50 in nominal value, so the level of victimization or resentment they can overcome is only about 50 to 60. So, even though people in other countries are not affected much by the sense of victimization or resentment (about 50 to 60), for Koreans, it exceeds the threshold of 100. In particular, even a feeling of victimization or resentment that seems insignificant to a third party, can easily exceed the threshold of self-restraint if it causes resonance with the accumulated grudges.

As a result, the Han (恨, grudge) being ingrained in the mind of Koreans has now caused a generalized statement that says "Koreans are sometimes extreme." For Koreans, as mentioned above, they are docile under the influence of the environment. Also as the people of a peninsular, they enthusiastically enjoy "excitement" and are active. On the other hand, they are strongly influenced by the Han (恨) inherent in their mind, which has been passed down from generation to generation, and can easily express extreme emotions. In the eyes of a third party, even with a trivial displeasure or insulting remark, or a situation that is completely unworthy of concern, they feel a tremendous sense of victimization or insurmountable resentment. When the hot-tempered emotions explode into a fit of rage, an extreme choice is made. This is the reason why Koreans have the highest suicide rate among OECD countries, in comparison to the peoples from other peninsular countries such as Turkey, Spain, and Italy, who also have hot-tempered personalities. It is believed that the reason why Koreans have the highest suicide rate is because they have lived in the small peninsula as a base for many generations, have been influenced by the environment, and have Han (恨, grudge) as an inherent component of their hearts.

The maturity of Koreans' human relationship is determined by Jeong (情, affection).

One of the most frequently used word by foreigners living in Korea to describe Koreans is "Jeong". They say that the Korean culture of giving generously and sharing even when one does not have much in possession, is a spiritual foundation that supports Korean society. In Korean language, the word 'Jeong' is exceptionally commonly found in words such as injeong (sympathy), mojeong (motherly affection), bujeong (fatherly affection), mujeong (no affection), yujeong (full of affections), loosing affection, affectionate hometown, lovely and hateful affection, etc. Regarding the word jeong, there are various ways of using it. Records of using the word jeong appeared from hundreds of years ago. Jeong by Koreans refers to the working state of the mind that indicates the degree of closeness to another person. For Koreans, jeong is formed through the experience of 'being together'. When a jeong is formed, there are no secrets and no gaps. It becomes a relationship where there is no need for boundaries in the mind because there is no hostile feelings between them. Jeong is derived from family relationships. The humane love that parents and siblings feel for each other is jeong. If you ask Koreans what kind of people are hard to get along with, they generally answer in three ways; "those who are not honest, those who only boast about themselves, and those who do not want to make concessions or accept losses at all." This fact shows that jeong starts from family relationships. Earning jeong in a relationship with a Korean means that the other person's defects are accepted or even positively perceived.

France's J. G. Le Clezio, who received the 2008 Nobel Prize in Literature, described Korean literature as being jeong (情, affection). He said "The concept of jeong is very subtle and unique. I searched English and French dictionaries, but there is no way to translate it." He assessed that Arirang and overall Korean culture are deeply influenced by jeong. Jeong represents all the emotions a person feels, and it is closely related to time.[49] It is because it takes a time to be bound by jeong, just as you do not say that you feel an affection to someone you just met for the first time. Don't they say that they are being or are bound by jeong? Jeong (情, affection) presupposes the passage of time to some extent. The logical opposite of "getting jeong" is "loosing jeong". But Koreans don't say that. They say "jeong has been detached." It takes a time to get jeong, but when jeong leaves, it does not leave gradually, but instead detaches at once. Jeong can be detached in a split second. However, like lingering feelings and thoughts that cannot be cut off, jeong is not completely erased and a trace remains.

When one expresses jeong, there is not only 'lovely jeong', but also 'hateful jeong.' This means that Jeong encompasses all the good feelings, bad feelings, and strange feelings. What is hateful jeong? It refers to the accumulated affection even when there is hostility between them. It is not simply the feeling of loading, hating, or jealousy of the other person. It is an incomprehensible and unique feeling of thinking and worrying about the other person's perspective. Jeong as the most representative emotional characteristics of Koreans is a characteristic of Koreans which cannot be judged rationally .

However, what is interesting, is that 'hateful jeong in Korean people' represents the concept of 'Koreans being people with no after grudge'. Above, it was said that Koreans are socially relational and have a strong sense of community called 'us'. These are all related. In a society based on jeong, people are classified as 'we' or 'others' according to whether they share jeong or not. In other words, they become as close as family or they are seen as others who have nothing to do with us.

A hateful jeong is the affection that can be felt for their boss who bully them at work and for their mother-in-laws who are mean to them. This concept shows the distinctiveness of jeong in which the victim feels a sense of care for the perpetrator, instead of hate, jealousy, or dislike. This is only possible when rational mentality of profit and loss are not considered. Because jeong begins with an attitude of acknowledging the other person before profit or loss, it does not call the other person cheap.

Jeong is an attitude of acknowledging the other person before profit or loss. It is based on a caring heart. Jeong occurs when one tries to accept the other person's position rather than only one's own. Socially, it becomes even more powerful when it is bound by a sense of community called "we." Koreans often say at the gathering with friends, "We are not like others!" This means that the other person is a part of me, and 'we' as a collective identity includes the two of us. Therefore, jeong is a keyword to maintain 'we' indicating that the other person feels like family, while also being an intimate feeling that Koreans feel between family members. As a result, there are many side effects caused by jeong. There are many times when it is difficult to refuse an unreasonable request from the other person who is part of 'us'. This is because there are times when you have to do something with fear of breaking the bond of jeong. There are some cases in which you cannot get money back after you lend it. This is because telling them to pay back can sometimes be an action that breaks the jeong with the other person. This is an example of how Koreans' 'Jeong' works in a negative way.

"Eat and live well!" is a phrase that Koreans use to comfort themselves when they feel resentment caused by others. it's not a blessing but a curse. "Give another piece of rice cake to the one you hate." It means that you will think positively and forget about it, telling yourself how desperate they must have been to do such a hateful thing. The two examples presented above are Koreans sublimating the injustice they suffered into a unique form of affection rather than trying to get payback seen through the concept of 'a tooth for a tooth'. This is one of the key traits of Koreans. For that reason, although many pieces of art in China, Japan, and around the world deal with 'revenge' as a basic subject matter, in Korean art works, the 'revenge' is very uncommon subject and does not appear often.

Jeong (affection) is a heart that feels love and friendliness. Compared to foreigners, Koreans in particular are said to be particularly vulnerable when it comes to jeong. How exposed must have they been to have an expression like 'because of that damn jeong?' Korean society is said to be less calculating and less dreary than Western society. This is because it is still a society where human affection remains. It was said that Korean pastors' missionary activities in the world are the expression of Koreans' jeong culture, which is kind and emotional to help the less fortunate. Jeong is an affection that is conveyed without wanting something back from the other person. It is a strange concept for Westerners who like to be logical and rational. That is why it is quite difficult to express jeong in their own languages. There is a significant difference between the meaning of love and jeong. Jeong is an emotion given unconditionally between colleagues, from superiors to subordinates, and from parents to their children. Looking at the history of the Korean people, as they have lived in poverty for generations, endured constant foreign invasions, and recently experienced violence during the era of Japanese colonial plunder and economic development, are embedded with the emotions of Han (恨) and Jeong(情).

Then, why do Koreans have strong character traits of Jeong? First, it is sensitivity of the Shimjeong (心情, mind) of Koreans. Here, Shimjeong is a state of mind that arises in relation to the other person's words, behaviors and situations. This is the fluid state of the mind, which varies according to time rather than the mind itself. The fact that Koreans are sensitive to their feelings means that they are good at empathizing with the other person's misfortune, such as a sick heart or unpleasant feelings. This is because, historically, Korean ancestors have had many unfortunate experiences. For that reason, the Shimjeong (mind) that arises from empathy for the state of mind and emotions of another person has developed. Here, what kind of relationship is there between Shimjeong (心情) and Injeong (人情), that is, human emotion towards other people? Injeong is formed during the process of empathizing with the mind of the other person. As a result, in order to form Injeong, you must first read the flow of the other person's heart, that is, Shimjeong, and sympathize with it. In this way, it is inferred that Koreans have developed Jeong because Injeong and Shimjeong are always expressed in a mutually correlated manner.

The second is because of the old social system of Koreans. The Samgangohryun and Hyangyak, which were guidelines for life in Joseon's Confucian society, are 'ethics that must be observed between king and servants, parents and children, husband and wife, adults and children, between friends and neighbors in human society.' It is believed that this was formed naturally as our ancestors had followed it for a long time as a way of life. Samgangohryun and Hyangyak are ethics that prioritize one's duty to the other person before the other person's duty to themself. In the process of fulfilling my duty, the feelings that has been accumulated with complain, hate, and resentment, and, at the same time, with praise, liking, and gratitude toward the other person are the hateful and lovely parts of Jeong.

In particular, the relationship between parents and children, that is, the family relationship, presented in Korean's Samganggoryun is unique. Family relations in Korea have been greatly influenced by the development of the long-standing genealogy and clan family rule systems. As a result, it is different from the rational and independent familial relationships that exist in the West. It is a state in which the self-undifferentiated relationship[110] is generalized in jeong (affection) of empathy and time. As such, unity and solidarity

---

110) Self differentiation is a central concept in family systems theory, and its degree is an individual's emotional maturity, indicating the degree of autonomy and dependence on the family system.

are emphasized rather than autonomy in one's family among parents and children. Their relationship and interaction are based on jeong, so the child's psychological attachment to their parents is very high. As a result, a parent's jeong for their children is internalized by the child as well. In this way, Korean children grow up as they accumulate jeong through close contact with their parents from an early age. It is said that there is a social condition where a child inevitably grows into an adult with a lot of jeong after being raised by parent's jeong. As a result, the maturity of Koreans' human relations is determined by jeong (情).

The third is because of the living conditions in which they have to embrace and cooperate with each other rather than against each other. It is the view that the living conditions in which Koreans lived for generations naturally led to the formation of a special personality trait called Jeong. Koreans lived in a peaceful agricultural society, almost cut off from the outside world, except when continental or maritime powers invaded. Moreover, the Korean Peninsula, the home of life, has four distinct seasons, so if they miss the timing, they have no choice but to ruin their farming as well. In order to farm in harmony with nature, intense labor is required during sowing and harvesting seasons, and at this time, it was crucial for neighbors to help each other. In addition to this, natural disasters such as droughts and floods that occur frequently were situations that no individual could face alone. Cooperation between neighbors was an absolute necessity. The agricultural living environment in which Koreans lived in an agricultural society for thousands of years sometimes required concentration of labor and sometimes close cooperation to overcome disasters. In addition to this, due to the nature of an agricultural society based on naivety, even if there were trivial disputes between neighbors, there would not have been many fights to the extent of resentment. In this way, Koreans have formed an agricultural society on the Korean Peninsula, where the four distinct seasons, and have survived in living conditions in which it is impossible to live without helping each other's neighbors. For many years, they had lived in an environment where they had to cooperate with each other, even with neighbors they disliked, did not want to see, or did not want to deal with. It is the logic that because of such a living environment, there was no choice but to have not only lovely jeong but also hateful jeong as well. In addition, as the founding ideology of Hongik Ingan suggests, it is my opinion that Koreans are naturally kind, meaning they have the characteristic of embracing even people they hate.

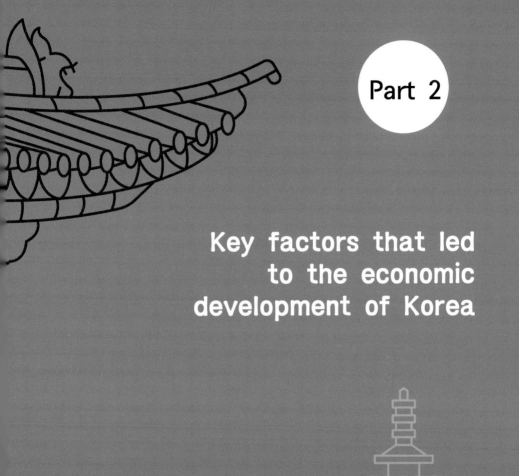

Part 2

Key factors that led to the economic development of Korea

The Korean Peninsula was liberated from Japanese colonial rule with the Allies' victory in World War II. However, as the country was divided into north and south based on the interests of the great powers, a country called the Republic of Korea was born in the south. In the process of establishing its status as an independent nation, the Republic of Korea was attacked by surprise attack by the communist regime in North Korea. Through the three years of the Korean War, the country had been turned into ashes. It has been over 70 years since the people of the country have been making all-out efforts for national survival and economic prosperity. In the 1950s and 1960s, Koreans shouted the slogan, "If united, we live, if scattered, we die," as an expression of anti-communism. It tells us that the survival of the country was so desperate. In the 1960s and 1970s, people shouted the slogan "Let's Try to Live well!", showing how desperately we needed to overcome poverty.

During such a difficult environment, national leaders presented a future vision to the people where all elements of the national power were mobilized to focus on economic development. That's what made Korea grow into an economically rich country. In 2021 it ranked 10th in the world in GDP, and ranked 1st in semiconductor exports and shipbuilding orders, and Bloomberg Innovation Index.[50, 51] This is the result achieved by the strategy to prioritize economic development, reflecting the nation's rallying call of "Let us try to live well, too" in order to escape from being one of the poorest countries in the world during the 1960s and 1970s. This economy-oriented national strategy has achieved great economic results at the national level. On the other hand, in the process of promoting the prioritization of economic development, politically, an anti-democratic national governing system was established. They also resorted to the violence during these times. Such incidents kindled anti-government demonstrations, and since the late 1980s, Korea has been devoted to political democratization. As a result, Korea today has achieved political democratization both in its name and reality. In the meantime, Koreans have been running, only looking forward, with the determination to live well. So, to some extent, they got what they wanted. Now they obtained a bit of spare money and time in their lives. That leeway served as the driving force behind the creation of their own culture called Hallyu. As Hallyu created a craze all over the world, Korea has now emerged as a soft power powerhouse.

Soft power refers to the ability to move people psychologically or emotionally.[52] It means having the power to lead people around the world by exerting a positive influence through the appeal of Korea's institutions, culture, and foreign policies. Until now, the world order has been dominated by hard power with economic and military strength. However, in today's world order, as interdependence among countries increases, business activities transcend national borders, and the science and technology development and its dissemination are transferred quickly to developing countries. It has become an environment where soft power exerts much greater influence than hard power.

A prime example of soft power is science and technology. The United States has been able to dominate the world because it has been able to overwhelm the world with science and technology. Thanks to this, pop cultures such as American Hollywood movies, Coca-Cola, and McDonald's have become popular all over the world. Science and technology are definitely the basis of a hard power, but can also be an important means to move the world as a soft power.

So, how are South Korea's soft power capabilities today? Korea's semiconductor, automobile, battery, shipbuilding, and nuclear power technology is leading the world. That's not all. The safety of Korean society, which is said to indicate the status of the people of that country, is also considered to be world-class. It is a society that is so safe that women can safely walk around the city wearing casual clothes even after 9 pm. It is said that there are few countries in the world that are as safe as Korea. To that extent, Korean society is an extremely safe society. The reason why Korean society is so safe is that it is a society strongly influenced by ethics before the institutional system of state laws. This is possible because Koreans have a high level of civic consciousness. In addition to this, cultural aspects, which are synonymous with soft power, are also greatly loved by people around the world. haven't K-dramas, K-pop, and K-movies been dominating the global market since the late 2010s? That's not all. Now, they add prefix "K" to anything related to Korea such as K-construction, K-shipbuilding, K-defense, etc., and are enthusiastic about anything Korea does. It shows how powerful Koreans' soft power is as much as hard power is.

Today, Korea's achievement of political democratization, Hallyu, and K-construction / shipbuilding / defense achievements can be said to be the output driven by economic development. As the economy developed and the food, clothing and shelter issues were resolved to some extent, the people wanted political democratization, they were able to create their own unique culture, and make concentrated investments in the field of technology. Maslow's 5-level theory of needs is proof of this. Under the premise that Korea's leap forward as an advanced country was possible because of its economic development, in Part 2, 'Leadership of National Leaders' and 'Environment/ Social conditions' which served as the foundation of Korea's development, and 'Korean's Unique Characteristics (K-DNA)', which is also made Korea prosperous today, are classified as key elements and summarized.

Leadership of national leaders

It can be said that the prosperity that Korea has achieved today was only possible thanks to the leadership of great national leaders who loved their country with all their heart. They laid the foundations for Korea's prosperity today. On the other hand, unfortunately, in later years of their regime, they planned to hold on to power for too long, making wrong political moves or leaving painful scars on some people. Resentments still remain in the hearts of those who suffered at the time, so their contributions are not recognized. I have no doubt that someday they will be remembered in Korean history as great politicians who played a decisive role in building today's Korea by clearly defining their merits and demerits.

President Syngman Rhee's leadership laid the foundation for economic development

In liberal democracies, election systems under pluralism, separation of powers, rule of law under open society, market economy under the recognition of private property, equality of human rights, and political freedom are guaranteed. On the other hand, in a liberal democracy, people need to have the intellectual level to understand the political and social systems guaranteed by the state, and take responsibility while demanding their rights. Otherwise, they cannot sustain a liberal democracy. In addition, capital, technology, manpower, and energy are required for industrialization as the foundation of national economic development. However, no leadership would be able to achieve economic development through industrialization if there were no capital, no technology, and no intellectual manpower and energy.

The political and social conditions at the time of the founding of the Republic of Korea in South Korea were, in a word, disastrous. Mountains and rivers, which were destroyed by the Japanese colonial plunder for 36 years, were divided into South Korea and North Korea along the 38th parallel with the agreement between the United States and the Soviet Union. South Korea under the US military government was in a state of social confusion due to the conflict between the politicians who advocated the establishment of a single government and the nationalist politicians who opposed the division between the two Koreas. In the end, thanks to the persistent efforts of politicians who insisted on the establishment of a single government, and had an accurate grasp of the international situation at the time, obtained the

United Nations approval for independent elections in South Korea. Through the general election on May 10, 1948, 196 members of the constitutional National Assembly and the first president were elected. With that, the establishment of the government of the Republic of Korea was officially declared on August 15, 1948. With the declaration of the Democratic People's Republic of Korea in North Korea on September 9 of the same year, the division of the Korean Peninsula between South and North Korea became official.

On August 15, 1948, the Republic of Korea, a liberal democratic country, was established in South Korea. However, traces of Japan's 36 years of land and forest exploitation, deliberate obscurantist policy by Japan, extortion of rice production, conscription for war mobilization, and the policy of annihilating Korean culture remained intact in Korean society. In addition to this, the society was in a very unstable situation due to severe conflicts between right and left political groups. More than 80% of the population was illiterate and there were only a few with higher education. During the aftermath of Japan's policy to strengthen colonial landlords, most of the farmers, who made up the majority of the population, were extremely poor tenant farmers. In April and May of the lunar calendar during the spring cessation period, there were many people who starved to death. No matter how hard they worked, there was no hope for tenant farmers under the social system in which only landlords were able to keep their bellies full. Society was in a gloomy and chaotic condition due to schemes of the communists who secretly operated under North Korea's orders in every corner of South Korea. In a word, it was too insufficient to be called as a liberal democracy. Intellectual level of the people was too low to utilize a fair electoral system, separation of powers, rule of law, market economy, equality of human rights, and political freedom. That's not all. None of the capital, technology, manpower, and energy required for industrialization to become a rich country was available. In a word, it was a newly established country with conditions of one of the world's poorest countries and low level of education its people.

How could economic development through industrialization be possible when there is no capital, no technology, and no manpower when there is a the required intellectual level and energy? However, there was a great politician in the Republic of Korea, where there was no hope at all on a pan-national level. He led the founding of the Republic of Korea under UN approval with an acumen for looking into the future. He established the education system required for the people to raise the intellectual level as citizens of a liberal democracy, and established the foundation to promote industrialization and economic development strategies. It was Rhee Syngman, the first president of the Republic of Korea.

For Koreans living in Korea today, President Syngman Rhee is a man who can be called the founding father of the country. I believe that any Koreans will sympathize with him if one day they understand his little-known true patriotism and achievements as a political leader. He built the first democratic republic in Korean history, the Republic of Korea, on the land of South Korea, where the illiteracy rate reached 80% with a per capita GNP of $50. It is common for new dynasties or independent states to emerge through civil wars. However, he succeeded in founding the Republic of Korea under UN approval through difficult political efforts in the United States under the belief that 'Korea should not become a puppet state, acknowledged by a single country, the United States'. This was completely devised by President Syngman Rhee. And he was elected as the first president by winning 180 out of 196 votes in the Constituent Assembly, which was formed through a general election with a turnout of 95.5%. It was an honorable founding of the Republic of Korea achieving UN approval, which is difficult to find in world history. In my opinion, because the South Korean government was established with UN approval, the UN Security Council could make a decision to promptly dispatch troops to defend Korea during the Korean War. At that time, if the former Soviet Union had exercised its veto power in the Security Council, would the decision to dispatch troops have been made? In less than two years after the establishment of the country was approved by the UN, the former Soviet Union could not exercise its right to veto without justification. With the abstention of the former Soviet Union, the dispatch of UN forces to Korea was carried out quickly. His assertion that Korea should not be founded as a puppet state had been justified.

As a founding figure, he thought that a newly established nation needed strong leadership. That is why he changed the constitution from parliamentary system to a presidential system. After the Korean War, he prevented war on the Korean Peninsula by signing the 「Korea-US Mutual Defense Treaty」, which the US did not want at the time. By requesting military aid from the United States, Korea grew into a military powerhouse by increasing the military power from 50,000 at the time, to 100,000 during the Korean War, and to 700,000 after the end of the war. It is said that it was possible because of his political acumen looking into the future.

In terms of the economy, President Syngman Rhee made a great contribution. As mentioned earlier, President Syngman Rhee carried out land reform to rationalize agricultural production and distribution. Although consequential, by carrying out land reform right before the outbreak of the Korean War, it also contributed to convincing South Korean farmers to not side with the North Korean People's Army during the war. Above all, his land reform provided a great opportunity to work for themselves by making tenant farmers, who accounted for nearly 70% of the people at the time, into self-employed farmers. Land reform was significant in that it provided an occasion to change the habits and inclinations of Koreans, who had been exploited by landlords for a long time and went from lazy, indolent and irresponsible people, into diligent and sincere people who work for themselves. It also gave Koreans a spirit of frugality, which has become a basic spirit of Koreans today. The impact of land reform at the time was so profound that it could be said that it was a social revolution in Korea.

Above all, his greatest achievement was the revitalization of national education. He had a strong belief that the nation could develop only by educating the people and nurturing talented people. Because he had such a belief, he played a decisive role in instilling a strong passion for learning into the DNA of Koreans. He was also the first president of the Provisional Government of the Republic of Korea established in Shanghai after the March 1st Movement of 1919. In the process of struggling under Japanese oppression for Korea's independence, he must have been keenly aware of the fact that the people must learn and be smarter. He must have felt strongly that the new country should never be allowed to be ruined again due to the stupidity and ignorance of the people like the Joseon Dynasty. The education policy he implemented represents this. On May 10, 1948, for the first time in Korea, elections for members of the Constitutional Assembly were held nationwide under the universal suffrage system from the founding of the Republic of Korea. The implementation of universal suffrage, which guarantees the right to vote for citizens over a certain age regardless of gender, religion, rich or poor, or class, was a revolutionary means to break down the inequality of social class that still remained in Korean society at the time. It provided a decisive opportunity that could lead Korean society into a free democratic society. This was because the election provided an opportunity for the people to think that they were sovereigns who could exercise their rights by being able to vote. However, the fact that each individual citizen correctly exercises his/her right to vote in universal elections presupposes that the people are equipped with the ability to make sound judgments accordingly. However, in 1948, when Korea was founded, the illiteracy rate of the people reached 80%. President Syngman Rhee must have judged that with such a level of education of the people, it would be impossible for the Republic of Korea to build a true democratic republic that pursues liberal democracy. For that reason, the Syngman Rhee government introduced a compulsory education system for free six-year elementary education from 1949 despite the poor government financial conditions. Universal suffrage led to compulsory education. The strong passion for learning from political leaders down to general populations was such that during the Korean War, compulsory education was conducted in open-air education sites in rural areas where there were no buildings.

After the Korean War, the country was in complete ruins. Human assets were the only resource in the country. President Syngman Rhee recognized that the advancement of human assets was necessary above all else for a wealthy country. He put more than 10% of the national budget into the education of the people even with being the poorest country in the world.

As a result, such implementation of educational policies at the national level led the development of Korean society into an open society through public education. During the reign of President Syngman Rhee, not only the public education to improve the overall intellectual level of people, but also the education to nurture high-quality human resources were carried out strongly. After liberation in 1945, there were only 19 universities, but in 1960, the number more than tripled to 63, and the number of university students alone increased to 100,000.

Even though the country was so poor, studying abroad was encouraged, and in the 1950s, an average of more than 600 people every year went to study abroad in developed countries including the United States. In 1956, he established a plan to support cutting-edge science and technology, giving many professors at Seoul National University the opportunity to study in the United States. They were the central force that led the Korean science and technology field in the 1960s. That's not all. Hankuk University of Foreign Studies was established in the form of a partial government subsidy in order to nurture international relations experts who would engage in global affairs. In addition, with the will to nurture talented people in the field of science and technology, breaking away from the traditional subjects of humanities and social education, Inha Institute of Technology was established on June 4th 1953. In addition, President Syngman Rhee promoted the elite education of the armed forces for the future development of the Korean military. The ROK military grew during the Korean War and in 1954 became a huge organization with 650,000 troops and took up 40% of the government budget. He confidently requested a great deal of aid from the United States because South Korea was at the forefront under the Cold War confrontation, and he maintained a huge army with said aid. As a part of the military aid plan, more than 1,000 officers were dispatched to the United States every year to learn about advanced military technology and organizational management methods of the US military. As a result, it greatly contributed to the development of Korean society by promoting the advanced elite of the Korean military and spreading American-style planning capabilities and organizational management concepts to Korean society. That's not all. About 10,000 technical non-commissioned officers were dispatched to the United States to learn about advanced technologies related to American-made weapons. Most of them became technicians who handled cutting-edge scientific equipment at the forefront of Korea's industrialization process in the 1960s and 1970s. They also contributed to the development of the defense industry.

In fact, in the 1950s, when agriculture was still almost the only industry even though land reform was carried out, there were still tenant farmers working under landlords of the past. Old-school elites with Japanese education and experiences dominated important social positions. Even so, the implementation of national education policies for the transition to an open society and the strong passion for learning of Koreans who wanted to become a dragon in a stream created a synergistic effect. In the short period of 10 years of President Syngman Rhee's reign, Korean society had rapidly changed and developed into a free democratic society. A new elite group with American education was formed to replace the old elite. In the 1960s, the level of consciousness of the people improved. They no longer tolerated rigged elections and corruption by political bureaucrats. They began to ask the state for workplaces where they could demonstrate their abilities as much as they had learned. However, Korean society at the time could not accommodate such social demands, so society became extremely unstable.

In 1959, 10 years after the founding of the Republic of Korea, the illiteracy rate of the Korean people fell to 22.1%.

The level of national education improved to such an extent that the number of middle and high school students, and university students has increased more than 10 times. This was achieved through the combination of President Syngman Rhee's policy of prioritizing the public's education to build an open society and a strong passion for learning that is firmly rooted in the hearts of the Korean people.

The process of transforming Korean society into an open society, where social status rose through education, became a prerequisite for creating the labor force necessary for the national industrialization policy that began in the 1960s. Fortunately, this was possible with the insight of Korean political leaders. Indeed, in the 1950s, the Korean people were so poor and ignorant that they could not do anything. Such people were treated as capable members of an open society through the implementation of educational policies at the national level. It laid the foundation for Korea's economic development in the 1960s.

As a result, the illiteracy rate, which reached 80% of the people after the Korean War, had fallen to less than 10% in the 1960s when he had to step down. 90% of the people had acquired the literacy skills. That's not all. It aroused Koreans' desire for education. It aroused Korean's desire for education.

"Knowledge is power, learn to live well." Despite the difficult living environment, they sent their children to school. It is said that the percentage of people going to university also exceeded that of England, an advanced country at the time. Thus, many Koreans received higher education. This is the result of President Syngman Rhee's strong conviction that 'nurturing human resources must be a priority for national development'.

In addition to this, President Syngman Rhee's revitalization of national education enabled Koreans to have a concrete 'idea of equality' based on democracy. The Saemaul movement, which was implemented later on, was able to succeed because Koreans were equipped with the meaningful idea of equality. After the success of the Saemaul movement that fulfilled the needs for food, clothing and shelter to some extent, they began to wish for political democratization, which was sacrificed in the process of economic development, and eventually achieved it. The revitalization of national education by President Syngman Rhee allowed Koreans to have concrete ideas of equality based on democracy. I believe that it laid the foundation for the success of the Saemaul movement and political democratization.

President Rhee Syngman devoted his whole life to building Korea into a true democracy. Nevertheless, in his later years, he failed to prevent corruption against democracy by his subordinates, leaving a stain, though a very small one in my opinion. However, it was an indisputable fact that he built the Republic of Korea with democratic ideology, on a foundation where the country and the people were not mature enough to build a nation on. And he protected the country from communist invasion. He led the signing of the ⌜Korea-U.S. Mutual Defense Treaty⌟ on an equal footing with the United States, which has deterred war on the Korean Peninsula and enabled Korea to focus on economic development to this day. Requesting military aid from the United States, Korea has grown into a military powerhouse with 700,000 troops. Through land reform, he also provided an occasion for people to have a spirit of frugality, which is a basic spirit of Koreans today. In addition, through education, he enlightened and fostered people to become advocates of democracy with a universal sense of equality.

In this way, President Rhee Syngman played a decisive role in helping President Park Chung-hee successfully develop the country in the 1960s by building a solid foundation for national prosperity. President Syngman Rhee's groundwork to overcome obstacles preventing national development, such as poverty, ignorance, and feudal remnants, enabled President

Park Chung-hee's economic construction to succeed. It is the logic that because he had sufficiently nurtured highly educated human resources and laid the foundation required for economic development, President Park Chung-hee's national development plans were able to succeed.

President Park Chung-hee's leadership led Korea's economic development

If President Syngman Rhee built the foundation for Korea's prosperity, it was President Park Chung-hee who built prosperity on that foundation. It is very fortunate that Korea has a great national leader like President Park. It was because of his leadership that Korea was able to achieve prosperity that other people of the world envy today. The land reform alone implemented by the Syngman Rhee government in 1950 did not lift the general state of poverty in society. However, the sense of social equality formed as a result of land reform was enough to arouse people's collective passion for modernization. The strong patriotism and possessive desire of Koreans gave them a collective will to escape from poverty and destitution under the national slogan of "Let's live well!" After the Korean War, the vast majority of the population was farmers. Under such conditions, education provided the base for modernization, industrialization, and urbanization. The city's population began to soar with migrant farmers and Vietnamese immigrants. Due to the lack of industrialization, most of the city's residents were poor except for a few groups of people. Under the Syngman Rhee administration, the number of education nurturing institutions of high school and above increased nearly 10 folds. Equal access to education has created a large number of students and scholars. However, the reality at the time could not offer any hope to them other than the severe hardships of life and an unstable future.

In the early 1960s, when per capita income was $76, 80% of the government's annual budget was supported by the United States. Quite a few people starved to death during the spring hardship season. This was a country where such scenes of dead people on the streets didn't even make the news. The student revolution on April 19, 1960 led to the establishment of the Democratic Party's interim government. People of the same beliefs formed factions and flocked to the streets to assert their interests. It had become a country of demonstrations. Society had become extremely unstable. It was a world of lawlessness that made it impossible to go outside at night. Even the North Korean live radio broadcast of the demonstration in Gwanghwamun could be heard in South Korea. Many North Korean spies were scattered throughout society. The national security was in a precarious situation like a candle in the wind. Kim Il-sung even said in his autobiography that he regretted not having invaded the South at the time. At that time, it was a dangerous situation where Korean society was on the verge of becoming communist country or dying of starvation. It was a desperate situation in which anyone with power had to make a decision to save the country. Under such circumstances, then General Park Chung-hee initiated a military revolution. After seizing power, he, as a national leader, presented a vision of a prosperous future to the Korean people, who had accumulated poverty, disappointment, and dissatisfaction. He planted hopes and dreams in them and embarked on extensive renovation work for national development. He had the insight, wisdom, and conviction to look 100 years ahead. Based on that belief, he laid the foundation for building today's Korea by demonstrating cool-headed judgment, determination, and driving force.

One of the key achievements of President Park Chung-hee was that he presented a 'Korea of a prosperous future' to Koreans who were in despair and guided them in that direction. At that time, the main agents of the economy were the members of farming and fishing villages. His candid yet powerful leadership gave them hope and a sense of ownership that 'if I get an education and learn skills and work hard, I can get out of poverty.' He kept his promise to the people, 'I will reward you if you follow the government policy.' This created belief in national policy and led the active participation of the people. By doing so, the 'Saemaul movement', a national community development movement based on the 'spirit of diligence, self-help, and cooperation', became successful. He laid the foundation for national development with both physical and mental aspects. Entrepreneurs who led exports were also rewarded at the national stage commensurate with their performance. It induced voluntary technology development and played a key role as a driving force in national development. Above all, it was a truly great achievement to have leaders in various fields of society envision developing plans for the future, even under the harsh conditions of sharp confrontation between the two Koreas at the time.

For economic development, social infrastructure must be in place. First of all, public facilities such as roads, ports, railways, telecommunications networks, electricity, and waterworks, which are the basis for industrial development, must be established. To this end, President Park established the National Land Construction Plan in 1966 for the first time in Korea, promoting the establishment of a self-sufficient economy and the modernization of the industrial infrastructure. It included projects such as the construction of one million housing units, comprehensive development of four major rivers, construction of ten ports in the West and South Seas, construction of highways connecting Seoul to Incheon, Gangneung, Mokpo and Busan, construction of railroads connecting the East, South and West Seas, and so on. First, the Gyeongbu Expressway between Seoul and Busan was built. Growth and regional development methods were adopted to promote the development of large-scale industrial complexes such as Ulsan and Gumi, by expanding the scale of gross national product. It also promoted the expansion of the transportation, communication and energy supply networks that connect large cities with regional and industrial centers in order to improve productivity. Such plans were incorporated into the Comprehensive National Development Plan in the 1970s. Establishment of industrial infrastructure, expansion of transportation and communication network maintenance, urban development, improvement of living environment, and development of water resources, and etc. were promoted under the leadership of the state with emphasis in land preservation. As a result of such efforts, they succeeded in conservation and development of mountains and rivers that will go down in history. This was the background that enabled Koreans to have a rich and beautiful living environment beyond economic development.

When it comes to 'President Park Chung-hee', people first of all think of the 'Saemaul movement'. The Saemaul movement was a "rural modernization project" that was promoted to raise the income of rural areas to the level of cities, following the urban-centered economic development in the early 1960s. The Saemaul movement, based on Hyangyak in the Joseon Dynasty, was centered on the people, and began in the late 1960s with 'farm household income increase projects' including simple farm road widening, bale weaving, roof improvement, and forest reclamation projects. However, considering that almost 80% of the Korean population at the time were farmers, it was a movement that almost everyone participated in. The true achievement of the Saemaul movement was that it awakened the potential of Koreans and gave them confidence. The Saemaul movement forced Koreans to work from dawn until their hands blistered without even having enough to eat. Nonetheless, it was very meaningful, that for the first time since the beginning of history, it made general population of Korea feel confident that "we can do it too." It gave them hopes and dreams that they could live well tomorrow, and filled them with the will to live. It made everyone feel enjoyment and happiness. The Saemaul movement was a successful project that promoted both a consciousness reform movement that encouraged cooperation, voluntary participation, competition based on a strong sense of community, and an income increase movement. The following is the successful process of the Saemaul movement.

In the process of promoting the Saemaul movement, the government limited the materials provided to villages to be used only for community projects. It allowed residents to choose the types of projects themselves. It adhered to the "principle of self-help," in which it supplied additional materials only to villages with successful results. It encouraged competitive participation among villages and awakened the competitive spirit of Koreans. It led to a change in the consciousness of rural villagers. At the time, the government estimated that it invested 551.9 billion won between 1971 and 1978, and achieved a result of 1.999 trillion won. 85,000 km of farm roads were built, so the tractors could have access. Self-reliant and self-help villages that required little or no additional government support had reached 90% within 5 years. During the non-farming season, they were encouraged to focus on Saemaul projects. Trends of drinking and gambling during the off season were gone. Each village was induced to have a strong desire to 'let's live well!' So, it gave people hope that if they worked hard, they could live well. As such, the Saemaul movement was both an economic and a mental reform project. The Saemaul movement revived the rural economy. With the opening of the Gyeongbu Expressway, logistics transportation was accelerated. The national economy began to grow. This Saemaul movement and the 5-year economic development plan became the starting point, and today's 'Miracle on the Han River' had been achieved. The forest reclamation project for bare mountains was also successfully carried out. They had overcome the droughts and floods that they experienced every year. Now, it had become a dense forest country, and the government had to spend money on thinning it out instead.

It is acknowledged by the world that Korea's prosperity today was possible because of President Park's leadership. For example, in China in 1993, 『Park Chung-hee』, the Chinese version of the biography of former President Park Chung-hee, was well perceived, became a bestseller, and was used as a training material for high-ranking officials of political parties and government.[53] In other words, it means that high-ranking party and government officials of China learned the excellent leadership of President Park. At the time, the Chinese people compared President Park Chung-hee to Qin Shi Huang, who unified China for the first time in its history, and highly praised him. Now is the time to properly evaluate the merits and demerits of President Park Chung-hee. How long will we not recognize his great achievements only with recognizing the seizing power through a military revolution and establishing the Yushin Constitution to hold on to it longer? There are still people in Korea who denigrate him as a dictator and try to discredit his achievements. The more people suffered damage during his regime, the more severe their dislike is. It's natural. However, now is the time that they, as developed citizens, should recognize his achievements objectively. In the early 1960s, the Philippines, North Korea, Malaysia, Thailand, and Pakistan were countries that lived several times better than South Korea at the time. How do you compare those countries to Korea now? While in public office, I had opportunities to visit Southeast Asian countries. They were genuinely envious of Korea, saying, "Korea has developed beyond comparison to their own country thanks to having such a great national leader."

President Park's outstanding leadership gave Koreans the conviction that "We can do it too." He planted hopes and dreams and made them happy. In conclusion, he gave today's Koreans the confidence that if we do our best, we can become the best in the world. It also played a decisive role in making Korea's economic prosperity into what it is today by igniting Koreans' peripheral character and competitive spirit. He achieved miraculous economic growth on the foundation laid by President Syngman Rhee, leaving behind an achievement that raised Korea's national status to an unprecedented level in the world.

President Park Chung-hee left Koreans with his spirit of "I can do it." ⌜Without Park Chung-hee, there would be no Korea today. Park Chung-hee was dedicated, hard-working, and did not engage in personal embezzlement. He was a leader who devoted himself to his country. (Ezra Vogel)⌟. ⌜Among the achievements that mankind has made since World War II, the most amazing miracle is the Republic of Korea, which gave birth to the great leadership of Park Chung-hee. (Peter Drucker)⌟. ⌜It was practically difficult for democracy and economic development to occur at the same time. We are all aware of what happened to Russia when they pursued these two things at the same time. It can be seen that President Park Chung-hee's judgment at the time was correct. (Henry Kissinger)」. 「Democratization is only possible when industrialization ends. Freedom should be limited according to the level of the country. It makes no sense to condemn Park Chung-hee as a dictator with this. (Alvin Toffler)」. 「It was the most shocking and surprising thing throughout the 20th century that Korea overcame poverty and became one of the world's leading industrial nations in just one generation. (Lawrence Summers)」. 「President Park Chung-hee focused his energies solely on work and left the rest to history. If President Park had focused only on the immediate reality, today's Republic of Korea would not have existed. (Lee Kuan Yew)」. These are the evaluations of President Park by the prominent figures of the 20th century.

Environmental / social conditions

The geopolitical conditions of the Korean Peninsula, the resulting division and confrontation between South and North Korea, and the compulsory military service system are also major factors contributing to the economic development that forms Korea's prosperity today. In the past, the Cold War system provided a structure in which South Korea and North Korea were in harsh confrontation with each other at the forefront of the East and West camps. The Cold War situation induced an economic inflow of political and military support from the United States and technology and capital from Japan. As a result, it was possible for South Korea to conclude a ROK-US Mutual Defense Treaty due to the geopolitical conditions of the Korean Peninsula. Also, North Korea's continuous provocations have always kept the people in suspense, preventing mental relaxation and encouraging them to work harder. In addition, the national compulsory military service system of 「Universal Conscription System」 provided a proper educational place for the young people of Korea who will lead the country's development. They were given the importance of national security and the high sociability that advanced democratic citizens need to live a sound and sincere life. It rapidly advanced Korean society, and is still doing so.

The ROK-US Mutual Security Alliance that guaranteed the people's survival and safety

The ROK-U.S. mutual security alliance is one of the key factors that has made Korea's economic growth possible today. During the Korean War in 1950, South Korea handed over operational control of the Korean military to the UN Commander, citing a lack of military power. After the end of the war, the ROK-US Security Alliance was signed with the United States on October 1, 1953 to deal with the military threat of North Korea. This was the result of President Syngman Rhee's excellent international political knowledge and insight. Since then, the ROK-US Mutual Security Alliance has faithfully performed the role of guaranteeing US support for South Korean security in response to North Korea's continuing threat of military provocations. In the early 1960s, South Korea's economic and military power was far inferior to that of North Korea. Even in such a situation, South Korea was able to use the "strategy of first economic development, then military construction" because of the ROK-US mutual security alliance. Because it could rely on the United States for security, it was able to focus its efforts on economic development at the pan-national level.

Now, as Korea emerges as the world's 10th largest economy in the world, criticism of the 「Korea-U.S. Mutual Defense Treaty」 is rising. The criticism is that the continued stationing of US forces in Korea and the failure to retake operational control are "Degrading the credibility of the South Korean military's deterrence against North Korea's military adventurism. It gave birth to defeatism and passivity that prevented us from decisively responding to external military threats or terrorism."[54] Nevertheless, we must admit the observation that the ROK-US mutual security alliance played a decisive role in Korea's economic development today.

The year 2022 marked the 69th anniversary of the ROK-US alliance. Now, in 2023, the ROK-US alliance is celebrating its 70th anniversary. Looking back, we have gone through many trials, glory, joys and setbacks. The ROK-US alliance prevented another invasion by North Korea after the Korean War. It is a clear fact that it has contributed to the growth of Korea in becoming the world's 10th largest economy. Since World War II, Korea has become a symbol of American pride as the best "security and economic honor student" that the United States has fostered. In response, most Koreans feel infinite gratitude to the United States. Nevertheless, around the year of 2,000, anti-American slogans in some parts of Korean society had gone too far and shaken the foundation of the alliance. 「The death of a middle school girl by a US armored vehicle」 and 「Anti-American candlelight protest against the import of US beef」 took place in the middle of Seoul. Anti-American protests began to be criticized in the United States as well.

Now, as time passed, both sides regained their sanity. By gathering wisdom and finding a way to coexist, the ROK-US alliance has passed the 60th birthday and soon will have its 70th birthday.

The ROK-US alliance did not go smoothly from the beginning. This was because the US did not want to be bound by an alliance with South Korea. South Korea demanded an alliance, but the United States was negative about it. It was because 'the United States had not been bound as an ally in a treaty document with any country since President Jefferson.' At the time, President Syngman Rhee, who majored in international politics, seemed to have thought that the only way for Korea to survive was through an alliance with the United States. During the Korean War, the United States tried to force a ceasefire despite South Korea's opposition. At this time, for post-war security guarantees, President Syngman Rhee demanded the ROK-US alliance, economic construction, and build-up of the Korean military. At the end of the war, the only legacy left in Korea was "the hopeless division of the South and the North and the devastated land." Under such circumstances, President Syngman Rhee thought that the only way for Korea to survive was to "guarantee security through an alliance with the United States, receive economic help, and survive through post-war restoration." But America didn't want to. President Syngman Rhee pressured the United States by carrying out the 「release of anti-communist prisoners of war」 as the final winning move. In retaliation, the United States even established a plan to remove Syngman Rhee. Through such a difficult process, the 「Korea-U.S. Mutual Defense Treaty」 was concluded. President Syngman Rhee established the ROK-US alliance with the equal footings between the US and Korea. Although Korea was founded in 1948, it did not have the economic ability to arm its own military. So, at the time, President Syngman Rhee had the perception that the only way to secure Korea's defense was through combined defense. President Syngman Rhee's initiative came to be in 1953 with a ROK-US security alliance.

The 「Korea-US Mutual Defense Treaty」, the legal foundation of the ROK-US alliance, was very weak in its early days. If either party chose termination of the treaty, it was to be automatically terminated one year later. The ROK-US alliance has grown like a living tree. While Syngman Rhee and President Eisenhower established the ROK-US alliance, President Park Chung-hee solidified the ROK-US alliance. The decision to deploy the ROK military to the Vietnam War played a decisive role in institutionally supplementing the legal weaknesses of the ROK-US alliance on a relatively equal footing with the US. It was these institutional supplementary measures that enabled the ROK-US alliance to overcome crises such as the withdrawal of US forces in Korea and the anti-US movement over the past 70 years. In 1968, when the ROK Army was fighting on the Vietnam front, the 「Korea-U.S. Annual Security Consultative Meeting (SCM)」 started. In 1976, the "Korea-U.S. Combined Exercise" began. In 1978, the 「ROK-US Combined Forces Command」 was established. These are examples of institutional supplementary measures. North Korea's provocations, such as the 1968 Blue House terror attack and the 1976 Panmunjom ax murder, also played a significant role in encouraging the ROK-US alliance to be institutionalized.

Through the Annual Security Consultative Meeting, the defense ministers of the ROK and the U.S. have been meeting every year to analyze the North Korean threat and devise a wide range of countermeasures. This is something that cannot be seen in any other country in the world. The ROK and the U.S. analyze the enemy's threats every year and have actively responded to them.[55] The ROK-US Combined Forces Command and ROK-US combined exercises preparing for an all-out surprise attack by North Korea, through a wartime command system and ROK-US joint exercises. Despite the "nuclear blackmail and threats" that have continued since North Korea's third nuclear test in 2013, the South Korean people have not been shaken up and have engaged in their livelihood. This is because they believe in the role of the ROK-US security alliance. This is the result of President Syngman Rhee's international political foresight. The Korea-U.S. Mutual Security Alliance is recognized by the world as the best exemplary alliance in the world. It has contributed greatly to the survival and economic prosperity of the Korean people today. For nearly 70 years, it has neutralized North Korea's relentless provocations and contributed greatly to the stability in Northeast Asia. This is a fact no one can deny.

Sharp confrontation between South and North Korea

After the end of World War II, President Truman of the United States presented a vision of the future world. It is the "grand strategy to blockade the Soviet Union" by forming an alliance against the Soviet Union through the reconstruction of Europe and Japan, and the spread of democracy. The 『Strategy of Containment Against the Soviet Union』 became the core of the US national strategy for the next 45 years and served as a leading strategy in all fields including US politics, economy, military, and diplomacy.[56] The core of US foreign policy was "to protect Europe against the expansion of the Soviet Union, a communist state." In the process of establishing the Containment Policy, the United States did not intend to wage any large scale conflicts against the Soviet Union on the Korean Peninsula. The U.S. Navy and Air Force are much more capable than the Army. This is because the continent of Asia or the Korean Peninsula, which is connected to the continent, was not suitable for an all-out war with communist forces. At that time, the island defense strategy of the US Joint Chiefs of Staff was the idea of defending along the "line connecting the Aleutian Islands, Japan, Okinawa, and the Philippines," called the "Far East Defense Line." From the US point of view, South Korea is outside this line of defense. After liberation, the USFK stationed in South Korea began the process of withdrawing after August 1948. On January 12, 1950, US Secretary of State D. Acheson announced the "Far East Defense Line" of the US that excluded Korea. The Korean War broke out on June 25th that year. South Korea's exclusion from the line of the United States' "containment strategy against the Soviet Union" provided an excuse for North Korea's Kim Il-sung's ambition to communize and unify the Korean peninsula. After the war, the ROK-US Mutual Security Alliance was concluded, placing Korea at the forefront in Northeast Asia for the US blockade of the Soviet Union. In this way, the geopolitical uniqueness of the Korean Peninsula made Korea an arena of power struggles between the great powers in the 20th century. Korea came under Japanese colonial rule. It also made them go through the fratricidal Korean War, and after the war, it even played a role in drawing support from the US and Japan.

According to the 2012 South Korean Defense White Paper, a total of 1,959 North Korean infiltration provocations have been made since the armistice agreement in 1953. More than half of them (1,011 cases) occurred in the 1960s. The surprise attack on the Blue House on January 21, 1968, and the infiltration of armed guerrillas in Uljin and Samcheok are the leading examples of infiltration provocations. Entering the 1970s, the number of infiltration and local provocations by North Korea decreased remarkably. On the other hand, other types of provocations continued, such as digging infiltration tunnels across the demarcation line and invading the Northern Limit Line in the West Sea. It seemed to settle down somewhat in the 1980s and 1990s, but increased again after the 2000s. In particular, the Cheonan sinking incident by a

North Korean submarine in March 2010 and the Yeonpyeong Island shelling incident in November were unprecedented high-intensity provocations. Moreover, North Korea's recent provocations and threats have sometimes seemed willing to go to war. Despite the international community's concerns and dissuasion, North Korea carried out its first, second, and third nuclear tests in October 2006, April 2009, and February 2013. In response to the South Korean Joint Chiefs of Staff's "preemptive strike" remarks regarding the nuclear test, North Korea did not hesitate to use blackmail equivalent to a declaration of war, such as "nullifying the armistice agreement, completely nullifying the non-aggression agreement between South and North Korea, and declaring the beginning of a war situation." Since the Korean War, North Korea has been constantly provoking South Korea.

Over the past 70 years, South Koreans have experienced North Korea's local armed provocations or infiltration attempts through espionage at least once a week on average. Koreans have lived without being able to let go of the tension. North Korea has created an atmosphere in which South Koreans have no choice but to think of the country that will protect them before their own interests. It played a role in creating an atmosphere that no one could disobey in front of the great cause of 'for the sake of the country.' This consequently did not allow for social relaxation in Korea. It kept Koreans from losing their focus. It pushed Koreans to focus on the 'right' policies of the government. It gave them a reason to live well. It also gave them a strong urge to escape from the reality of always being harassed and being chased. It also reminded them that theie country must become rich in order to have independent national defense. It also made them understand that their development is fundamental to the development of the country. The harsh confrontation between South and North Korea also made Koreans, who are the back-bone of Korea's economic development, into hard-working and sincere people.

National compulsory military service system

The compulsory military service system for national defense has also contributed greatly to the prosperity and development of Korea today. It is my opinion that it has contributed greatly to building today's bright and just Korean society by instilling a sense of democratic citizenship in young adults who are about 50% (male) of Koreans prior to entering the society. Recently, as the advanced civic consciousness of Koreans has been published in the world media, there have been frequent attempts by famous foreign media outlets to cover the civic consciousness of Koreans. Thanks to such attempts, the advanced civic consciousness of Koreans has recently been widely known as it has been proven through social experiments in actual Korean society. Currently, 26 countries around the world are using a conscription system based on the 「Universal Conscription System」, in which all citizens are obliged to serve in the military. Under the conscription system, military service is treated as a citizen's duty. It demands personal burden and contribution to national defense. Several disadvantages of the Universal Conscription System are pointed out, such as huge training costs, difficulty in securing professional manpower, possibility of personal freedom infringement, impediment to the continuity of learning of young manpower, and consequent adverse effects on national industries.

In Korea, the legal age of youth is between 19 and 34, which is specified in the Youth Basic Act. The age of enlistment is between the ages of 18 and 28. Those eligible for active duty enlistment who have received a grade 1 to 3 in physical evaluation with a middle school diploma or higher can apply for active duty in the Army, Navy, and Marine Corps online every month. This way, young men in Korea enlist in the military before returning to society as adults after completing their mandatory service period (24 months in the Army, 26 months in the Navy, and 27 months in the Air Force). To Korean adults, the experience of military life is a topic of conversation that never fails to appear. It can be seen that experiences in the military organization at a young age have a tremendous impact on people's lives.

In the long history of mankind, sacrifice for the sake of one's country or people has always been recognized as a precious value. It can be seen from the fact that many foreign state guests visiting Korea visit Seoul National Cemetery as their first destination to pay their respects. Due to such a universal perception, young men's military service in Korea has been recognized as the minimum self-sacrifice every man must make for the country. Nonetheless, everyone in Korea can relate to the saying, 'I went to the army and came back as a man.' This means that the Korean conscription system has been widely recognized as an effective character training process for young men. If they enlist in the military, they will learn how to behave while fulfilling their role as a member of a specially organized society called the military under equal conditions. In order to maintain an organizational culture that meets the needs of a military organization, it is important to learn the basic social skills required of their members. As a member of the organization, they learn basic words and behaviors to be followed, basic etiquette to be observed with colleagues and superiors, and by observing the words and behaviors of seniors and superiors, and learning what is right and wrong, they pay attention and view them as role models. Naturally, as a member of society, they get the opportunity to learn about the mentality they need to have.

The military has established norms and procedures that must be followed in order to achieve the goals of the military organization regardless of the will of its individual members. In the military, individuals are not free to act, and words and behaviors driven by desire are greatly restricted. That is why young people who have grown up as precious sons in their families find it hard and difficult to serve in the military. For that reason, the emotional self who always wants to resist the restrictions imposed on them and the rational self who has to overcome these difficulties are always in conflict. By the time they are discharged from the military without falling out of the continuous struggle within themselves, their unsocial minds, words and behaviors would be refined, and they would have grown as a member of society equipped with the knowledge of a model citizen. Young people who have completed their military service for a short period of about two years will become true democratic citizens of advanced Korean society. An honorable discharge puts an end to teenage wandering and resistance to the social order. As a mature person in an organized civil society, it helps him to cooperate and play the role that he is expected to perform. It has served as a confirmation that he has become a man responsible for supporting his family.

In the military, people are reorganized by the hierarchical order within the military regardless of their places of origin, the gap between the rich and the poor, and their academic background. The performance of national defense missions within the armed forces requires intense individual sacrifice. A certain hierarchical order of the military itself and desocialized equality are maintained. This provides the members with an opportunity to objectively reflect on their existence. It also provides an opportunity to form unique bonds with colleagues in organizations that do not have personal interests. In the process of overcoming intensive and difficult training together, the experience of limitations of one's ability and the sense of solidarity formed with colleagues also allow them to have a new sense of values. It also humbles himself. It also lets him know the responsibilities and obligations that he has to keep in his position and creates a sense of noble comradeship within the organization. It plays the role of nurturing him with the characteristics required by the advanced free democratic society.

Currently, Korea is operating a military service system that combines occupational soldiers and the recruitment based on the 「Universal Conscription System」. Due to the nature of the military society, any military service inevitably provides an occasion for character development for young people who are in the process of establishing their views of life. In the process of taking responsibility for the duties assigned to him as a soldier, it allows him to grow into a righteous and independent person in society. Young people who were inexperienced before joining the military return to society as mature citizens after honorable discharge.

The Korean military was established on August 15, 1948. As society developed, the barracks culture also developed along with the flow of the times. A culture is formed under the influence of the ideas, philosophies, and values that flow through a society. The barracks culture of the Korean military was also formed by professional soldiers who were ingrained in Confucian ideology and lifestyle, as seen in Korean society from the beginning of its establishment, and has been handed down for many years. Confucian ideology and lifestyle in Korean society are not much different. These are the beliefs that people must abide by as members of society, such as the cause and duty to be followed, the conditions of moderation in life, and how to maintain harmonious interpersonal relationships. These are just the guidelines of life that are the basis for the improvement of individual sociability. This is the background in which the barracks culture of the Korean military was naturally formed and developed based on Confucian ideology. As a result, Korea's barracks culture has promoted the sociability of Korean young people under the influence of Confucianism since its the establishment. Moreover, as Korean society developed into an advanced country and the level of education and awareness of Koreans increased, the barracks culture also developed into a training hall that fosters advanced citizens wit high sociability. For that reason, it is the view that young people who return to society after completing

military service in Korea among many countries that currently use 「Universal Conscription System」 naturally change their consciousness and return as advanced citizens. In this way, the Korean national compulsory military service system has played a positive role in building an advanced society in Korea from the early days of the establishment of the Korean military to the present.

These days, it has become a society where most people have only one or two children. As a result, juvenile delinquency and moral hazards in society are increasing. Various youth problems such as lethargy and loss of sense of belonging[111] among young people is increasing. These are common phenomena in countries that abolish or do not operate the conscription system. Korea's mandatory military service system has played an important role in reducing the factors of recent youth problems in Korean society. These days, in general, young people grow up free, precious, without any restraints, and lack nothing. Life as a member of an organization with a clear hierarchy from top to bottom, makes them feel responsible for their behaviors. It allows them to learn that everyone is equal regardless of being rich, poor, noble or not noble. It fosters a regular lifestyle with no exceptions. It plays a role in nurturing young people with self-confidence, moderation, and independence in Korean society that continues to evolve.

Recently, a South Korean official said that in response to the COVID-19, as of April 4, 2022, 96% of adults were vacci-

---

111) The tendency of young people to prefer part-time jobs instead of jobs that require restraints

nated twice or more, and in particular, about 63% of the entire population received the third vaccination. In addition, the cumulative fatality rate at the time was 0.12%, which was the lowest level in the world, significantly lower than the United States (1.22%), the United Kingdom (0.79%), and Japan (0.44%). CNN reported that the number of daily confirmed cases of Corona 19 in Korea is rapidly increasing, but the fatality rate is low, due to having the world's highest level of vaccination. Considering the high vaccination rate of Koreans, trust in the national public health system and high health awareness among the people, led global media outlets to expect that Korea will be the first country in the world to transition from a pandemic to an endemic. I believe that the fact that Korean society is cautiously overcoming the COVID-19 pandemic is also due to the influence of the people being nurtured as advanced citizens by the compulsory military service system. The level of consciousness of Koreans is the highest in the world, as explained in several sections above. Most Korean men have acquired the mentality to actively respond to the correct policy of an organization (government) through military service. As a result, when Korean people agree that the government's policy is correct, they actively participate in the government policy itself. That is why despite the late start of COVID-19 vaccination, a high vaccination rate was recorded in a short period of time that was not achieved in any country. In addition to this, it was assessed that the COVID-19 pandemic in Korea would be overcome in the shortest time in the world by actively complying with the government guidelines such as distancing, mask mandates, and washing hands. I believe that the national movements, such as government-led garbage separation and collection, implementation of non-smoking areas, and maintaining of clean public toilets, which were implemented in the 1990s and settled in a short period of time, were able to succeed in the same context.

Korea's mandatory military service based on the "Universal Conscription System" is also one of the main factors that has played a large role in Korea's prosperity today, and I have no doubt that it will continue to nurture young Koreans into advanced democratic citizens with sincere characters in the future.

A strong national consensus on the Saemaul movement

Based on Maslow's hierarchy of needs, the prosperity of today's Korean society was possible because of the success of the national economic development plans from the 1960s to the 1990s. The reason why the national-level economic development plans were successful was that all citizens actively participated in the government-led Saemaul movement. Citizens who actively participated in the Saemaul movement obtained the confidence that 'we can live well as much as we work hard' while reaping the results of the movement. The sense of confidence of the people served as a key factor in a virtuous cycle in which the people led economic growth. It accomplished a transformation in reforming the consciousness of the people. As a result, people-led political democratization and the creation of Hallyu culture were followed.

「Saemaeul Day」 on April 22 was established as a legal anniversary based on the Saemaul Movement Organization Promotion Act on March 3, 2011. Now, the Saemaul movement, well known worldwide, has become a national awareness reform and a national transformation. When presidents, prime ministers, ministers, and members of the National Assembly from developing countries in Asia and Africa, who want to achieve economic development just like Korea, go visit Korea, they always visit the Saemaul Federation located in Bundang, Seongnam-si, Gyeonggi-do. As of the end of

April 2011, it was said that the cumulative number of leaders and civil servants from developing countries who visited the Saemaul Federation to learn about the Saemaul movement reached 50,000 in 84 countries.

It has been over 30 years since the Saemaul movement was introduced to the outside world. There were a lot of national leaders who have learned about the Saemaul movement. However, I have not yet heard of any news that the Saemaul movement has led to economic development in other places similar to that of Korea. Why don't those countries achieve national economic development through the Saemaul movement like Korea? I have long wondered why. To understand this, I first analyzed the causes of the success of the Saemaul movement in Korean society from various angles, from social conditions to the characteristics of Koreans. Because if you know what made it a success, you will know why it didn't succeed elsewhere. The success of the Saemaul movement in Korea was because the basic ideology and implementation method of the Saemaul movement matched the character, habits, and inclinations of Koreans. On the other hand, if a country has attempted Saemaul movement but has not succeeded, it may be that it was because the environment in which Saemaul movement could succeed, was not created in that country. In particular, it can be said that the reason is that the social conditions at the national level were not suitable. The Saemaul movement was able to succeed in Korea because the conditions for promoting the Saemaul movement and a national consensus were formed at that time. It is described in detail below.

As mentioned above, the Saemaul movement was also a consciousness-reshaping campaign for Koreans. Through the Saemaul movement, it made people feel confident that 'if I work hard, I can live well, and I can do anything I want.' To do so, first, the level of consciousness and education of the people must be at a level where they can understand and coordinate with the policies promoted by the government. Since 1949, Korea has implemented a compulsory education policy of six years in elementary school. Later, in the 1950s, many schools were established at the pan-national level to give people higher education opportunities. As a result, the illiteracy rate, which was over 80% in 1948, was reduced to less than 20% in about 10 years in the early 1960s. It means that the level of consciousness and education of the people has risen to the level of fully understanding the government's policy and following its guidelines within a short period of 10 years. This means that by the time the Saemaul movement was promoted under the leadership of the government, the level of awareness and education of Koreans was at the level of fully understanding the plans and benefits proposed by the state.

Second, social conditions must be created in which the individual is rewarded properly for his or her efforts. In order for the Saemaul movement to be successful, all participants must be equally rewarded for their efforts. To do so, it is necessary to universalize the civic consciousness of liberal democracy that all members of society are equal. In 1910, Joseon, which had existed for more than 500 years, was annexed by Japan. Living under colonial rule for 36 years, the social class system of scholars, farmers, artisans and tradesmen that existed in the Joseon Dynasty completely collapsed. After liberation from Japan in 1945, as they went through a period of political and social confusion, remnants of class convention in society disappeared further. After the Korean War, the class consciousness of the past that remained in society disappeared completely as they lived together with strangers who emigrated from North Korea, without knowing each other's status. In addition, as opportunities for higher education increased after the 1950s, the understanding of Korea's national ideology of the time, a liberal democracy, deepened and the sense of freedom and democracy increased.

As a result, in the late 1960s when the Saemaul movement began, there was no sense of privilege left in Korean society. The perception that anyone who works hard should be compensated fairly for the amount of work was taken for granted by all citizens. In the late 1960s, when the Saemaul movement began, Koreans were strongly conscious of the idea of equality, one of the key requirements of the Saemaul movement. Only when there is a strong sense of equality among members, true cooperation between members is possible. On the other hand, in a society where a sense of privilege exists or a sense of equality is not embodied, true cooperation between people does not take place. It only frustrates eager members who are actively participating. This is because it incapacitates the principle that each person can be guaranteed a reward as much as he or she works. Who would actively participate in the Saemaul movement when there is no guarantee of compensation for the amount of work done? At the time of Saemaul movement, no exceptions such as 'I am the headman of this village, or a local public servant, so I do not have to participate in the local cooperative work' were recognized. Koreans, who are conscious of the Hyangyak Guidelines and have a strong sense of competition and comparison, never tolerated exceptions, which were the most critical impediment to the Saemaul movement. This is one of the reasons for the success of the Saemaul movement.

Third, the government, which led the Saemaul movement, accurately kept its promises to implement the policies presented to the people. It was the biggest factor that led to the formation of national consensus. Even those people, who were dubious about the government's implementation plan, came to actively participate in policies later with trust by accurately following through the promises of the implementation plan announced by the government. Initially, the government promised to provide cement and reinforcing steel rods free of charge if the villagers cooperated to plan and carry out the necessary tasks for the Saemaul movement. In addition, 100% support was provided to villages that implemented as planned, and support was stopped to villages that did not. That's not all. Support was further expanded for villages that performed well as planned if they came up with new projects. In this way, the Saemaul movement was able to succeed because the government induced active participation of the people by making sure that all the support and compensations promised in the process of planning and implementation of the Saemaul movement are provided.

Fourth, the motivation for the participants in the Saemaul

movement was clear. When the Saemaul movement was first initiated by the Korean government, Koreans had a strong desire to 'live a better life by working hard and eating well.' As mentioned several times above, most of our ancestors lived poorly in an agricultural society with very limited farmland for a long time. In the process, from the 15th century onward, as the population of the Korean Peninsula increased, they had to sustain a very poor lives to such an extent that "Have you eaten a breakfast?" was a morning greeting towards adults. I believe that as the life of poverty has been passed down from parents to children for hundreds of years, the earnest desire for a life of abundance in food, clothing, and shelter has been ingrained in the DNA of Koreans. One of the prime examples is the attachment of Koreans to 'own their house'. At the time of the Saemaul movement, Koreans were strongly motivated with the slogan'I want to live well by working hard.' For them, the motivation for a better life and the trust built by keeping the promises of the government to the people was converted into a strong hope. In this way, a strong national consensus on the promotion of the Saemaul movement was formed. With a strong consensus, the Saemaul movement became successful in Korea as the people actively participated.

Unique characteristics of Koreans (K-DNA)

I have been living in Korea from the time when Korea was one of the poorest countries in the world until now when Korea has risen to the ranks of developed countries. Born in a quiet rural village, I studied in Seoul away from home and finished high school there. At a young age during my second year at the Air Force Academy, I went on a field trip to the 3rd Military Academy in the United States and actually experienced how small and shabby we Koreans are in comparison. After graduating from the military academy, I became a pilot and worked as a vanguard of air defense during the period of sharp confrontation between the two Koreas, and I realized the country's need for self-defense before pride. In the 1980s, while studying in the United States to obtain late education, I personally experienced the unfair treatment toward Koreans by foreigners. From the 1990s to the mid-2000s, as a high-ranking officer in the ROK Air Force, when I visited allies around the world for official business, I felt the growing status of Korea from the visiting countries. Overall, I am one of those who experienced the joys and sorrows of Korea's growth process more directly than anyone else. These days, while experiencing the soft powers of Korea, I can't help but to admire and be amazed. In addition, I am grateful for the fact that Koreans are truly great people.

In addition to the leadership of national leaders and environmental/social conditions described above as key factors in national economic development, this section describes the unique characteristics of Koreans (K-DNA). Among the various characteristics of Koreans described in Part 1 above, the ability to devise, peripheral character and fluidity, the spirit of scholars and patriotism, sincerity and diligence, and putting public interest first before private matters, democratic equality, passion for learning, adaptability to environmental changes, high sociability, and Hongik Ingan ideal, have led Korea's economic development and prosperity today.

Koreans' outstanding devising capabilities

Compared to foreigners, Koreans have many peculiarities. Here are a few of those examples. Koreans still call the people of Japan, an economic powerhouse that no one in the world can ignore, 'Japs' in denigrated terms, even though they were colonized by them for 36 years. Despite living in the gap between huge continental and maritime powers and being invaded countless times, they maintain a single ethnicity, which is rare in the world. Koreans are shamefully ranked third in the world in cancer mortality, alcohol consumption, liquor import rate, traffic accidents, and youth smoking rates. Nevertheless, in the face of the financial crisis, which was refinanced by the International Monetary Fund (IMF), Koreans are the only people in the world who have overcome such a crisis in just over two years. In the World Cup soccer game, where Korea's reputation was at stake, even people who didn't normally watch soccer came out to cheer. The team advanced to the semifinals with tremendous support from the people.

The only resources in Korea are human resources with unique characteristics. Nonetheless, Koreans achieved phenomenal economic growth and political democratization in the second half of the 20th century. Now, the Korean wave is taking the world by surprise. This is due to the excellent devising capability of Koreans. As the only resource in Korea, Koreans rank 25th in the world in terms of population, which is relatively not small. It means that Koreans' outstanding devising capability as a resource has brought about Korea's economic development and prosperity today. People with an inferiority complex cannot do anything, while people with self-confidence are confident even during difficult times. They try to create a favorable situation for themselves. When the conditions are right, they try to make their dreams come true.

As long as Koreans have a dream of becoming a true advanced country, Koreans will achieve it. So far, Koreans' display of their superior devising capabilities are enough to convince us that they will.

The following are prime examples of Koreans demonstrating their outstanding devising capabilities recently. According to the "World Intellectual Property Index 2020" published by the World Intellectual Property Organization (WIPO) in 2021, the number of patent applications per million Koreans was 3,319, ranking first in the world. Japan ranked second with 1,943 people, Switzerland ranked third with 1,122, and Germany ranked fourth with 884.[57] Another example is the performance achieved in the World Skills Olympics, which can be said to indicate the level of technical ability or talent of Koreans. First held in 1950, the International Skills Olympics, which has been held every two years since 1971, is where young people between the ages of 17 and 22 participate and compete in their job skills. Korea first participated in this competition in 1966. The Korean team, which participated in the 17th in 1968, won 3rd overall at the second participation to them. Since then, by participating in a total of 29 times, up to 45 competitions in 2019, they won 19 championships, placed 5 times as the runners-up, and earned three 3rd place prizes, letting the world know the excellencies of Korean on technical abilities and talents in the fields of such as machine, metal, crafts, electricity, electronics, information, architecture/ wood, and fine arts. In particular, at the 43rd International Skills Olympics held in Brazil in August 2015, the Korean national team won their 19th championship and set a record of five consecutive victories.[58] The continuous efforts of Koreans to develop their technical skills and talents in the relevant fields led to Korea's economic development today.

In fact, there are countless examples of achievements made by Koreans' excellent devising capabilities today. In the meantime, Koreans have developed their country from one of the world's poorest countries to one of the world's 10th largest economy by demonstrating their excellent devising capabilities, and have put them in the ranks of advanced countries both in name and reality. Now, following political democratization, it is sweeping the world like a tsunami by creating Korean Wave (韓流), which symbolizes Korean culture. In the early 2010s, singer 'Psy' made known his name and Korea to remote parts of the world with just one song, 'Gangnam Style'. Now, even in the field of cultural content, Koreans are showing their outstanding devising skills. The global popularity of the boy group BTS, the movie Parasite, and the TV show Squid Game are examples of Koreans' devising capabilities in the field of entertainment industry. I wonder if the dignified performance of Korean artists on the world stage is the image of Koreans living hard, by demonstrating their excellent devising capabilities in the world today!

Fluidity and peripheral character that achieve the goal without fail

In Part 1 above, it was said that Koreans are characterized by fluidity, which is the property of adapting to unfolding situations, and peripheral character, which is the property of completing work by being flexible according to the situation. These are characteristics that have been internalized in the process of adapting to the times for survival against foreign pressures and aggression for a long time.

Some say that Koreans have no principle from these outward fluidic appearances. Some criticize them for having a peninsular temperament represented by fluidity and peripheral character. However, the peninsular temperament represented by the fluidity and peripheral character of Koreans, which they say, was a characteristic that was inevitably formed by the geopolitical influence between maritime and continental powers. These social characteristics which had been formed to cope with the forces in the oceans and continents that are relatively larger than themselves, were internalized. This is neither being heteronomous, nor a tendency of following others blindly, but is a wise survival strategy.

In particular, the colonial view of Japan denigrated the fluidity and peripheral character of Koreans from a different perspective in order to make them take their colonial rule for granted. It stressed the negative interpretation of Joseon history, saying, "Koreans have a clear understanding, are weak in unity, and strong in factionalism." As a result of such colonial education, there are still some old generation Koreans who see the National Assembly and say, "We can't do anything because of partisan conflicts like that." However, from a optimistic perspective, one can see that this is not the case at all. In the past, factional conflicts of the Joseon Dynasty were perceived as a vicious political disease. But now, as a very advanced and democratic political institution, some argue that it was an excellent system that had continued healthy politics for hundreds of years through mutual criticism and checks and balances within the large frame of coexistence.[59] Koreans sometimes fought in unity against the strong powers that exerted influence towards the weaker side between the continent and the sea. If necessary, they depended on strong forces to guarantee their survival. This is reflected by the fact that Korea has not been broken or absorbed by the military, ideological, and cultural pressures of neighboring countries, except for the 36 years of Japanese colonial rule. Fluidity and peripheral character, which are the temperamental characteristics of Koreans, are social inclinations to wisely adapt to. The fluidity and peripheral character of Koreans accepted ideas that were seen to be suitable for them and developed them as their own, using them as a new driving force for imitation, improvement, and creation. The creation of Hangeul between Chinese characters and Japanese Kana, and the development of Korean fast food after seeing McDonald's in the United States are examples of this. Koreans' fluidity and peripheral character are also the ability of Koreans to respond flexibly to changes in their surrounding environments. For that reason, Koreans were able to preserve their own livelihood, culture of food, clothing, and shelter without being subjugated to the culture of surrounding powers.

Due to their fluidity and peripheral character, which were embedded in them in order to survive among forces relatively stronger than themselves, Koreans demonstrate few negative behavioral patterns and life attitudes such as "they are weak to those who seem powerful, they behave differently depending on the situations, they would go through any means to achieve their goals, and they try to solve their own problems with the hands of others, etc." However, this is not being heterono-mous, nor a tendency of following others blindly, but is a wise survival strategy and one's own development strategy. Thanks to such strategies for survival and development, Korea was able to grow from one of the world's poorest countries in the 1960s to the world's 10th largest economies in just 50 years. I do not deny that there are some negative views about Koreans' fluidity and peripheral character. However, the attitude of Koreans to do their best by mobilizing all available means to achieve their goals, had a positive effect on the construction of an economic powerhouse. Maybe if they insisted on everything that people say was the right path and pursued economic growth, Korea might not have achieved such economic growth as seen today. How difficult would it have been for them to jump into the global market as a latecomer, which was already established and to build a world market for exports and imports as large as it is today? It is clear that the construction of today's economic powerhouse of Koreans is clearly the product of their characteristics of fluidity and peripheral character.

Seonbi Spirit and Patriotism embedded in Koreans

One of the main factors that enabled Korea to achieve phenomenal economic growth is the 'Seonbi spirit and patriotism in Korean people'. As explained earlier, Koreans have been exposed to Confucian thought through their ancestors for more than 2,000 years. For that reason, the scholarly spirit based on Confucianism is still strongly rooted in Koreans. For Koreans, the righteous spirit of a scholar is still flowing. It awakened their minds to actively participate in policies for national development, such as the Saemaul movement. It also helped to reduce privilege and corruption among bureaucrats, which acts as one of the biggest obstacles to national development in underdeveloped countries. I believe that it has contributed significantly to promoting economic development.

For a long time, Koreans have lived on the foundation of Confucianism, which regards the spirit of scholars as a value of life. For that reason, they had a perception that 'bureaucrats must have the minimum of the scholarly character' at the base of their minds. Koreans generally believe that "if you are a bureaucrat, you must do what you say and be polite and prudent in your words and actions. You should be ashamed of your mistakes and you should not disgrace your country in a foreign country. Even in difficult circumstances, you must not commit injustice. You must not harm others or covet others' possessions." These are virtues required of scholars imprinted on Koreans and are the minimum quality required of bureaucrats. Such an upright scholarly spirit continues to flow in the consciousness of Koreans to this day. Because of this, I think that even in the ruins of the Korean War, bureaucrats silently endured difficulties together with the people without a sense of their privilege. In the early 1960s, even in front of the national vision of "Let's achieve national economic development and live well!", they took the lead and actively induced the people to participate in national policies. Their active participation is one of the key factors that led to the success of economic development policies. The positive function of the scholarly spirit is, above all, to prevent corruption by bureaucrats. It serves to remind the consciences of bureaucrats who secretly take bribes that they should not accept by making them have a sense of guilt, saying, "I shouldn't be like this!" It is the view that Korean bureaucrats were not completely corrupted even under the difficult living conditions of the 50s and 60s because of this scholarly spirit.

Also, I mentioned earlier that world-class patriotism is

inherent in Koreans. Koreans have been constantly invaded in the gap between continental and maritime powers based on their rise and fall for many generations. In the process, they had to endure the hardships because of weak national power. Recently, they experienced the Han (恨, grudge) of loosing their country under Japanese colonial rule and the Korean War, suffered the pain when their homeland could not provide the protection. It was a painful experience of the need for a homeland that could protect them. That's not all. Through the Samgangohryun, which had been taught by parents or elders in the family for generations, the idea that "it is the basic duty for the people to serve the country, and when the country is in danger, you must risk your life to protect" has been clearly embedded in their minds. It is the view that such complex factors are the source of the great patriotism that erupts from Koreans today. Koreans' patriotism has made them devote themselves to national development, sometimes even sacrificing themselves. The 「National Debt Redemption Movement」 in 1907 and the 「Gold Collection Movement」 that helped to overcome the foreign exchange crisis in 1997 represent this. Koreans favored domestic products, out of such patriotism, instead of high-quality foreign products. It was to enhance the quality of Korean products by vitalizing the domestic market.

This has allowed them to take the lead in enhancing the image of Korea and improving the quality of Korean brands. Such collective aspirations made it possible to export Korean products by breaking through tough foreign export barriers. The patriotism of Koreans was also one of the factors that played a big role in today's economic development.

Koreans' patriotism has made them recognize that 'my development is the development of the country, and the development of the country is my development'. It made each citizen diligent and sincere, while encouraging self-development. It also encouraged them to actively participate in ⌜reforestation and erosion control projects⌟, ⌜water control and disaster prevention projects⌟, and ⌜nature and cultural heritage conservation projects⌟ for national territory conservation. As a result, Korea, along with Israel, has become one of the successful countries in the representative greening project of the 20th century as selected by the United Nations. The patriotism of Koreans has played a decisive role in establishing an affluent living environment in Korea today. A typical example of this, the forest reclamation project, is described in details below.

A US congressman visited South Korea on a plane immediately after visiting North Korea in the summer of 1997. In the plane, he exclaimed, "I came from hell to heaven," and it became a well-talked about topic. It is said that the reason he made that comment was because of the stark differences in the appearance of 'forestry greening' between North and South Korea. North Korea's mountains were all red, while South Korea's mountains were all green. Until the early 1960s, the situation between the two Koreas was exactly the opposite. At that time, the mountains of South Korea were as bare as North Korea today. Since then, it was only about 20 years after that they were dressed up with green clothes. According to the 「1984 Forestry Statistics Manual」, 84% of the total tree areas in South Korea are covered with trees of 20 years or younger, which means that more than 8 out of 10 trees were planted after the 1960s. Korea's forest reclamation movement was able to succeed thanks to the strong will of the national leader at the time. 'We will make green mountains just like developed countries', and the active participation of Koreans who sympathized based on their patriotism. The will of the national leader was materialized and promoted as a pan-national action plan and campaign. Promotion of the forest reclamation plan (1973-82), cows' grass-feeding campaign, rural residents furnace renovation project (1973), proclamation of the ban on leaf collection, and campaigns to encourage the use of briquettes (1975), were all parts of forest rehabilitation campaigns. Koreans believed in their national leader and actively participated in those forest reforestation campaigns. Such efforts have reaped great results, and achieved today's green mountains. Koreans sympathized with the pan-national vision of the leader, "Let's have green mountains and fields." In order to achieve the vision, they actively participated in 'Arbor Day' in the spring and 'Forestry Day' in the fall every year. Regardless of who owned the mountain, they worked together to plant and care for the trees. This is how Korea succeeded in the forest reclamation campaign. During the first 20 years of promoting the forest reclamation campaign, there were many difficulties. The soil in the mountains was so barren that trees could not take root. Even the surviving trees were washed away due to soil erosion during the rainy season. Rural residents without alternative fuel were so desperate, that they even had to cut down trees planted on Arbor Day to use them as fuel. Nonetheless, Koreans' love for their country and patriotism eventually made them create today's rich environ-ment. In any difficult situation, Koreans believed in the vision of the national leader. In addition, they had a patriotic spirit that made them devote themselves to the cause of national development, helping them to achieve their goals in the end.

Pan-national concentration based on such patriotism is what made today's Korea.

Embedded sincerity and diligence

The sincerity and diligence of Koreans are also important factors that have driven Korea's economic growth today. The sincerity and diligence of Koreans are at a level worthy of being presented to the world. It is a habit that has been ingrained in the process of living through generations by settling down on the barren Korean Peninsula and forming an agricultural society. Evidence of this is that even ethnic Chinese and Jews, famous for their hard work and strong viability among the peoples of the world, could not take root in Korea as they did in other parts of the world.

The occasion to awaken sincerity and diligence to Koreans can be said to be the land reform led by the Syngman Rhee regime. There are still people who dismiss the land reform implemented by the Syngman Rhee regime in 1950 as a very incomplete reform compared to that of North Korea. However, looking at the process that unfolded, one can see that this is not the case at all. Immediately after liberation, 80% of the Korean population were farmers. At that time, land reform was the number one task at the time. Farmers had been exploited by landlords and bureaucrats since the Joseon Dynasty. For them, the principle of 「Kyungja Yujeon(耕者有田[112])」 was a long-cherished wish and ideal. In 1950, Syngman Rhee's regime deprived land aristocrats of their inheritance of land. Land reform was carried out to limit the amount of land owned by each farming family. The tenant farmer was required to pay 15% of the annual yield to the landlord for 5 years as land price, and the land ownership of the self-employed farmer was limited to 2 jungbo.[113] The sale of farmland and leasing for tenancy were prohibited. These were the main points of the land reform bill. During the process of land reform, the Korean war broke out. The legal price of rice was only 30-40% of the market price, and the inflation rate was close to 1,000%. The value of the cash that landlords were compensated for after the transfer of ownership from tenant farmers became almost the price of toilet paper. As a result, immediately after the war, the landlord class completely collapsed and more than 90% of the farmers became independent farmers.

This was a revolutionary change for the peasants who had been exploited by landlords. Nearly 70% of tenant farmers,

---

112) The farmer who cultivates owns the land.
113) As a unit of area, 1 jungbobo (町步) corresponds to 2.45 acre.

who were the majority of the Korean people at the time, turned into self-employed farmers. Their spirit of frugality, 'I also want to escape from poverty through frugality, and live well', had become the national spirit of Korea. Land reform allowed farmers to have their own land. They can now put their efforts in the service of their families rather than the landowners. In order to increase their income even a little, they cultivated the land day and night. They educated their children with the surplus agricultural products they harvested. It allowed them to dedicate themselves to the success of their children. It awakened the latent diligence of Koreans. Even during the Japanese colonial era, in the eyes of foreigners, Koreans were usually incompetent, lazy, and inferior people who had nothing to do but take a nap. Such Koreans have changed into the exact opposite. It has transformed them into a person who is active and diligent in everything. The impact of land reform was so great that it could be called a spiritual revolution in Korean society.

As one of the external factors that made Korea's economic development possible, people mention the construction of the Gyeongbu Expressway. The Gyeongbu Expressway was built in 2 years and 5 months from February 1, 1968 to July 7, 1970. During construction, 77 people lost their lives. In order to commemorate their sacrifice, 「Gyeongbu Expressway Memorial Tower for those who sacrificed their lives」 was built near the Geumgang Service Area on the Gyeongbu Expressway. In the epitaph of the memorial tower, poet Lee Eun-sang wrote condolences that read "they are indeed industrial warriors of the national march toward modernization of our country, and have become the holy cornerstone for the construction of a welfare society for our descendants. How can we forget the grace and dedication of their blood and sweat!" When Koreans promise to do something, they do their best to keep it. Such strong sincerity is a personality trait and an advantage. The following is the testimony of the director of the construction at the time. The justification for the construction of the Gyeong-bu Expressway was "for the future development of the country." The government divided the construction of the Seoul-Busan highway into several sections and set the opening date for each section. In order to meet the opening date for each section set by the government, workers worked in two shifts of 12 hours each day. As we tried to proceed with the construction without a delay, there was no choice but to overpace ourselves and have other troubles in the process. It was an unavoidable situation where one had to sacrifice noble lives. Due to such sacrifices, the project was able to be completed as scheduled. Thanks to the construction of the Gyeongbu Expressway, it was possible to build large industrial complexes such as the Pohang Iron and Steel Company and Ulsan Shipyard, which played a large part in Korea's economic development. For national development, the construction of the Gyeongbu Expressway at the time was an essential infrastructure construction. Even so, the opposition leaders at the time said, "How many cars will use it? Why do you make such wide roads when you don't have money?", and they objected vehemently. Assuming that today's opposition for the sake of opposition and occasional outside protests are derived from senior politicians of the past, one can easily imagine the extreme protests of politicians against the highway construction at the time. Even so, the people did not hesitate to sacrifice themselves in front of the grand cause of national development. In my opinion, the diligence and sincerity of Koreans is what drove the economic growth in today's Korea.

A strong sense of responsibility of Seongong-Husa as a member of the organization

Seongong-Husa (先公後私) means public works come first and private matters later. As a member of an organization, it also means that the responsibility for public affairs takes precedence over any private affairs. This is a four-character idiom in Samacheon's Sagiyeoljeon 「Yeompa-Insangyeo Yeoljeon」. This is an anecdote between Yeompa, the general of the country of Zhao, and Im Sang-yeo, the chancellor, during the Spring and Autumn Warring States Period in China. The country could be in jeopardy if a personal conflict erupted between the chancellor and the general, who were the leaders of the country. So, it comes from Insangyeo's reason for avoiding conflict with Yeompa, "because national affairs come first and private matters come later." The exemplary contents of biographical records of Han China, which were widely read in the Confucian society of Joseon, have been embodied as guidelines for life in the consciousness of Koreans. One of them is the spirit of Seongong-Husa (先公後私). Since some time ago, Seongong-Husa, which means that public works take precedence over private matters, has been firmly established as a basic virtue required of members of organizations, including public officials. In particular, it has become similar to an obligatory clause for officials who receive pay from the government. It has become a natural virtue that high-ranking bureaucrats and political leaders must have.

In the case of an author who served 34 years as a military officer, I do not remember taking a vacation normally during my whole career. When I was young, I was unable to apply for a normal leave because I had to fill additional duties of the combat personnel who were always in short for the air defense mission. As a high-ranking officer, I gave up my normal vacation because I always had a lot of responsibilities in front of me. As an official who receives government pay, I thought it was a natural thing to do. I never complained once because I thought it was normal. It wasn't an issue exclusive to me. This is something that anyone who has lived as a member of an organization in Korean society in the 1970s until 1990s can relate to. It was the basic attitude of Koreans at the time and the organizational culture of Korean society.

The Russia-Ukraine War, which broke out with the Russian invasion on February 20, 2022, provided an opportunity to widely publicize the excellence of Korean defense equipment to the world. Korean weapon systems such as self-propelled artillery, tanks, fighter jets, and anti-aircraft defense weapons have received evaluations that their performance is not inferior to those of the world's best-known weapon systems, and their cost to effectiveness is relatively good. As a result, in preparation for the threat of war, many countries are ordering Korean-made self-propelled guns, tanks, fighter jets, and air defense weapons. However, it is surprising why they chose to purchase Korean-made defense weapon systems. Korean defense weapons are relatively cost-effective. But most of all, it is because they can secure defense weapons on the contracted delivery date when they need it. In the case of countries with advanced defense weapon systems, their weapons may have slightly better performance compared to Korean weapons. However, it was said that the price was relatively high and that it could not be guaranteed to secure contracted weapons at the required time.

In liberal democracies, it is the right of the members of an organization to take vacations. In Western society, members of an organization take a vacation, which is their right, regardless of their duties in the organization. It is because they think that their job in the organization is important, but taking a vacation is equally important as well. That is the Western democratic way of thinking and their philosophy of life. In Korean society, even during the vacation season, members of the organization put off the vacation and perform their duties first if they have responsibilities to perform during the vacation period. But they don't think at all that their freedom has been taken away. They take it for granted. The mentality of Seongong-Husa is inherent in them.

The core reason why Korean construction companies are

selected in the process of bidding amid fierce international competition and Korean defense industries beat advanced countries in the weapon systems contracts is that they comply with contracts. They always faithfully abide by the terms of the contract. In other words, when they fail to deliver according to the contract, they do not blame environmental factors or unavoidable accidents, but rather take responsibility. By clearly keeping promises, they built that much trust in the international community. Korea, which has developed through international trade, has joined the ranks of advanced countries today because it has built trust in the international community. It is my view that it was possible because Koreans had a strong sense of responsibility of Seongong-Husa as members of an organization.

Inherent Free Democratic Egalitarianism

An important value in a liberal democracy is that members fulfill their responsibilities and obligations that are entailed by their freedoms and rights. The idea of equality in liberal democracy, "all people are equal before the law," refers to the idea that rights, duties, qualifications, etc. are constant and are applied to all people without discrimination. It is the idea that my rights and qualifications are important and as much as I want to be respected, the rights and qualifications of others are equally as important, so they must be respected, and my obligations must be fulfilled as much as the others' obligations. So, in a society dominated by the idea of liberal democracy and equality, people listen to other people's opinions. Even if the other person does not fit my interests or has a different opinion, I try to resolve it through dialogue or an exchange of opinions. At the end of a face-to-face discussion with the other party, a better alternative is sometimes created. If a conflict of opinion cannot be resolved until the end, a decision is made by majority vote based on the idea of equality, and everyone respects it.

Koreans have a high level of patriotic consciousness, such as, "Even if I feel uncomfortable, but if it is beneficial to the country, I should definitely participate." What is the level of democracy in Korea? In 2021, the British "Economist Intelligence Unit (EIU)" surveyed 167 countries around the world about the level of democracy. Korea ranked 16th with an average score of 8.16 out of 10 on the Democracy Index 2021. Following the 8.01 point in 2020, it has exceeded the average score of 8 points for two consecutive years, continuing to be classified as a "Full Democracy country group". Then, what level do Koreans actually feel? Looking at Korea's political culture today, can it be said that Korea is a mature democracy? I think the level of liberal democracy would be rated higher in Korea today if politicians were excluded. They often talk about the people, but because of the arrogant attitude of the National Assembly members who only insist on their rights, Koreans often ridicule themselves by saying, "We are still far away!" However, considering that politicians are also our friends, brothers and sisters, their images could also be a different images of ourselves. Therefore, it is my view that Koreans still need a consciousness reform campaign to promote citizens' consciousness of true freedom and democracy at the national level.

In the process of economic development since the 1960s, Koreans have been fiercely competing to survive as a strong person and foster themselves as better human resources. Koreans, who have lived in a fiercely competitive environment where only the winner can survive, tend to think that it is equal only when they can exercise their rights fairly and receive proper treatment. In order to survive in a competitive society, you must overcome your opponent. Consideration or concession to the other party means defeat. So such compromises and concessions are not accepted. This is the state of today's politicians in the Republic of Korea, a society where the development of a discussion culture was not possible and such conditions continued for long. Under the premise of a free democratic society, they strongly insist on their rights, but only hold others accountable. But that's just some of them. If only such people existed in Korean society, would it have been possible to obtain an average score of 8 or more out of 10 for two consecutive years in the democracy index for Korea, which continues to be classified as a "Full Democracy group"?

Fortunately for Koreans, in the first half of the 20th century, the vertical caste system of Sanonggongsang, which had maintained society for a long time, completely collapsed due to the policy of eradicating class status under Japanese colonial rule. With the establishment of a liberal democratic country, the implementation of compulsory education and the establishment of a higher education system, the level of education moved up in a short period of time. In addition, as most Korean men served in the military and experienced the fact that all people are equal regardless of status, the strong sense of equality in liberal democracy was established. As a result, the Saemaul movement in the 1970s was able to succeed because the idea of free democratic equality became clear early on although it was not perfect. In the late 1980s, as the Saemaul movement lifted people out of poverty and improved their standard of living, the people's desire to build a truly free democratic society exploded. Political democratization was achieved through such aspirations. I think that the high level of Korean awareness for free democratic equality is also the main DNA that has led to today's Korea.

Strong passion for learning

Above, I explained the backgrounds under the agenda that Koreans' passion for education is truly world-class. Koreans are proud of their "thousands of years of long history." Among them, being under Japanese colonial rule for 36 years from 1910 to 1945 was like 'a flaw on the precious stone' to Koreans. How can you not consider this a disgrace? At the end of the 19th century, when Joseon's fortunes were waning, the pioneers of Joseon felt the urgent need for national education for a wealthy country with a strong military, prepared a modern education system, and even promulgated the 「Modern Education Protocol」. In parallel, schools for modern education were established. With the goal of restoring sovereignty after the Eulsa Treaty with Japan, nationalists argued that "national education is the foundation and essence of the national movement." At that time, they established several private schools under the slogan, "Learning is power." The slogans they heard from their parents while growing up are still imprinted in the minds of older Koreans today. Koreans are thoroughly imprinted with the idea that "the only route to a rich and strong country is for people to learn and become intelligent", which the pioneers insisted when the country was in trouble. The reason Joseon was ruined by Japanese imperialism in 1910 was because, like a frog in a well, the people were completely ignorant of the world situation. The pioneers at the time realized this and they emphasized the need for national education in order to keep the people awake.

After the collapse of Joseon, Japanese imperialism implemented an educational policy to keep Koreans ineducated. Of course, workers, farmers, and urban poor in Joseon had a hard time getting the opportunity to get an education. In the 1920s, the illiteracy rate was so high, that 16 million people, or 80% of the 20 million people at the time, were illiterate. Concerned about this, the media took the lead in promoting literacy campaigns with slogans such as "Knowledge is power, learn to live." Even under the strict surveillance and control of Japanese imperialism, Korean pioneers deeply imprinted the idea that "education is the only way to live" to the people. This is the reason why Koreans had been imprinted with the consciousness that they must get an education to survive in a situation where the country was in a crisis like a candle in the wind. There was only brutal exploitation by the Japanese imperialism with no hope for the future. Pioneers had enlightened Koreans whenever the country was in crisis. It seems that the perception that they can overcome difficulties only by learning and developing their strength had been imprinted in Koreans and had been handed down.

The opportunity to realize the strong passion of Koreans for education had arrived. It was by the first president of Korea, Syngman Rhee, who had a strong belief that the nation could develop only when the people were nurtured as human resources through education. With the founding of the Republic of Korea, he played a decisive role in imprinting a strong passion for learning into the DNA of Koreans. On May 10, 1948, elections for members of the National Assembly were held nationwide for the first time in Korea, setting a landmark record of 95.5% participation in the election. However, at that time, the illiteracy rate of the Korean people reached 80%. The participation rate was extremely high given that all citizens could cast one vote under the same conditions. However, no leader would believe that building a truly liberal democratic nation was possible with 80% illiteracy. The Syngman Rhee government introduced a compulsory education system for free six-years of elementary education from 1949 despite the government's poor financial conditions. Universal suffrage eventually led to compulsory education. From this time, the strong passion of Koreans for education began to be displayed. The only viable resource in Korea was human capital. For a prosperous country, developing human resources was a top priority. This was the reason for prioritizing education by political leaders at the time. Parents thought that even if they did not have opportunity to learn, they could not let their children live like them. As the people devoted to the education of their children, a tremendous synergistic effect occurred. Through education, Korean society has developed into an open society in a short period of about 10 years.

In fact, in the 1950s, when agriculture was still almost the only industry, land reform was carried out. Nonetheless, as always, in some areas there were still tenant farmers, centered on landlords. Old-fashioned elites with Japanese-style education and experience still occupied most dominant positions in society. Even so, the implementation of national education policy for the transition to an open society was successful. The strong passion for learning of Koreans who wanted to become a dragon in a stream created a synergistic effect. As a result, in the short period of about 10 years under

President Syngman Rhee, Korean society rapidly changed and developed into a free democratic society. A new group of elites with American-style education was formed to replace the old elites. After liberation in 1945, the number of universities increased from 19 to 63 in 1960. Entering the 1960s through education, the level of consciousness of the people was improved so that fraudulent elections and corruption by political officials could not be tolerated. They began to ask the state for workplaces where they could demonstrate their abilities as much as they had learned. However, there were no workplaces in Korea at the time to accommodate the trained human resources. Society at the time, unable to accommodate the demands of the people, and was bound to become unstable.

What satisfied the people's demand was the implementation of the 5.16 military government's Saemaul movement in rural areas and the National Economic Development Plan. Koreans' strong passion for learning has developed further in the process of becoming a better human resource and surviving in the fierce competition for survival. Koreans' passion for learning has been a key factor in the virtuous cycle of Korean social development since the success of the Saemaul movement. After the mid-1980s, it led to political democratization in Korea, creating a more advanced and open society.

Korea was one of the world's poorest countries in the early 1960s, but in the 21st century, it joined the ranks of developed countries in 70 years. Now, Korea is creating a Korean Wave craze all over the world with economic prosperity, political democratization, cultural entertainment products represented by 'K-pop' and industrial technology. As a result, it is my opinion that Korea has now become a soft power powerhouse, both in name and reality in terms of culture and industrial technology that only appear in a highly advanced and open society.

I defined the "open society index" as an average value of the safety index of 「NUMBEO」, which is the world's largest cost-of-living database. The income index and education index which were used in calculation of the human development index by the United Nations Development Program (UNDP), and the democracy index of the British Economist Intelligence Unit (EIU). And this was set as the criterion for evaluating the level of an open society. As a result, Korea's open society index was 0.826, ranking within the top 10 in the world.

I asked myself the question, "What made Koreans produce world-class cultural products such as Squid Game and Pachinko?" The output of an attempt to find an objectively convincing reason is the open society index. The open society that K. R. Popper spoke of is a society in which the free

Nations	Income Index	Education Index	Safety Index	Democracy Index	Open Society Index
Korea	0.916	0.865	0.720	0.801	0.826
U.S.A	0.976	0.899	0.528	0.792	0.781
Britain	0.926	0.926	0.563	0.854	0.786
China	0.767	0.659	0.682	0.227	0.584
Germany	0.954	0.946	0.652	0.867	0.855
France	0.930	0.817	0.532	0.799	0.770
Sweden	0.952	0.958	0.529	0.926	0.841
Australia	0.933	1.030	0.586	0.896	0.861
Spain	0.909	0.832	0.680	0.812	0.808
Turkey	0.850	0.731	0.605	0.448	0.659
Japan	0.916	0.849	0.793	0.813	0.843
Italy	0.915	0.794	0.557	0.774	0.760
Russia	0.841	0.823	0.589	0.331	0.646
Canada	0.934	0.897	0.603	0.924	0.840
Israel	0.906	0.883	0.704	0.784	0.819

Table 1. The open society index of countries selected by the author

activities of reason are allowed, and a democratic society in which these characteristics are institutionally guaranteed. I believe that because Korean society has grown into a truly open society, it could produce works that people around the world can sympathize with. By the way, according to Maslow's hierarchy of needs, humans have five needs: physiological, safety, love and belonging, being respected, and self-actualization. When the needs are met in stages and the 4th stage, to be respected, is satisfied, self-realization needs appear last. This is a desire to develop one's self to the fullest and tends to expand further as the need is satisfied.

Based on this, today's world-class works by Koreans, such as K-drama, K-pop, K-movies, and K-food, are viewed as manifestations of Koreans' desire for self-realization based on their strong passion for learning. The open society index was defined based on objective data above, under the premise that those performances are possible only when an open society based on Maslow's 98 hierarchy of needs are satisfied. As expected, meaningful results were obtained in the open society index of Korea as shown in Table 1. Koreans' passion for learning is one of the aspects of DNA in Koreans that has led Korea's prosperity today. I believe that it will continue to lead the development of the nation in the future as a dominant Korean gene.

Strong adaptability to environmental changes

As mentioned earlier, Koreans have been influenced by geopolitical, historical, and environmental factors from generation to generation, and are characterized by excellent environmental adaptability and viability.

Until today's economic prosperity, the Korean economy faced a crisis at a key point after industrialization when per capita income reached 1,000 dollars, 10,000 dollars, and 20,000 dollars. At that time, the high adaptability of Koreans to change was really amazing. The Korean economy showed resilience, taking one step back and then taking two steps forward. In addition, Koreans took it as an opportunity to upgrade its weak economic constitution. The oil shock in the 1980s forced Korea to enter high value-added and high-tech industries such as semiconductors, home appliances, and automobiles. It provided an opportunity to become a middle-income country with the per capita income of $2,000. In the late 1990s, when the income exceeded 10,000 dollars, the IMF foreign exchange crisis hit. It drove Korea to the brink of bankruptcy. Nonetheless, the Korean economy took this as an opportunity to enhance the soundness and transparency of corporate management and national finance. It served as an opportunity to prepare a stepping stone for a new leap forward. In 2007, when the per capita income exceeded $20,000, the global financial crisis occurred. In the aftermath, it briefly returned to the $17,000 level. However, it has recovered to the $22,000 mark in three years, being regarded as a model country for overcoming the economic crisis. Even in the recent trade dispute between Korea and Japan, Koreans wisely coped with environmental changes and made it an opportunity to increase the localization of raw materials for Korea's flagship products.

The recent trade dispute between Korea and Japan is based on the South Korean Supreme Court's 2019 ruling on compensation for forced labor by Nippon Steel. On July 1, 2019, Japan's Ministry of Economy, Trade and Industry imposed export restrictions on key materials, such as hydrogen fluoride and film for panels in semiconductors and displays, Korea's main products, citing the South Korean Supreme Court's ruling on compensation for victims of forced labor by Japanese companies. Right after that, the second round of sanctions was enforced, excluding South Korea from the "white list" of the export partner management classification system. In response, at the government level, Korea pushed ahead with the "material, parts, and equipment self-sufficiency strategy." Local governments of Gyeonggi-do, where the semiconductor, such as Samsung Electronics industry, is concentrated, also carried out various support campaigns extensively while promoting 「materials and parts technology independence projects」 as one of the strategies for localization of materials, parts and equipment. As of 2021, two years later, the results of Korea's material, parts, and equipment self-sufficiency strategy and technology independence project were showing great effects. Based on import and export data, hydrogen fluoride decreased by 88% compared to import amount in weight before export restrictions, and photoresist also decreased by approximately 64%, overcoming Japan's dependence on semiconductor materials. In addition, contrary to the wishes of Japanese politicians, Korea's semiconductors ranked first in their export items in terms of value in 2020 and 2021 as well. Through this trade dispute with Japan, Korea continued to pursue countermeasures, such as promoting investment in research and development for materials, parts, and equipment. Rather, the opposite situation developed where Japanese semiconductor materials companies, which have been hit by Japan's export restrictions, are now investing in Korea to survive. As a result, Korea has earned an opportunity to become self-sufficient in key semiconductor materials while going through trade disputes attempted by Japan. In addition, localization of materials, parts, and equipment for major domestic products and diversification of import sources were simultaneously pursued.

As such, one of the strengths of Korea's economic growth today is due to its ability to quickly adapt to environmental changes. In my opinion, Koreans have an amazing ability to turn an impending crisis into an opportunity. The immediate adaptability or resilience of Koreans to such sudden environmental changes has received the world's attention since the global financial crisis. Credit rating agency Moody upgraded Korea's sovereign credit rating to A1 in April 2010. It explained the reason as "the Korean economy is showing exceptional resilience in the global crisis." At the time, the Korean ambassador to the OECD said, "The ability of the Korean economy to adapt to a crisis is no longer questioned by anyone in the world."[60]

A prime example of the adaptability of Koreans to sudden environmental changes is the gold donation campaign during the Asian financial crisis. One of the high-ranking economic officials at the time said, "When the enemy attacks, nomads think about whether to run away or go out and strike first. Koreans have a nomadic DNA that reacts sensitively to crises." This means that when Koreans face a crisis, they resolve it before it spreads with quick decisions and responses. Amazing adaptability is embodied in Koreans to deal with sudden environmental changes wisely. Korean's adaptability has contributed greatly to Korea's economic development today by turning a crisis into an opportunity.

High sociability of Koreans

「High sociability of Koreans」 is also one of the aspects of DNA of Koreans who led Korea's prosperity today. Sociability is a basic human tendency needed to live in groups. It is defined as an adaptation skill to maintain an individual's life and gain a sense of stability in the environment to which the individual belongs. Since humans are defined as social animals, sociability is a basic requirement. A common characteristic of people who adapt well to society is that they are highly sociable. They are people who have the aptitude, ability, and sociability to do well in relationships with others in a group. I mentioned above that many Koreans are relation-oriented in dealing with people in society, so they value their roles and strive to be faithful to their ethics and duty. Above all else, no one would hate a person who values a personal relationship with him or her. As such, Koreans have a strong tendency to value human relationships with others. This is why it is said that Koreans have high social skills. It can be said that Koreans are embodied with advanced civic consciousness with high sociability. Then, where does this high sociability of Koreans come from?

Historically, Joseon society was dominated by Neo-Confucian culture from the late 16th century to the early 20th century by Sarim who studied the human mind. The Sarim faction tried to build and maintain a society that followed the principles of Neo-Confucianism by making Confucian values a part of life. At the national level, Confucian ethics guide books were compiled and disseminated, and the practice of Confucian ethics was actively encouraged. As a result, Korea has been influenced by the basic principles and ideology of Confucianism represented by the Four Books and Three Classics, and Samgangohryun and Hyangyak life guidelines based on them for more than 300 years. Parents orally taught Confucian life guidelines to their children from an early age. As such good habits were handed down from generation to generation, it was an environment in which the teachings had no choice but to become deeply conscious. As a result, it can be seen that Confucian ethical awareness, life attitudes, and behavior patterns still appear in today's Korean society. It is also a proof that it is embodied in the consciousness of Koreans today. The following perceptions are still engraved in the consciousness of the majority of Koreans. Perceptions are that the state takes precedence over individuals, one should be filial to one's parents, one should use honorifics and respect for one's elders, one should maintain trust among colleagues and friends, there must be distinction between men and women, one should give advice when a friend goes down the wrong path, and one should help a neighbor in need. The above mentioned beliefs had been taught by the parents to their children over many generations.

Sima Qian, an ancient Chinese historian, evaluated Confucianism as follows in his book, 「The Legend of Shiji」: Confucianism teaches people about changes in world affairs, facts, and causes, so that people can live in moderation. It contains contents that create harmony in the mind and promote justice. The manners to be observed between ruler and the servants, father and son, the rank of the husband and wife, and the elders and the young are the rules of nature that people cannot change. Based on this, I think that the fundamentals of Confucianism are talking about what humans, as social animals, must abide by in society, that is, ways to enhance their social skills. Accordingly, over the past hundreds of years, the ancestors of Koreans had lived in the Joseon Dynasty, observing the Confucian teachings as the basic ethics of life to build a utopia of an upright civil society. For such reasons, I believe that the basic ethical awareness mentioned above as examples, that is, the high sociability of Neo-Confucianism pursued in the Joseon Dynasty that was imprinted in the DNA of Koreans living today. More recently as the level of consciousness was raised with higher education, a higher level of sociability is being expressed as an advanced civic consciousness.

These days, there are countless examples of high sociability of Koreans recognized by people around the world. Let's see some examples. The most preferred route by international flight attendants is the route to Incheon. They say it is because the manners of Koreans, who are the main customers on the route to Incheon, are kinder and more mannered. Also, wherever you go in Korean society, Koreans keep public order quite well, such as standing in line, is an example. Also, isn't it because Koreans are highly sociable that the recent K-movies and shows such as 「Squid Game」, 「My School」, and 「Pachinko」 are gaining worldwide popularity? The logic is that it is because of the excellent ability of Korean writers with high sociability to persuade people. In addition, it is also an example of a high level of sociability that Koreans generally underestimate themselves and pay more attention to what they do wrong than what they do well. What kind of a person do people hate? Isn't it the ones who claim to be good at something when they are not and show off themselves? Who in this world would not like a person who welcomes them, helps them when they are in trouble, and supports them?

The kindness of Koreans to foreigners visiting Korea is also an aspect of high sociability. People who have lived in Korea miss Korea. Famous celebrities who have been to Korea also like Korea, and say that they would definitely like to come back and they even promote Korea on behalf of Koreans. These are all effects obtained by Koreans' high sociability.

Hongik-Ingan spirit embodied in Koreans

This is a story I heard from my partner at the time when I visited a powerful country in Eastern Europe on official business in 2000. He said, "Korea uses science and technology developed by mankind to develop home appliances that help people in their daily lives, but it seems that we have only used it to develop weapons systems that kill people. The good quality of Korean home appliances proves this. There is no household in my country that does not use one or two high-quality Korean home appliances." He continued, "I heard that a vacuum cleaner for home use had been developed in my country a while ago, so I was happy to buy one, but once it operated at home, it made a lot of noise, just like a tank rolling, so I don't use it often. I really envy Korea."

The following is a story I heard from officials during my visit to countries in Central Asia. They said, "After the collapse of the former Soviet Union, Japan and China entered Central Asian countries before Korea. However, Koreans do not discriminate against us and they help us. That's not all. They never mind getting along with us. So, most of us like Koreans more than those who entered my country before."

Historically, Koreans never invaded neighboring countries to conquer. In addition, when Koreans feel resentment after suffering losses to others, they soothe themselves with the mindset of giving the person you hate one more rice cake. For that reason, although many cultural contents around the world have been using 'revenge' as a subject, it rarely appears as a material for Korean cultural contents. That's not all. Today, Koreans are helping others overcome poverty on their own by handing down the know-hows of overcoming poverty they had experienced in the past without requiring any conditions or costs. Even after 70 years, Korea has not forgotten the kindness of the countries that helped it during the Korean War, which was the most difficult time for Korea, and has expressed gratitude to the veterans every year.

I introduced the stories I heard from the locals during my visit and the habits of Koreans listed above which seemed to appropriately and metaphorically express the spirit of Hongik-Ingan embodied in Koreans. The Honhik-Ingan spirit of Koreans is also one of the aspects of DNA of Koreans that led to Korea's prosperity today. Above, I mentioned that Koreans are proud of being in unity with the Hongik-Ingan ideology, which has a long history with Dangun as their ancestor. Expanding on the contents mentioned above, Hongik-Ingan (弘益人間) in the dictionary means "to benefit the human world widely" or "to make everyone happy together." This concept is introduced as the founding ideology of Gojoseon, the oldest state on the Korean Peninsula, in 『Samgukyusa』 and 『Jewangungi』 that were compiled in the 13th century. It is also the current education philosophy of Korea. According to Article 2 of the Framework Act on Education, "Education enables all citizens under the ideology of Hongik-Ingan… Its purpose is to contribute to the realization of the ideal of human co-prosperity." It was the founding ideology of Dangun, who is recorded as the ancestor of Koreans in history books, and the Hongik-Ingan ideology, which is the current educational philosophy of Korea, seems to be embodied as the highest value of life in the minds of Koreans both in name and reality. Below are examples showing that the Hongik-Ingan ideology is inherent in the DNA of Koreans.

In the stark reality that there is only interest oriented

relationships between countries, Koreans today are contributing to the realization of the ideal of common prosperity for mankind by benefiting human society all over the world. If any country has colonized another country, I believe that it is the basic responsibility for them to share the pain experienced by the new country that became independent from the colonial rule. I think they would sympathize with them if they have even a little bit of Jeong (情, the innate affection). But the reality is different. Even now, despite being subjected to all sorts of exploitation under colonial rule from countries that pride themselves as advanced countries, how many newly independent countries are suffering because they did not teach them how to solve the most basic food problem for survival? In addition, the reality is that there are hegemonic countries that take for granted the act of trying to put a yoke on them again by lending money to the new countries and taking advantage of their many weaknesses. Ironically, due to such a reality, Koreans' Hongik-Ingan ideology is receiving better sympathy from people around the world.

Korea had to import rice due to a rice shortage until the 1960s. So, to reduce rice consumption, they were even told to eat food made of flour once every two days. When buying rice, it was mandatory to include 20% mixed grains. In parallel with the Saemaul movement, Korea focused on food self-sufficiency and developed a rice variety with a high yield of over 30% and resistance to disease and pests. And the government disseminated systematic farming techniques for the successful harvest of new varieties. Korea's Green Revolution, which solved the food self-sufficiency problem at once, became the driving force behind economic development. Entering the 21st century, the Rural Development Agency of Korea took the lead and set out to solve poverty in developing countries by handing down their experience of the green revolution. The following are two prime examples of international cooperation and support projects that the Rural Development Agency of Korea is taking the initiative to solve the food shortages in developing countries.

First, in 2009, it is the overseas agricultural technology development project (KOPIA)[114] led by the Rural Development Agency. The goal of the KOPIA project is '1. Poverty Eradication, 2. End of Hunger'. KOPIA centers were installed in developing countries and agricultural technology experts were dispatched as directors. It was a project to develop, demonstrate, and distribute customized agricultural technologies for each country. In cooperation with local agricultural

---

114) KOPIA; KOrea Program on International Agriculture

research institutes in developing countries under grant aid, the aim was to increase the income of local small farmers through the improvement of agricultural productivity. Instead of simply providing food, it was a project to go to the field and teach them how to actually increase food production. As of December 2021, Korea's agricultural technology, which has been localized in 22 countries around the world (8 in Asia, 7 in Africa, 5 in Central and South America, and 2 in Common-wealth of Independent States), played a role in driving the development of the agricultural industry in partner countries. In 2020, even under the constraints of COVID-19 around the world, the KOPIA project achieved many results by working on site. The Rural Development Administration plans to continue its efforts to address food security in partner countries through international cooperation in agricultural technology development. In this way, Korea is striving to make the world a better place by transferring agricultural technology to countries that truly need help.

The following is the activity of Korea-Africa Agricultural Food Technology Cooperation Council (KAFACI[115]).[61] KAFACI is also an international agricultural technology cooperation consultative body established under the leadership

---

115) KAFACI; Korea-Africa Food & Agriculture Cooperation Initiative

of Korea's Rural Development Agency. It is also an agricultural technology development project aimed at strengthening food security in Africa, jointly resolving agricultural issues, and narrowing the technological gap between countries. Projects carried out by KAFACI in Africa include basic agricultural science research support, development of rice that is resistant to disease in Africa, post-harvest management of horticultural crops, dissemination of small and medium-sized livestock breeding manuals, and establishment of an agricultural technology dissemination system in Africa. These projects help people in developing countries in Africa, who are in poverty because they are not yet self-sufficient in food, by passing on our experiences to help them get rid of their poverty. It is also an example of realizing the Korean people's Hongik-Ingan ideology, "We must pass on the experience of the Green Revolution to people in the global village who are still experiencing food shortages to benefit the human world." Established in 2010 under the Hongik Ingan ideology, KAFACI aims to improve agricultural productivity and poverty allevi-ation in Africa, discover sustainable agriculture, and improve agricultural structure through cooperation in African agri-food industrialization. To this end, projects that focus on distributing technologies for increasing food production and improving livestock in member countries are currently being implemented. A total of 23 member countries are currently participating. Four international organizations, including the International Livestock Research Institute, the African Green Revolution Alliance, the African Rice Research Institute, and the Center for Conflict and Development, are also contributing their strength. In this way, the sincere efforts of Koreans based on the Hongik-Ingan ideology are bearing fruit. This is evidenced by the unending request from the world to pass on the advanced agricultural technology achieved by Korea today. Koreans' experience of escaping poverty through the Green Revolution has become a benchmark for people in developing countries. South Korea's agricultural technology support for these developing countries was initiated to solve the food shortage, which is a basic human right. Who in the world would not like Koreans who help them for free? Korea's sincere and pure support for developing countries will now enhance Korea's energy, resource security, and global leadership. Furthermore, I am confident that it will develop into a cooperative relationship between countries in a virtuous cycle that induces economic growth in developing countries.

It is not just national level projects that realize the Hongik-Ingan ideology. There are quite a few Koreans who are currently putting into practice the Hongik-Ingan ideology. I will present just two examples of them. First, it is the story of Dr. Soon-Kwon Kim (78 years old), a proud Korean agronomist who has been contributing greatly to benefiting the world through research on corn, which is a basic food. Born as the son of a farmer, he joined the Rural Development Agency after graduating from college. After studying in the United States, he began research to develop high-quality corn of the United States. In 1979, while working for the Rural Development Agency, he received a research request from the International Tropical Agricultural Research Institute (IITA) to solve the food shortage in Africa. As a result, his corn research journey began in Africa for about 17 years. Through passionate research, he produced seeds of a new variety of corn that were resistant to weeds and pests in 1984 and succeeded in cultivation in 1985. At the time, the IITA[116] assessment team evaluated that "a corn miracle has occurred in West Africa." In addition, his key achievement was to find corn seeds resistant to 'Striga', so called the devil's weed, that is causing great damage to local crops. He solved this problem caused by deadly weeds on the African continent that no one could solve until then. For that reason, he was even nominated

---

116) International Institute of Tropical Agriculture

several times for the Nobel Peace Prize. He screened 10 striga-resistant corn cultivars and was able to reduce striga damage from 73% to 5%. He made it possible to produce corn, their main grain, without damage. He was recognized for his achievements locally and was the first foreigner to be appointed as an African honorary chief twice. That's not all. In 1994, he hurriedly returned home from Africa after hearing the news that "the North Korean people are suffering a great famine due to floods." After returning as a professor at Kyungbuk National University, he visited North Korea in 1998 to solve the food problem in North Korea. He discussed the corn support plan with high-ranking officials related to agriculture in North Korea and suggested solutions. Since then, he has continued to provide great help to North Korean farmers through the application of scientific cultivation methods and the farming of new corn varieties he developed. He said that if he could help solve the food problem, he would not give up or stop helping North Korea until the end of his life. This is the true identity of a Korean who practices Hongik-Ingan ideology.

The following is the story of Dr. Kwon Soon-young[62] (74 years old), who received the Asan Award for Social Service from the Asan Social Welfare Foundation in recognition of his contribution to saving malnourished newborn babies in Afghanistan in November 2021. As a Korean-American, he heard the news in September 2002 that "in the aftermath of the long civil war in Afghanistan, one in four babies die of malnutrition before the age of five." After graduating from a university in Korea and completing a doctoral course in food biochemistry in the United States, he joined Nestle, a global food company, in 1986 and was in charge of developing medical foods, including alternative milk powder made from soybeans for infants. Listening to the news, he thought, "Malnutrition is a field I know well⋯ , I think it's time to repay the help I've received so far" and he persuaded his wife and the company. In 2003, to help solve the food crisis in Afghanistan, he established a non-profit organization called "Nutrition and Education International (NEI)" at his own expense. He thought that soybeans could play a role as a source of protein helpful to Afghan women and children suffering from malnutrition caused by protein deficiency. When Dr. Kwon introduced soybeans for the first time and taught them how to grow and process them, Afghan people accepted them without any objection. Poppy farmers also plowed their fields and planted beans. He retired early from the company in 2008 and went back and forth between the US and Afghanistan in earnest to focus on businesses such as soybean cultivation, education, and establishment of a processing plant. Since then, his "Soybean Cultivation and Distribution Project" has been cruising, and the harvest of 300 kg in 2006 has increased 20,000 times to 6,000 tons in 2021. As the malnutrition problem has improved, the Afghan media called him "the father of beans." When he first tried soybean cultivation, few farms in Afghanistan grew soybeans. Dr. Kwon brought in seeds suitable for the Afghan climate and natural features, taught farming methods, and built various processing facilities such as soymilk manufacturing facilities. Thanks to such efforts, it was possible to localize the entire process of soybeans with 「production – processing – sales – consumption」. Dr. Kwon also taught them how to catch fish. He now says the goal is to increase Afghan soybean production to 300,000 tons by 2030. It is said that he has also made plans to start a second soybean project in the Philippines as early as 2022. He said that for NEI activities, although the financial loss was significant due to early retirement of 20 years, he was proud of helping to solve malnutrition in a country. What can be compared with the precious value gained by devoting himself to community service to save lives helping Afghans suffering from starvation? Even the Taliban, who occupied Afghanistan, demanded that the NEI activities led by Dr. Kwon continue. How proud are Koreans with Hongik-Ingan ideology?

Above, I explained the activities of the overseas agricultural technology development project (KOPIA), which aims to eradicate poverty, end hunger, and the Korea-Africa Agricultural Technology Cooperation Council (KAFACI), which aims to improve agricultural productivity and structure in Africa. I also introduced the story of Dr. Soon-Kwon Kim and Korean-American Dr. Soon-Young Kwon, who are putting into practice the Hongik-Ingan ideology through corn and beans. The cases of Hongik Ingan practices introduced here are just a tip of the iceberg. Including missionaries who are dispatched to various parts of the world, there are many Koreans who stopped by a country for the purpose of travel, saw the difficulties in the local area, and personally provided lifelong help. There are countless stories related to good deeds based on the Hongik Ingan ideology of proud Koreans who benefit the world by providing hope to the needy.

Korea's national economic development began in the late 1960s. At that time, the only available resource was human resources. However, Koreans have achieved today's economic prosperity by exporting the products they made. In the meantime, most of the products produced and exported by Korea had to break through the thick barriers of competing countries that were already dominating the export market. Through such ceaseless efforts, any products currently made by Koreans are gaining a reputation in the world market. How could that be? There is only one reason. This is because products made by Koreans were more beneficial to customers than products from competing countries. I have no doubt that as long as Koreans make products that are even a little more beneficial to customers by demonstrating their embodied Hongik-Ingan spirit, Korean products will find their way into the global market. I hope that the Hongik-Ingan spirit embodied in Koreans will further contribute to the prosperity of Korea in the 21st century.

End Notes

1 Britannica (Daum Encyclopedia), 'Soil of Korea', 'Geology and Terrain of Korea'

2 Edited by the Japanese Government-General of Korea/translated by Munhak Kim, "The Thoughts and Characteristics of the Joseon People", Booktime, 2010, pp. 153.

3 Kim Jong-gwon, "Overview of National Disaster History (Pre face)", Myeongmundang, 1993.

4 Edited by the Japanese Government-General of Korea/ trans lated by Munhak Kim, "The Thoughts and Characteristics of the Joseon People", Booktime, 2010, pp. 78-83.

5 Ham Seok-heon, "Korean History through Will", Hangilsa, 2003. pp. 181-390.

6 Edited by the Japanese Government-General of Korea/translated by Munhak Kim, "The Thoughts and Characteristics of the Joseon People", Booktime, 2010, pp. 36-43.

7 Edited by the Japanese Government-General of Korea/translated by Munhak Kim, "The Thoughts and Characteristics of the Joseon People", Booktime, 2010, pp. 116.

8 Joo Dae-hwan, 'Koreans who cannot tolerate favoritism, there is a possibility of a welfare state,' Pressian, 2010.

9 Edited by the Japanese Government-General of Korea/ trans lated by Munhak Kim, "The Thoughts and Characteristics of the Joseon People", Booktime, 2010, pp. 19-20.

10 Edited by the Japanese Government-General of Korea/trans lated by Munhak Kim, "The Thoughts and Characteristics of the Joseon People", Booktime, 2010, pp. 25, 209-214.

11 Edited by the Japanese Government-General of Korea/ trans lated by Munhak Kim,"The Thoughts and Characteristics of the Joseon People", Booktime, 2010, pp. 209-214.

12 https://olympics.com/ko/news/why-are-south-koreas-women-so -good-at-golf

13 https://economychosun.com/site/data/html_dir/2022/01/17/20220
11700015.html

14 Jangtae Geum, "Understanding Confucianism", Korea Halsul In formation
Co., Ltd., 2007, pp. 350.

15 Edited by the Japanese Government-General of Korea/trans lated by Munhak
Kim, "The Thoughts and Characteristics of the Joseon People",
Booktime, 2010, pp. 212.

16 Hwang Eui-dong, "Confucianism in Korea", Seogwangsa, 1995. pp. 14.

17 Hwang Eui-dong, "Confucianism in Korea", Seogwangsa, 1995. pp. 13.

18 Translated by Choi In-wook and Kim Young-soo, "Samacheon's Story of
Sagi Ⅱ", Dongseo Culture Publishing Company, 1975. pp 530-533.

19 Kim Byeong-il, Stop denigrating the 'spirit of Seonbi (scholars)', Chosun
Ilbo, pp. 30, editorial '100 Years of National Ruin', 2010. 9. 3

20 Junsu Han, "A Study on the Political History of Yulryeong in the Middle
Ages of Silla (Chapter 1, Section 1)", Seogyeong Munhwasa, 2012.

21 Edited by the Japanese Government-General of Korea/trans lated by Munhak
Kim, "The Thoughts and Characteristics of the Joseon People", pp.
126-127.

22 http://encykorea.aks.ac.kr/Contents/Item/E0015909: Encyclope dia of Korean
National Culture (Taoism)

23 https://m.blog.naver.com/PostView.naver?isHttpsRedirect=true&blogId=spp
0805&logNo=120210431258: What is Seonbi Spirit?

24 Gallup Korea, 'Korean family life and children's education', Gallup Korea
Research Institute, 1983, pp. 139, 142-143, 93-94, 58-59.

25 Choi Sang-jin, "Korean Psychology", Hakjisa, 2011, pp. 243-254.

26 Edited by Park Il-bong, "History of Chinese Thought", Yuk munsa, 1990.
pp. 12.

27 Han Mi-ra and Jeon Gyeong-sook, "Lifestyle of Koreans", Iljin sa, 2009, pp.
267-272.

28 http://contents.history.go.kr/front/km/view.do?levelId=km_030_0060_0020_
0010

29 http://www.bmceo.co.kr/mail/2016/pdf/160317_BookM orning CEO_2088.
pdf

30 Choi Sang-jin, "Korean Psychology", Hakjisa, 2011, pp. 10-18.

31 Han Mi-ra and Jeon Gyeong-sook, "Lifestyle of Koreans", Iljin sa, 2009, pp. 10-21, 55-58, 214-278.

32 Anes Kim·Sunhye Choi, "Korean History Special 2", Shinwon munhwasa, 2002, pp. 61-85.

33 Hwang Jae-soon, "The Secret of the Birth of Korean Surnames" christ59won Daum_cafe, 2009. Oct.

34 Hwang Jae-soon, "The Secret of the Birth of Korean Surnames" christ59won Daum_cafe, 2009. Oct.

35 Han Mi-ra and Jeon Gyeong-sook, "Lifestyle of Koreans", Iljin sa, 2009, pp. 272-273.

36 Han Mi-ra and Jeon Gyeong-sook, "Lifestyle of Koreans", Iljin sa, 2009, pp. 185-188.

37 Edited by the Japanese Government-General of Korea/ trans lated by Munhak Kim, "The Thoughts and Characteristics of the Joseon People", Booktime, 2010, pp. 211-212.

38 https://blog.daum.net/xlavksl/3385166

39 eun@chosun.com Reporter's viewing of other articles,' Kim Kyung-eun, 2010. Dec. 14

40 Choi Sang-jin, "Korean Psychology", Hakjisa, 2011, pp.46-48, 101-102, 117-128.

41 Park Ji-hyang, 'The Way to Eliminate Nationally Ruinous Regio nal Feelings', Chosun Ilbo, 2011. April 12.

42 Edited by the Japanese Government-General of Korea/trans lated by Munhak Kim, "The Thoughts and Charac teristics of the Joseon People", pp. 19-20.

43 Lee Sang-gyeong et al., '2011 National Security Awareness Survey', National Defense University Security Research Institute, 2011. Oct., pp. 208, 215-218.

44 Source: Google Earth; www.ilgok.es.kr

45 Source:Google Earth; www.ssamp.net

46 Source: www.tutormentorconnection.ning.com

47 https://namu.wiki/w/Suicide/Statistics

48 Edited by the Japanese Government-General of Korea/ trans lated by Munhak Kim, "The Thoughts and Characteristics of the Joseon People", Booktime, 2010, pp. 128-129.

49 http://www.ikoreanspirit.com/news/articleView.html?idxno=36 499

50 Yongseop Han, "Theory of Defense Policy", Parkyeongsa, 2012, pp. 2-3.

51 https://www.korea.kr/news/policyNewsView.do?newsId=14889 4061

52 https://www.mk.co.kr/opinion/contributors/view/2012/06/341 587/

53 https://www.joongang.co.kr/article/2831636#home

54 Yongseop Han, "Theory of Defense Policy", Parkyeongsa, 2012, pp. 25.

55 Kim Byung-ryun, 'The Achievements and Significance of the 60th Anniversary of the ROK-US Alliance', Bangbang Ilbo Special Project, 2013. Jan. 7.

56 Yongseop Han, "Theory of Defense Policy", Parkyeongsa, 2012, pp. 9.

57 Korea Policy Briefing(www.korea.kr)rk

58 https://www.youtube.com/watch?v=1kOhBzRH-ck

59 https://brunch.co.kr/@u842/332

60 Choi Kyu-min, 'one step back, two steps forward in every crisis··· Korea "Ottogi DNA"', Chosun Ilbo, 2012. May 29.

61 http://www.ezyeconomy.com, Heo Seung-wook, 'Journal of the Korea International Agricultural Development Society'(vol. 24, no. 5)', 2012, pp. 511-517.

62 https://www.hankyung.com/society/article/2021112898881

Korean Traits (K-DNA) That cultivated Korea's prosperity

the first edition	July 1, 2023
the author	Shin, Bohyun
an open book	Shin, Bohyun
an open space	DAEHAN publish
Report number	No. 302-1994-000048
Address	68, Wonhyo-ro 4-ga, Yongsan-gu, Seoul. Yeongcheon B/D 3F)
Phone	02)754-0765
fax	02)754-9873

price 28,000won

ISBN 979-11-85447-17-9(03000)